DOCTOR ANDROMEDA

AND THE KINGDOM OF LOST TOMORROWS

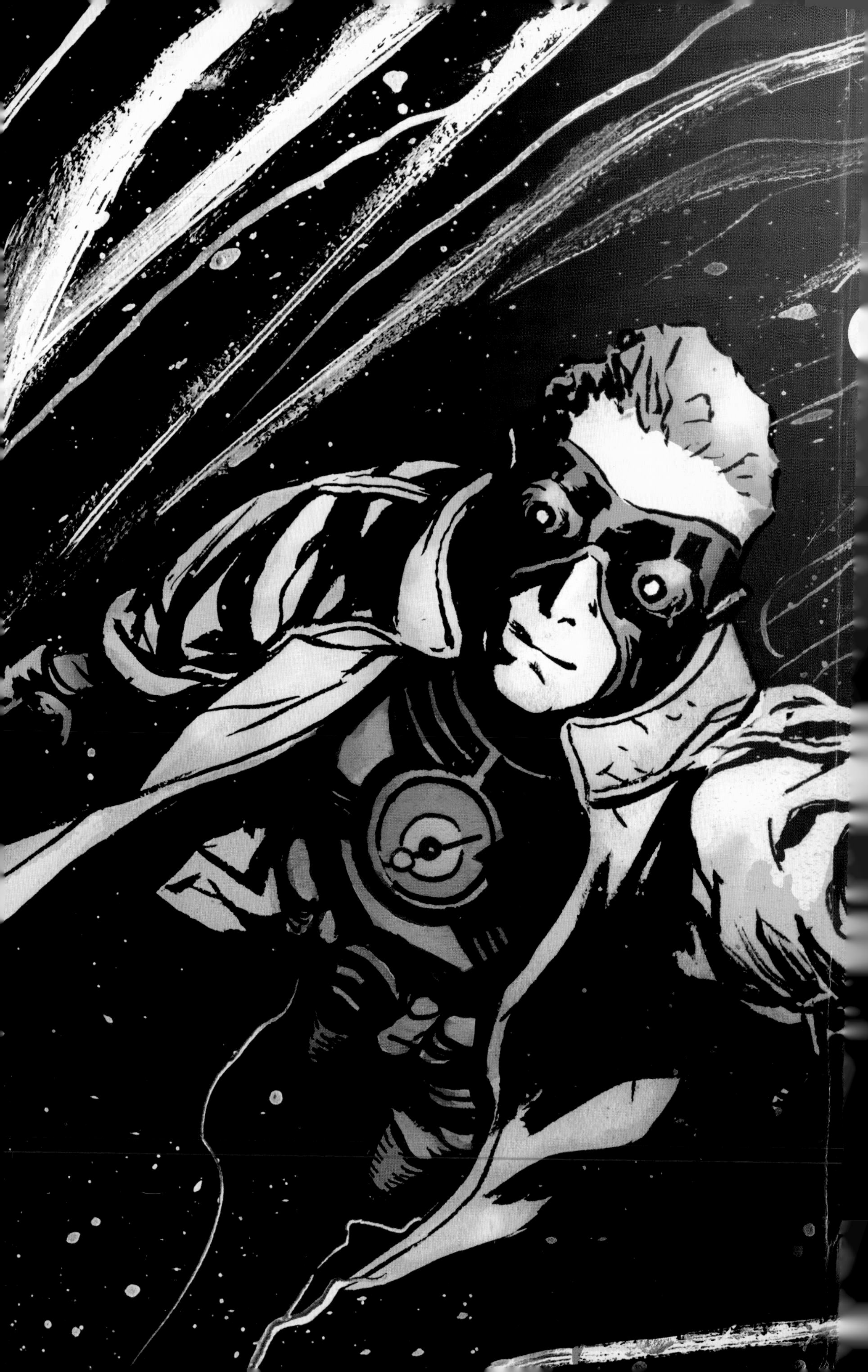

DOCTOR ANDROMEDA™

AND THE KINGDOM OF LOST TOMORROWS

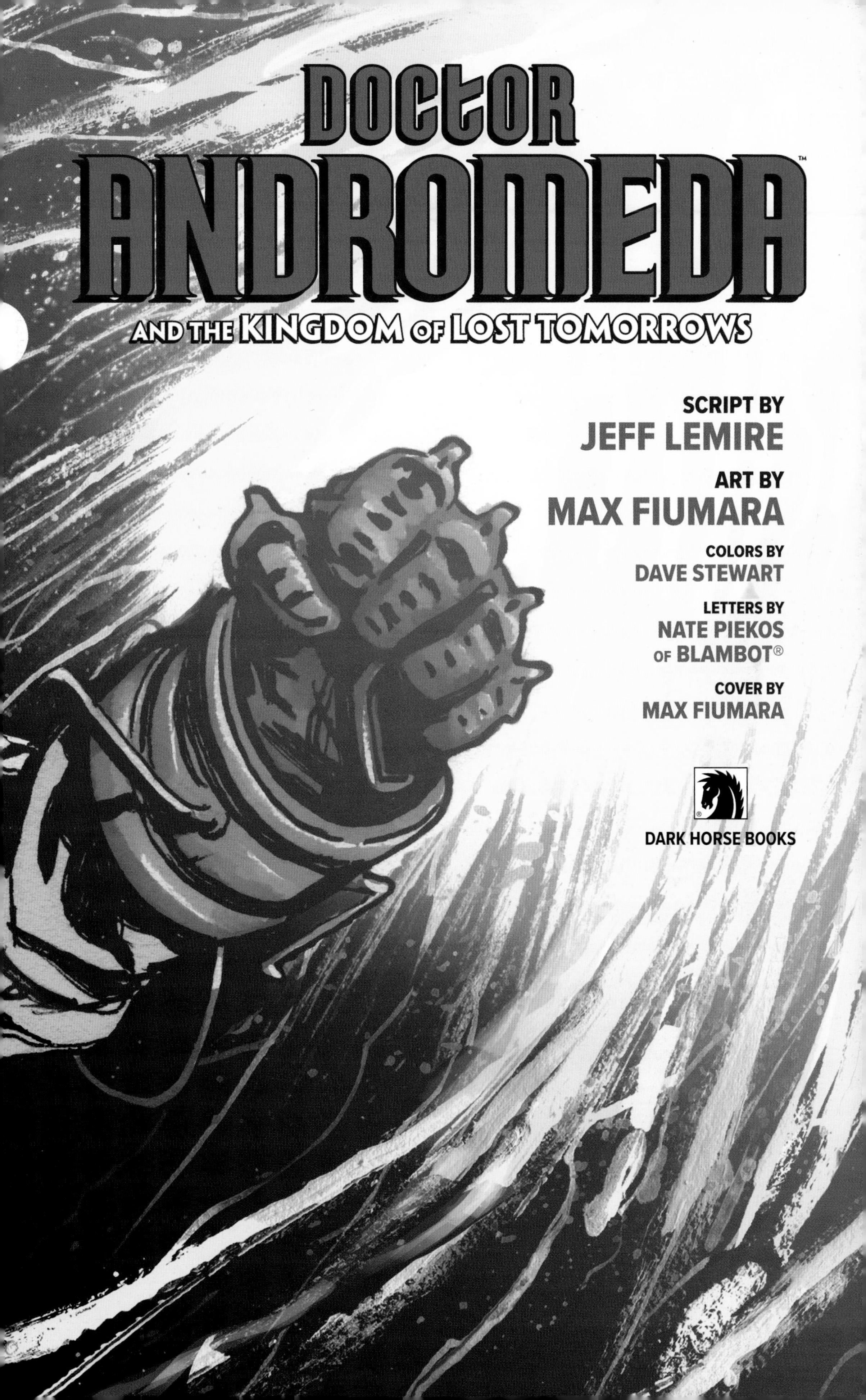

SCRIPT BY
JEFF LEMIRE

ART BY
MAX FIUMARA

COLORS BY
DAVE STEWART

LETTERS BY
NATE PIEKOS
OF **BLAMBOT®**

COVER BY
MAX FIUMARA

DARK HORSE BOOKS

PRESIDENT & PUBLISHER MIKE RICHARDSON

EDITOR DANIEL CHABON

ASSISTANT EDITORS BRETT ISRAEL AND CHUCK HOWITT

DESIGNER ETHAN KIMBERLING

DIGITAL ART TECHNICIANS CHRISTINA McKENZIE AND JOSIE CHRISTENSEN

DOCTOR ANDROMEDA AND THE KINGDOM OF LOST TOMORROWS

Collects what was originally titled *Doctor Star* #1–#4.

Published by
Dark Horse Books
A division of Dark Horse Comics LLC
10956 SE Main Street
Milwaukie, OR 97222

DarkHorse.com

To find a comics shop in your area, visit comicshoplocator.com

First edition: April 2021
Ebook ISBN 978-1-50672-330-3
Trade paperback ISBN 978-1-50672-329-7

10 9 8 7 6 5 4 3 2 1
Printed in China

CHAPTER ONE

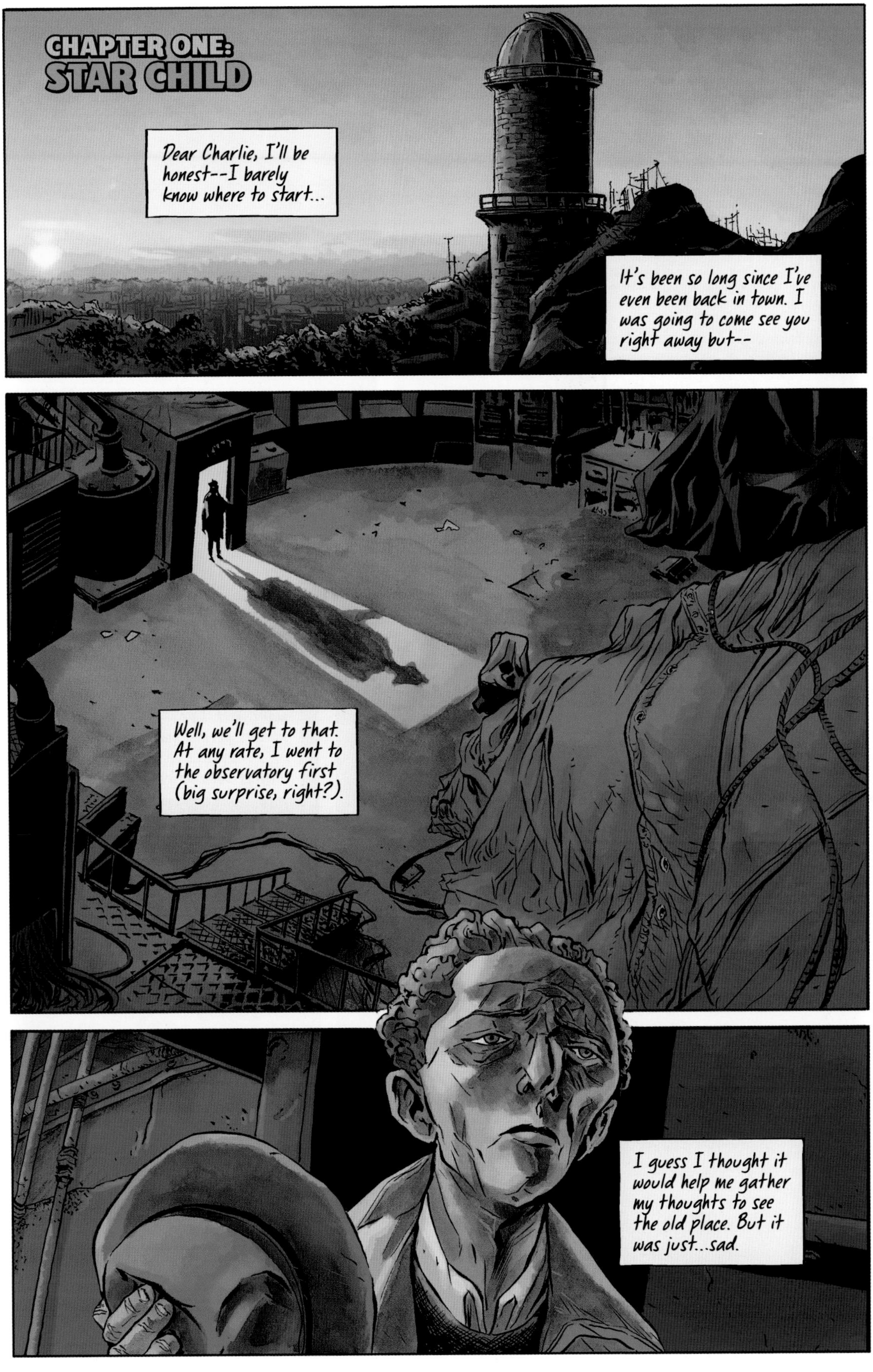
CHAPTER ONE:
STAR CHILD
Dear Charlie, I'll be honest--I barely know where to start...
It's been so long since I've even been back in town. I was going to come see you right away but--
Well, we'll get to that. At any rate, I went to the observatory first (big surprise, right?).
I guess I thought it would help me gather my thoughts to see the old place. But it was just...sad.

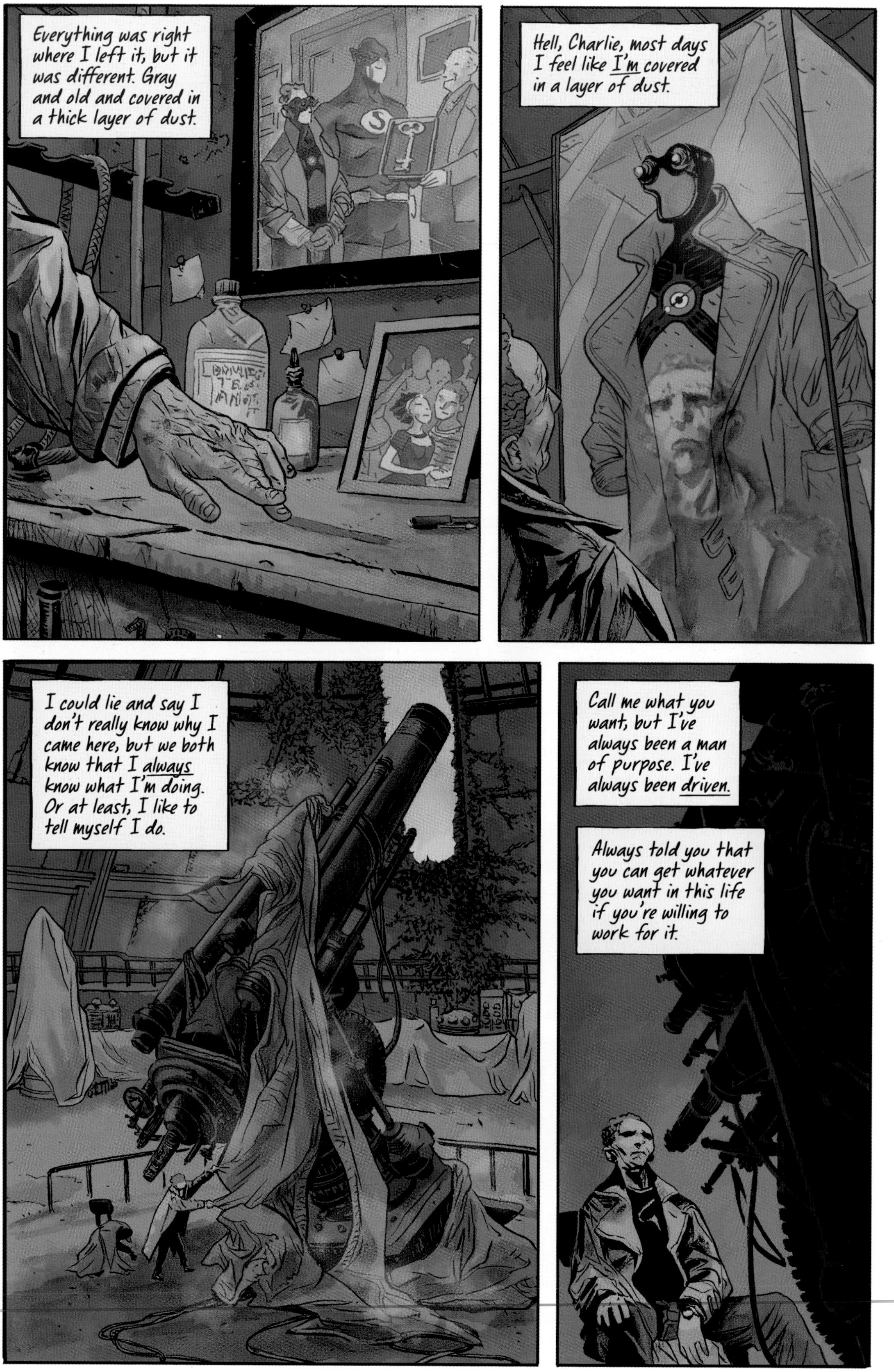
Everything was right where I left it, but it was different. Gray and old and covered in a thick layer of dust.
Hell, Charlie, most days I feel like I'm covered in a layer of dust.
I could lie and say I don't really know why I came here, but we both know that I always know what I'm doing. Or at least, I like to tell myself I do.
Call me what you want, but I've always been a man of purpose. I've always been driven.
Always told you that you can get whatever you want in this life if you're willing to work for it.

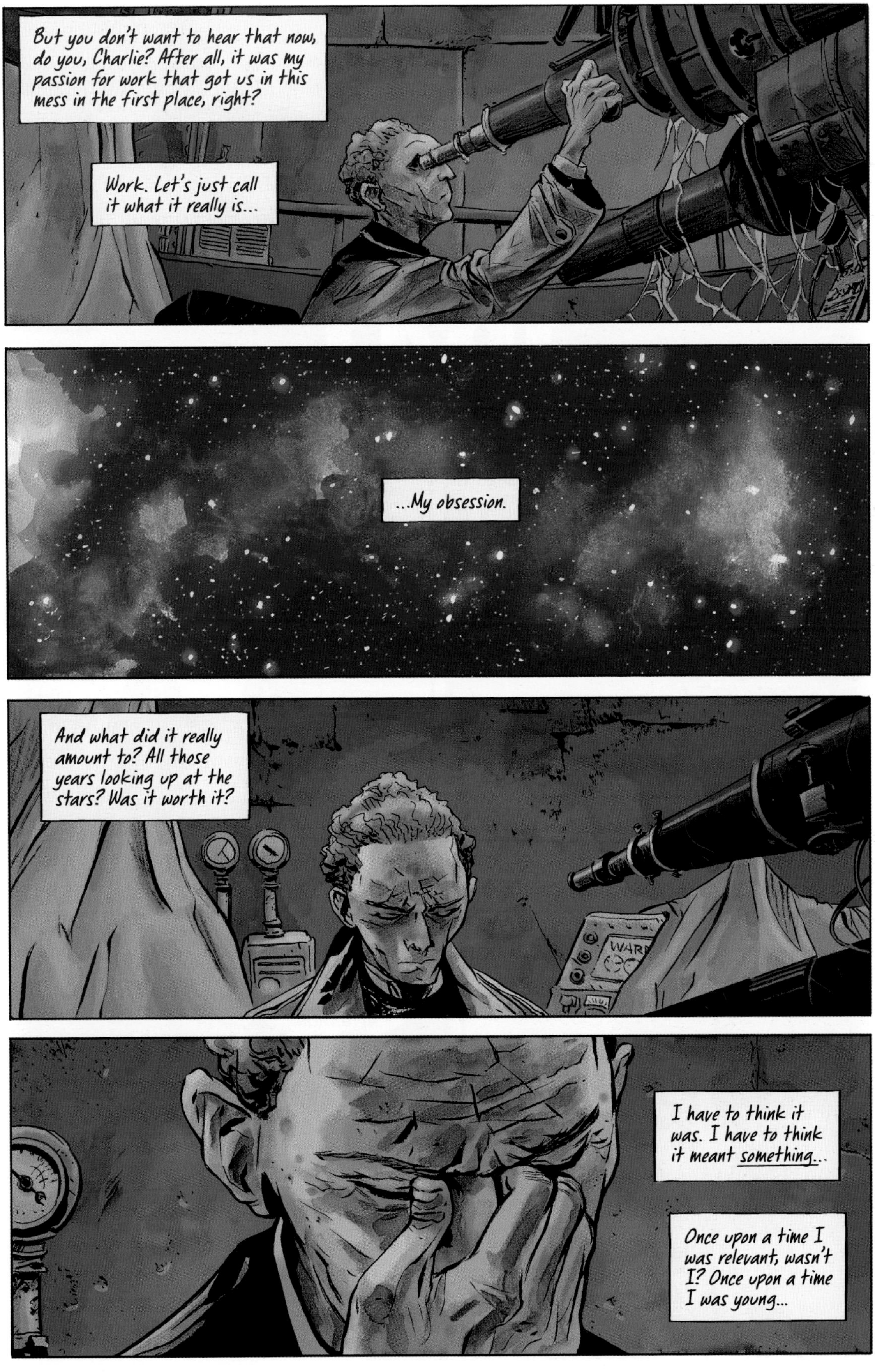

But you don't want to hear that now, do you, Charlie? After all, it was my passion for work that got us in this mess in the first place, right?
Work. Let's just call it what it really is...
...My obsession.
And what did it really amount to? All those years looking up at the stars? Was it worth it?
I have to think it was. I have to think it meant something...
Once upon a time I was relevant, wasn't I? Once upon a time I was young...

...and my sins were yet to come.

1941

MR. ROBINSON? JIM ROBINSON?

UH, *DOCTOR* ROBINSON.

DOCTOR. APOLOGIES. AT ANY RATE, DO YOU HAVE A MOMENT?

DON'T GET MANY VISITORS UP HERE. WHAT CAN I HELP YOU FELLAS WITH?

DOCTOR, MY NAME IS AGENT STERN, AND THIS IS AGENT MACAVOY. WE'RE FROM THE DEPARTMENT OF DEFENSE.

UNCLE SAM IN SPIRAL OBSERVATORY?! WELL, THIS DOESN'T HAPPEN EVERY DAY.

OKAY, AGENTS, YOU HAVE MY ATTENTION. WHAT'S THIS ALL ABOUT?

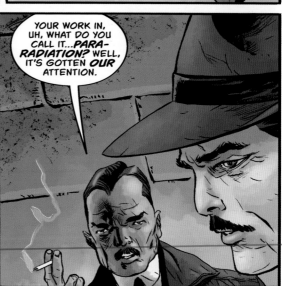

YOUR WORK IN, UH, WHAT DO YOU CALL IT...*PARA-RADIATION?* WELL, IT'S GOTTEN *OUR* ATTENTION.

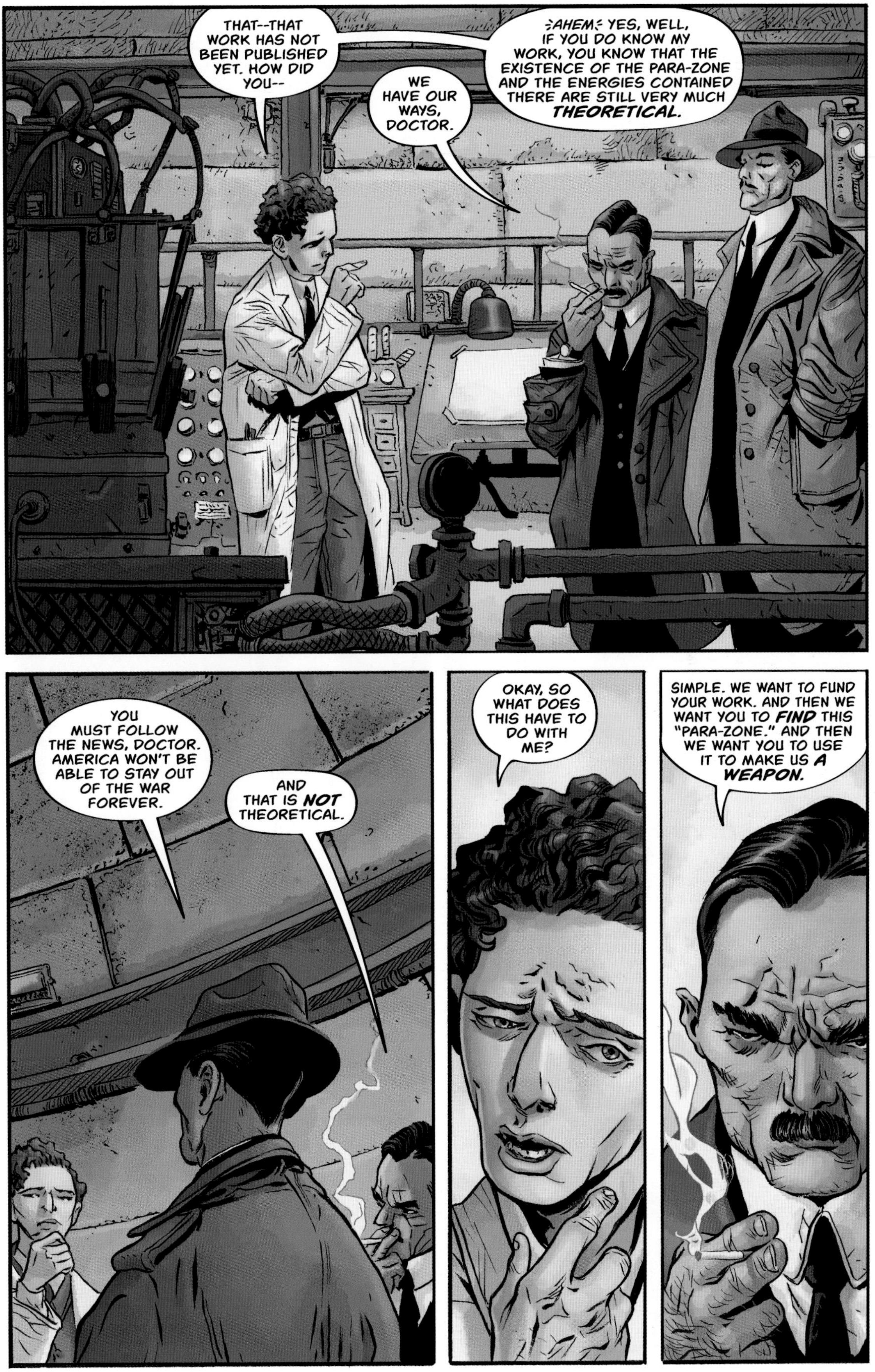
THAT--THAT WORK HAS NOT BEEN PUBLISHED YET. HOW DID YOU--
WE HAVE OUR WAYS, DOCTOR.
AHEM. YES, WELL, IF YOU DO KNOW MY WORK, YOU KNOW THAT THE EXISTENCE OF THE PARA-ZONE AND THE ENERGIES CONTAINED THERE ARE STILL VERY MUCH THEORETICAL.
YOU MUST FOLLOW THE NEWS, DOCTOR. AMERICA WON'T BE ABLE TO STAY OUT OF THE WAR FOREVER.
AND THAT IS NOT THEORETICAL.
OKAY, SO WHAT DOES THIS HAVE TO DO WITH ME?
SIMPLE. WE WANT TO FUND YOUR WORK. AND THEN WE WANT YOU TO FIND THIS "PARA-ZONE." AND THEN WE WANT YOU TO USE IT TO MAKE US A WEAPON.

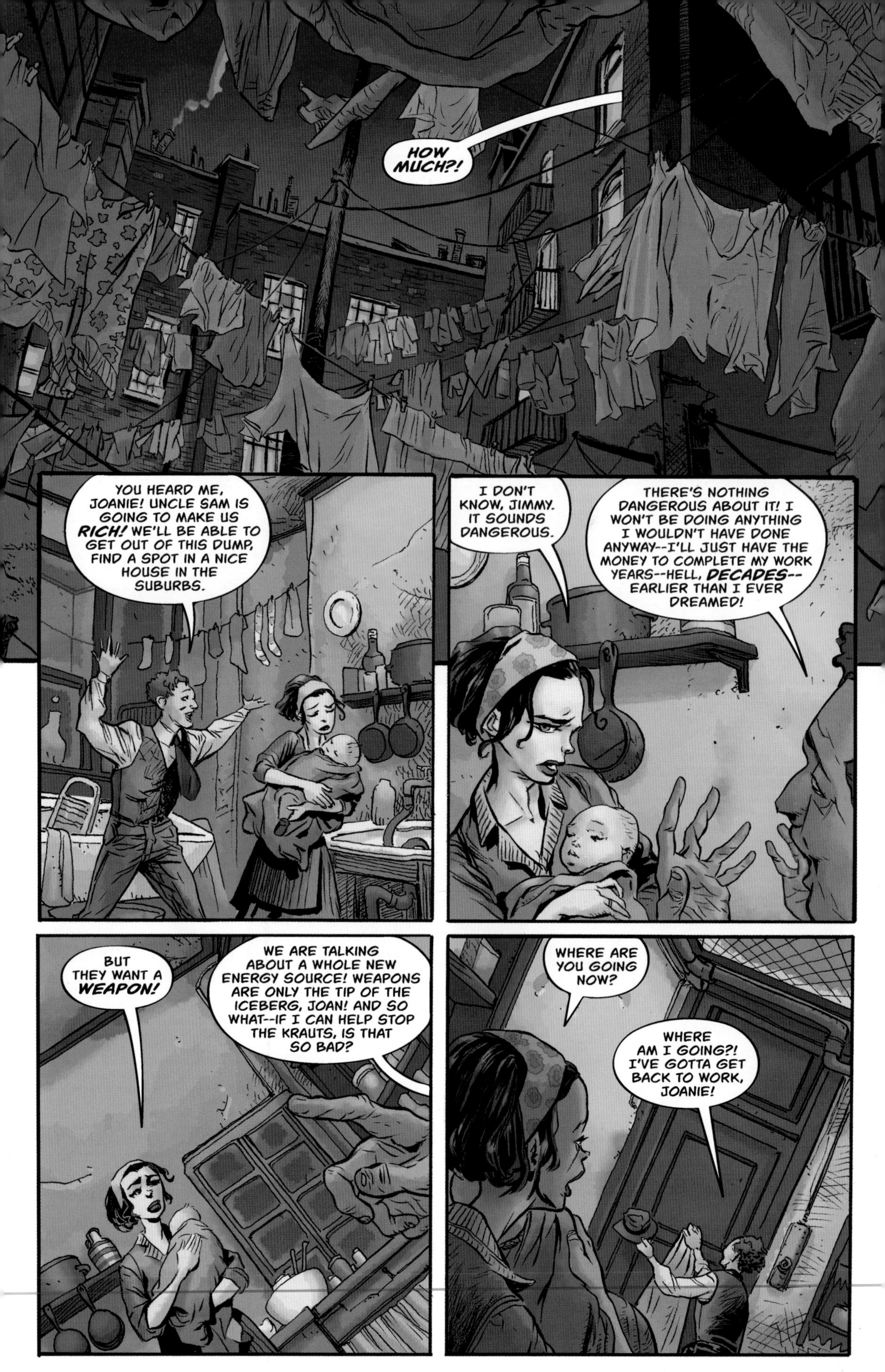
HOW MUCH?!
YOU HEARD ME, JOANIE! UNCLE SAM IS GOING TO MAKE US RICH! WE'LL BE ABLE TO GET OUT OF THIS DUMP, FIND A SPOT IN A NICE HOUSE IN THE SUBURBS.
I DON'T KNOW, JIMMY. IT SOUNDS DANGEROUS.
THERE'S NOTHING DANGEROUS ABOUT IT! I WON'T BE DOING ANYTHING I WOULDN'T HAVE DONE ANYWAY--I'LL JUST HAVE THE MONEY TO COMPLETE MY WORK YEARS--HELL, DECADES--EARLIER THAN I EVER DREAMED!
BUT THEY WANT A WEAPON!
WE ARE TALKING ABOUT A WHOLE NEW ENERGY SOURCE! WEAPONS ARE ONLY THE TIP OF THE ICEBERG, JOAN! AND SO WHAT--IF I CAN HELP STOP THE KRAUTS, IS THAT SO BAD?
WHERE ARE YOU GOING NOW?
WHERE AM I GOING?! I'VE GOTTA GET BACK TO WORK, JOANIE!

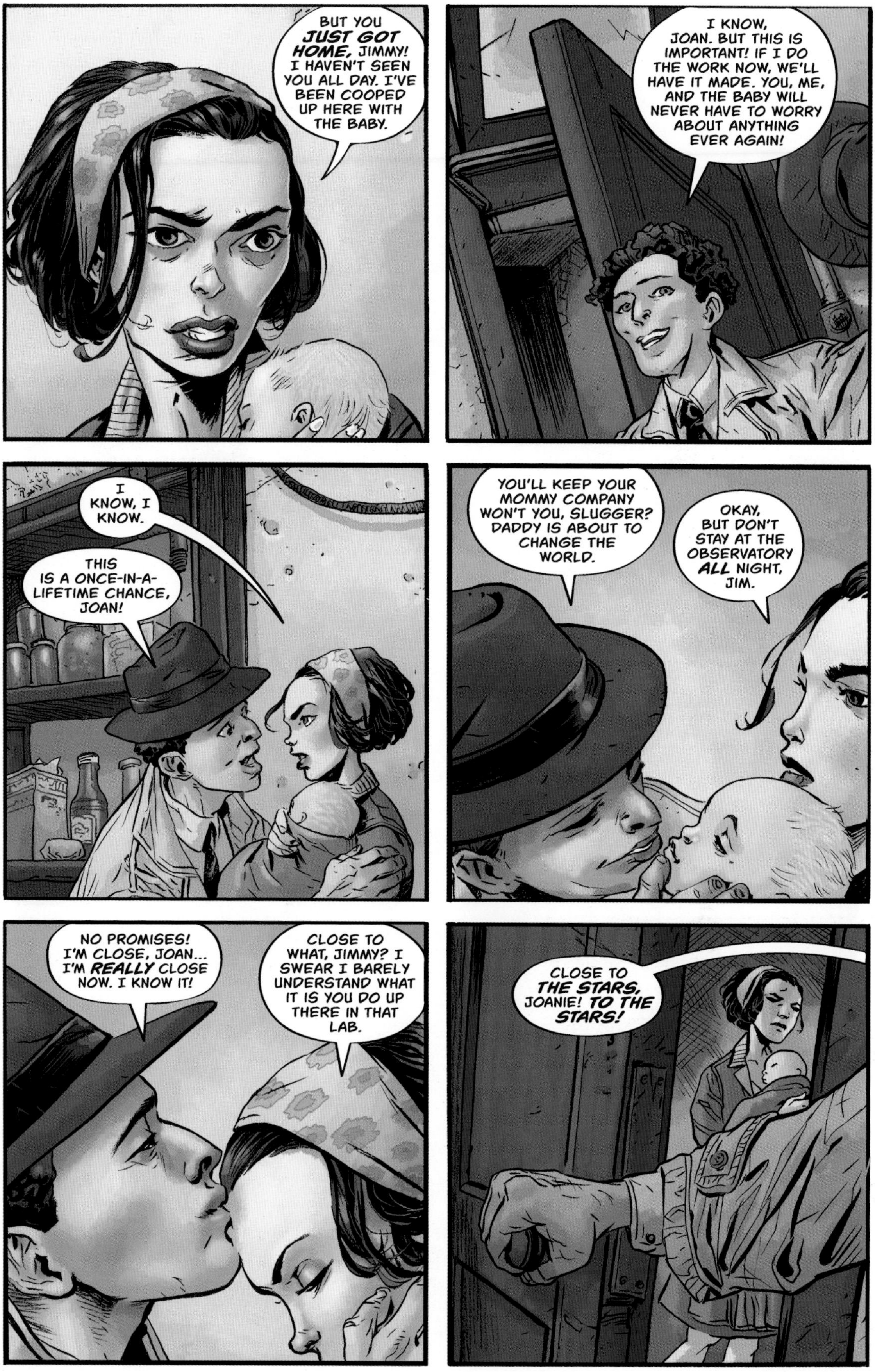
BUT YOU JUST GOT HOME, JIMMY! I HAVEN'T SEEN YOU ALL DAY. I'VE BEEN COOPED UP HERE WITH THE BABY.
I KNOW, JOAN. BUT THIS IS IMPORTANT! IF I DO THE WORK NOW, WE'LL HAVE IT MADE. YOU, ME, AND THE BABY WILL NEVER HAVE TO WORRY ABOUT ANYTHING EVER AGAIN!
I KNOW, I KNOW.
THIS IS A ONCE-IN-A-LIFETIME CHANCE, JOAN!
YOU'LL KEEP YOUR MOMMY COMPANY WON'T YOU, SLUGGER? DADDY IS ABOUT TO CHANGE THE WORLD.
OKAY, BUT DON'T STAY AT THE OBSERVATORY ALL NIGHT, JIM.
NO PROMISES! I'M CLOSE, JOAN... I'M REALLY CLOSE NOW. I KNOW IT!
CLOSE TO WHAT, JIMMY? I SWEAR I BARELY UNDERSTAND WHAT IT IS YOU DO UP THERE IN THAT LAB.
CLOSE TO THE STARS, JOANIE! TO THE STARS!

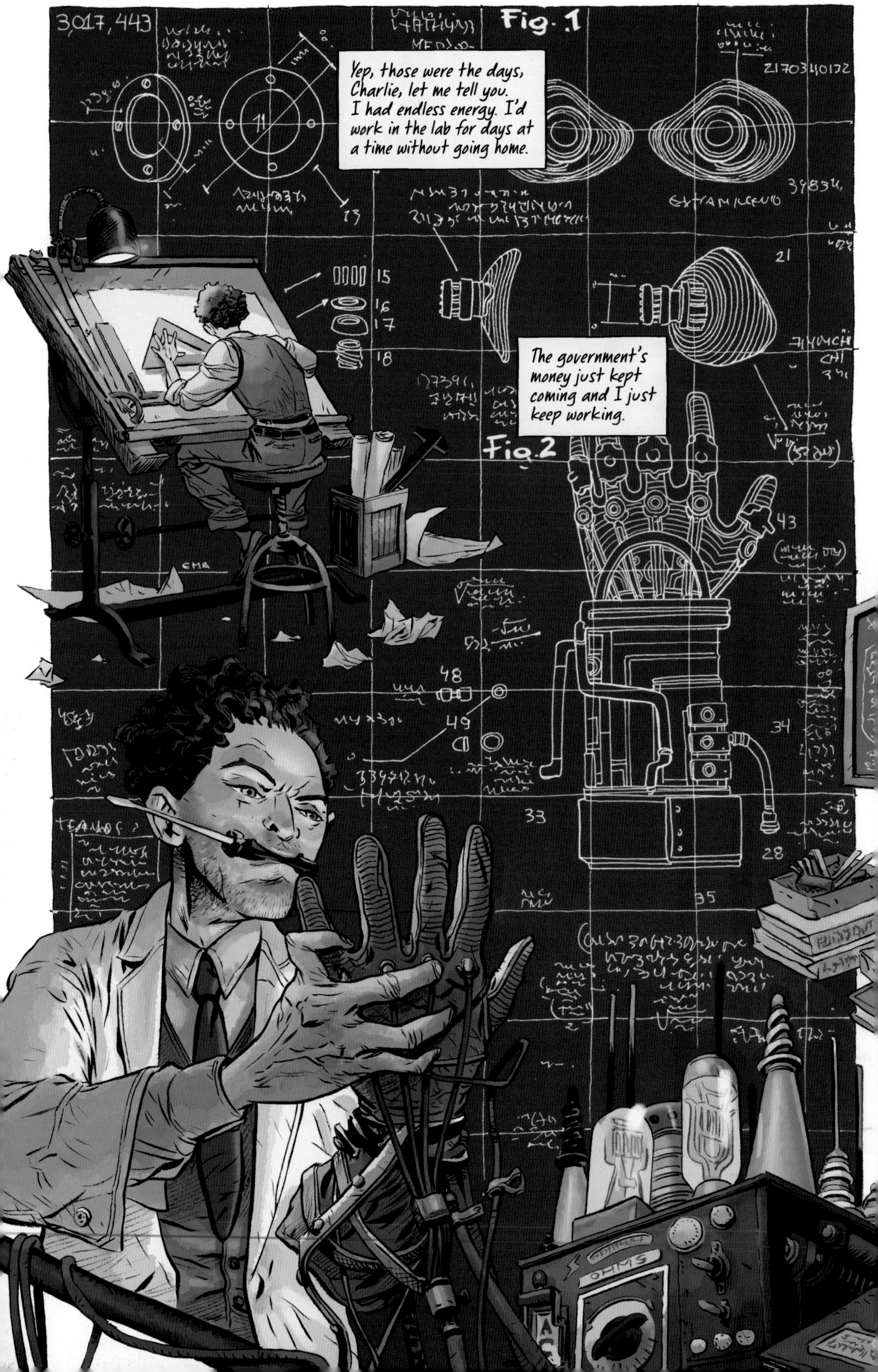
3,017,443
Fig. 1
2170340172
Yep, those were the days, Charlie, let me tell you. I had endless energy. I'd work in the lab for days at a time without going home.
15
16
17
18
21
The government's money just kept coming and I just keep working.
Fig. 2
43
48
49
34
33
28
35
OHMS

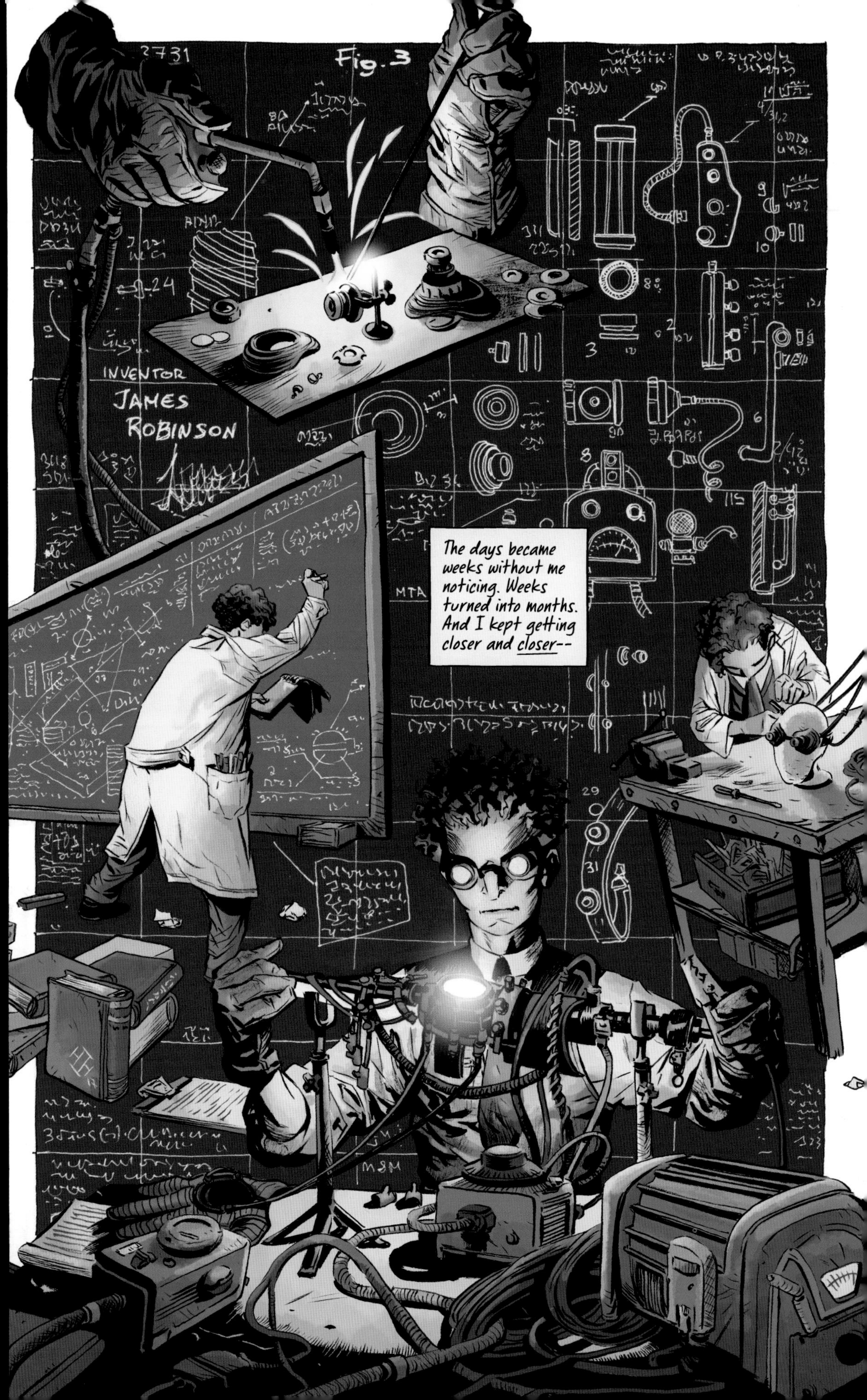
Fig. 3
INVENTOR
JAMES
ROBINSON
MTA
The days became weeks without me noticing. Weeks turned into months. And I kept getting closer and closer--

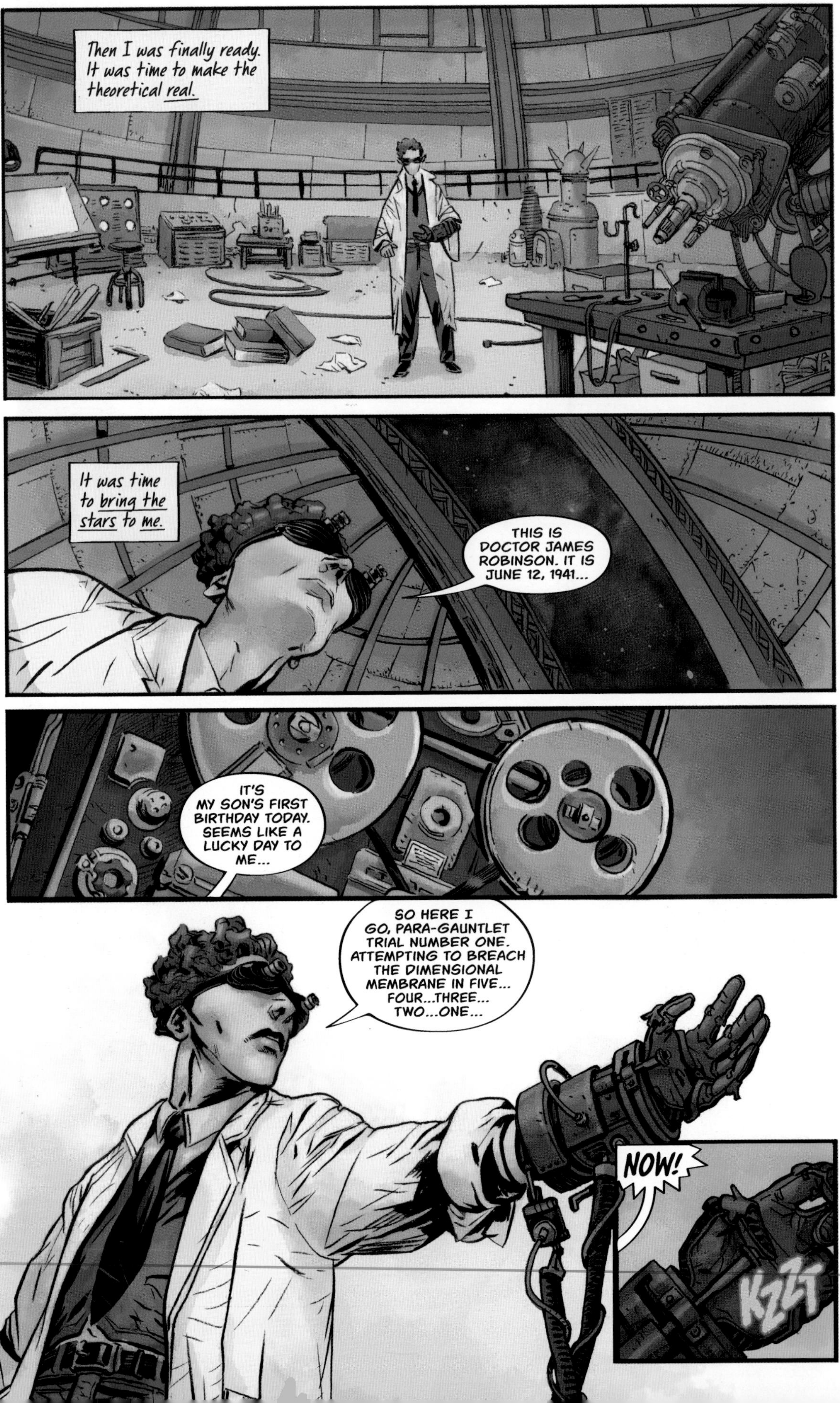

Then I was finally ready. It was time to make the theoretical real.
It was time to bring the stars to me.
THIS IS DOCTOR JAMES ROBINSON. IT IS JUNE 12, 1941...
IT'S MY SON'S FIRST BIRTHDAY TODAY. SEEMS LIKE A LUCKY DAY TO ME...
SO HERE I GO, PARA-GAUNTLET TRIAL NUMBER ONE. ATTEMPTING TO BREACH THE DIMENSIONAL MEMBRANE IN FIVE... FOUR...THREE... TWO...ONE...
NOW!
KZZT

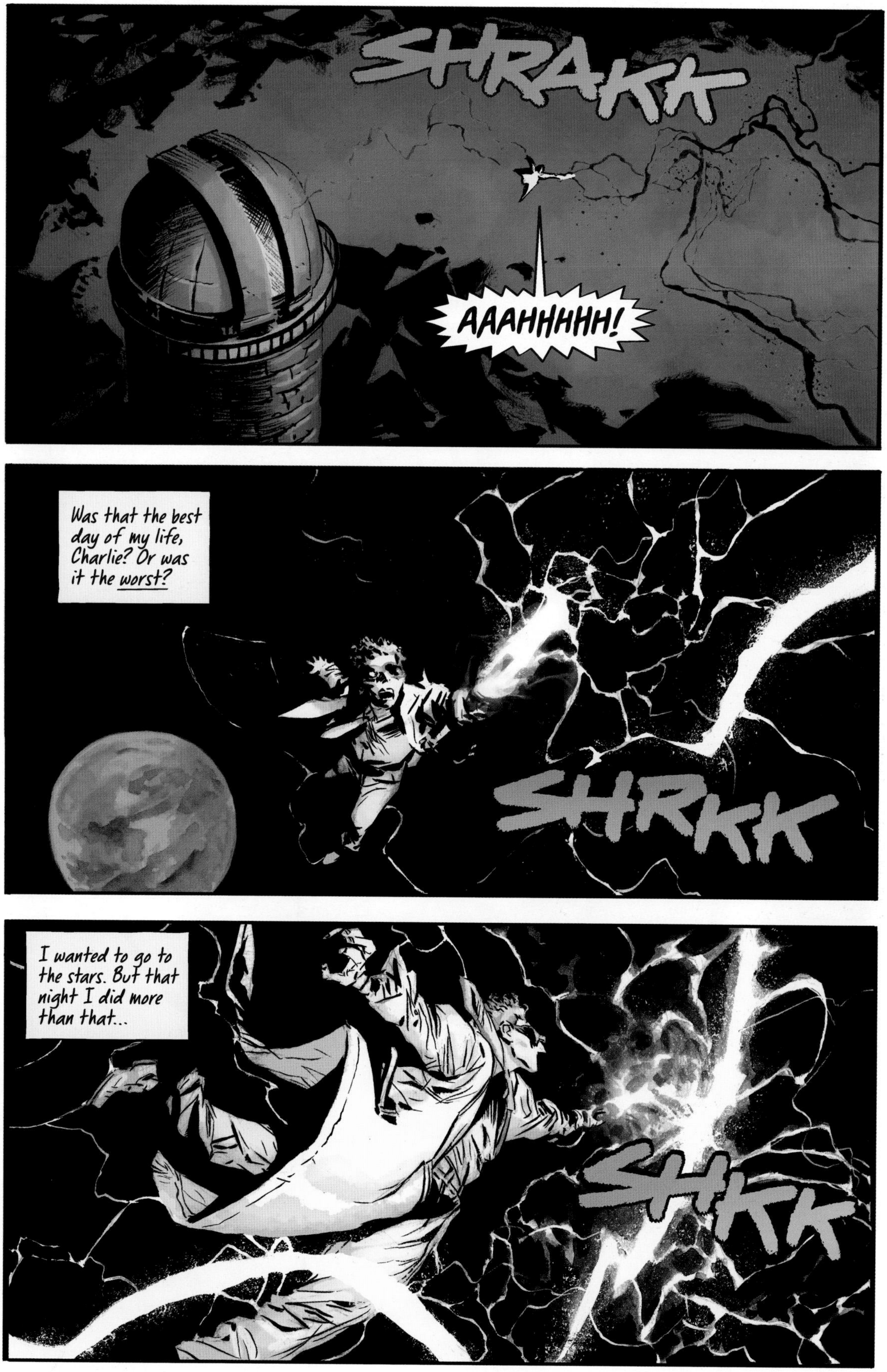
SHRAKK
AAAHHHHH!
Was that the best day of my life, Charlie? Or was it the worst?
SHRKK
I wanted to go to the stars. But that night I did more than that...
SHKK

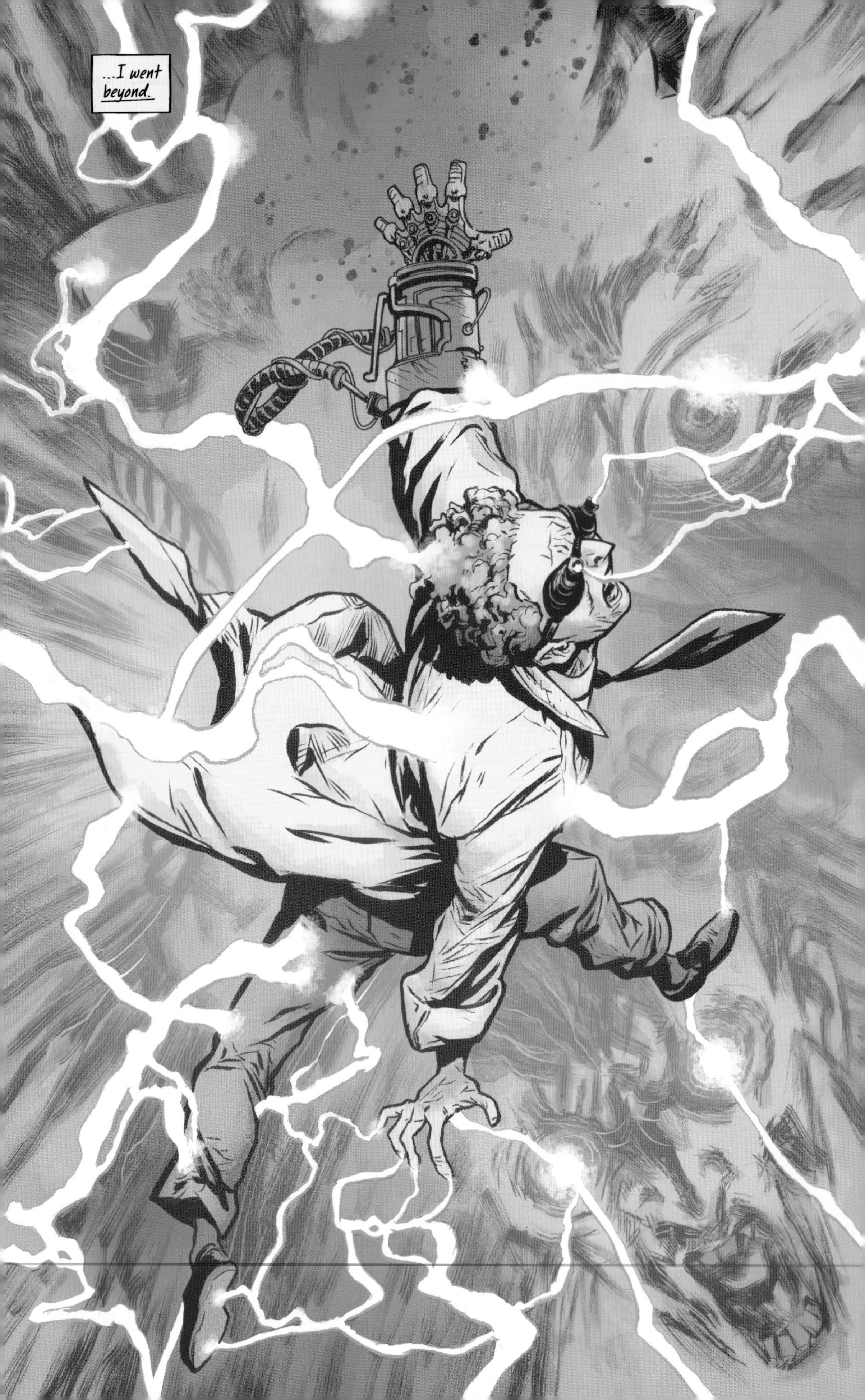
...I went beyond.

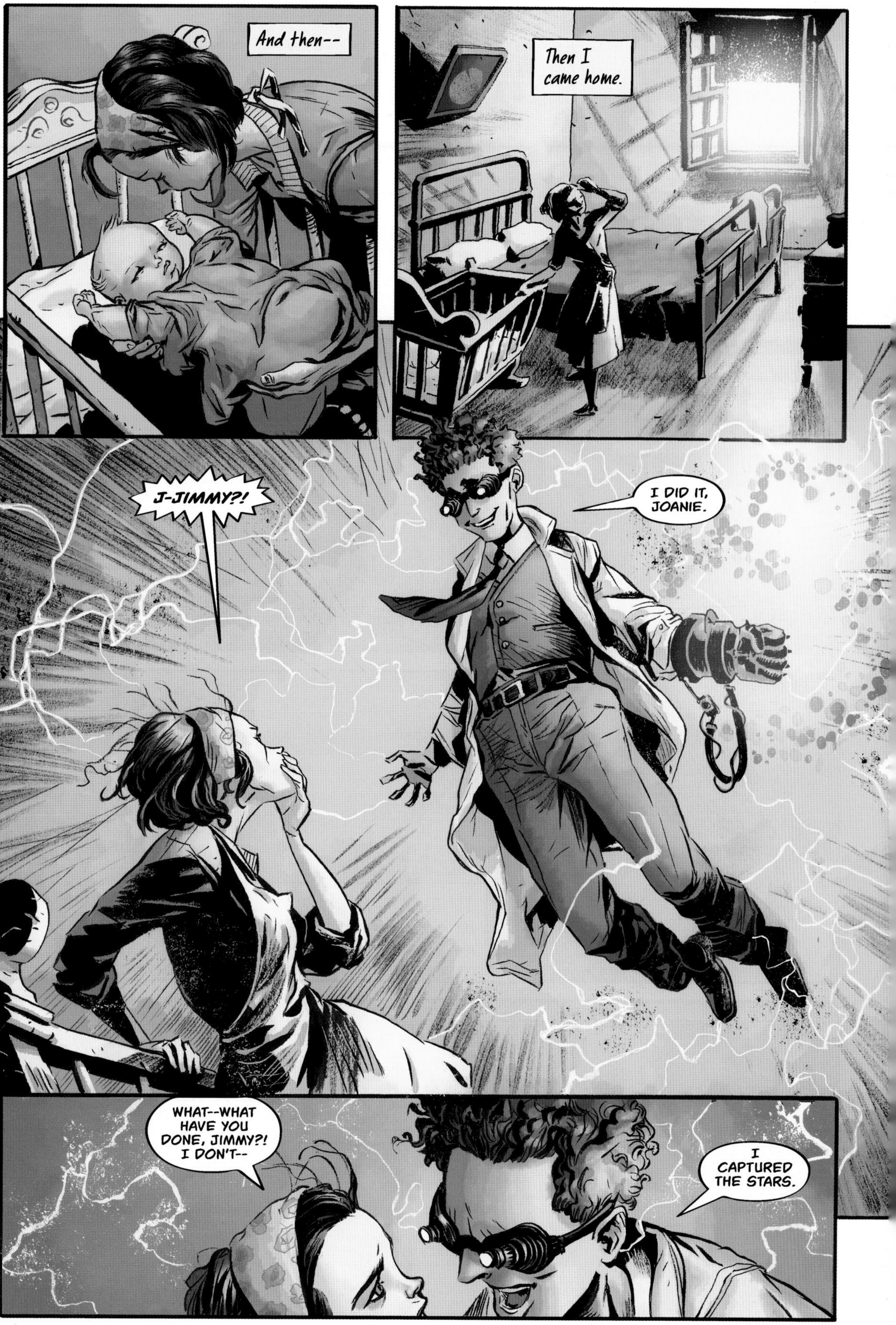
And then--
Then I came home.
J-JIMMY?!
I DID IT, JOANIE.
WHAT--WHAT HAVE YOU DONE, JIMMY?! I DON'T--
I CAPTURED THE STARS.

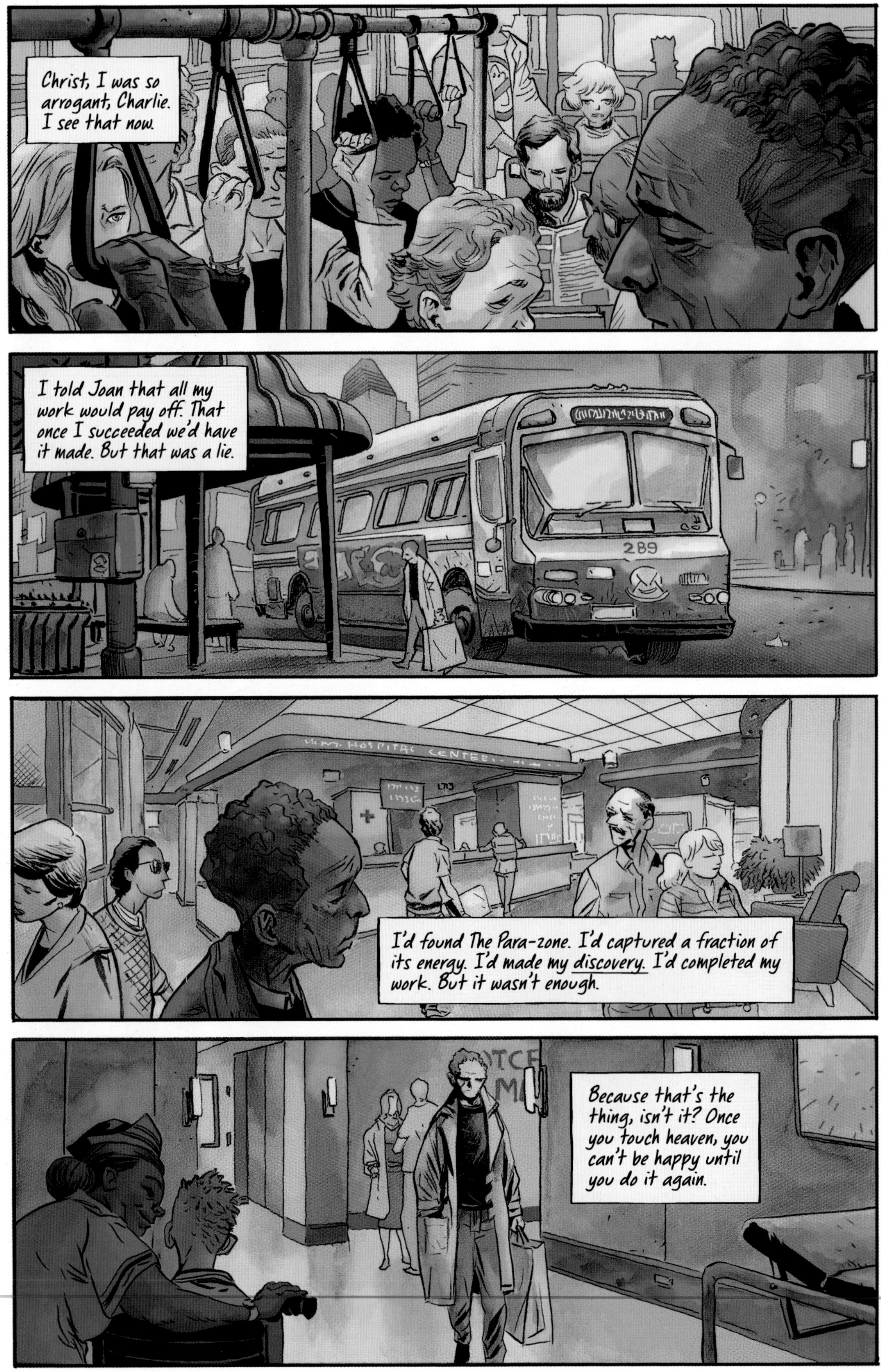
Christ, I was so arrogant, Charlie. I see that now.
I told Joan that all my work would pay off. That once I succeeded we'd have it made. But that was a lie.
289
I'd found The Para-zone. I'd captured a fraction of its energy. I'd made my discovery. I'd completed my work. But it wasn't enough.
Because that's the thing, isn't it? Once you touch heaven, you can't be happy until you do it again.

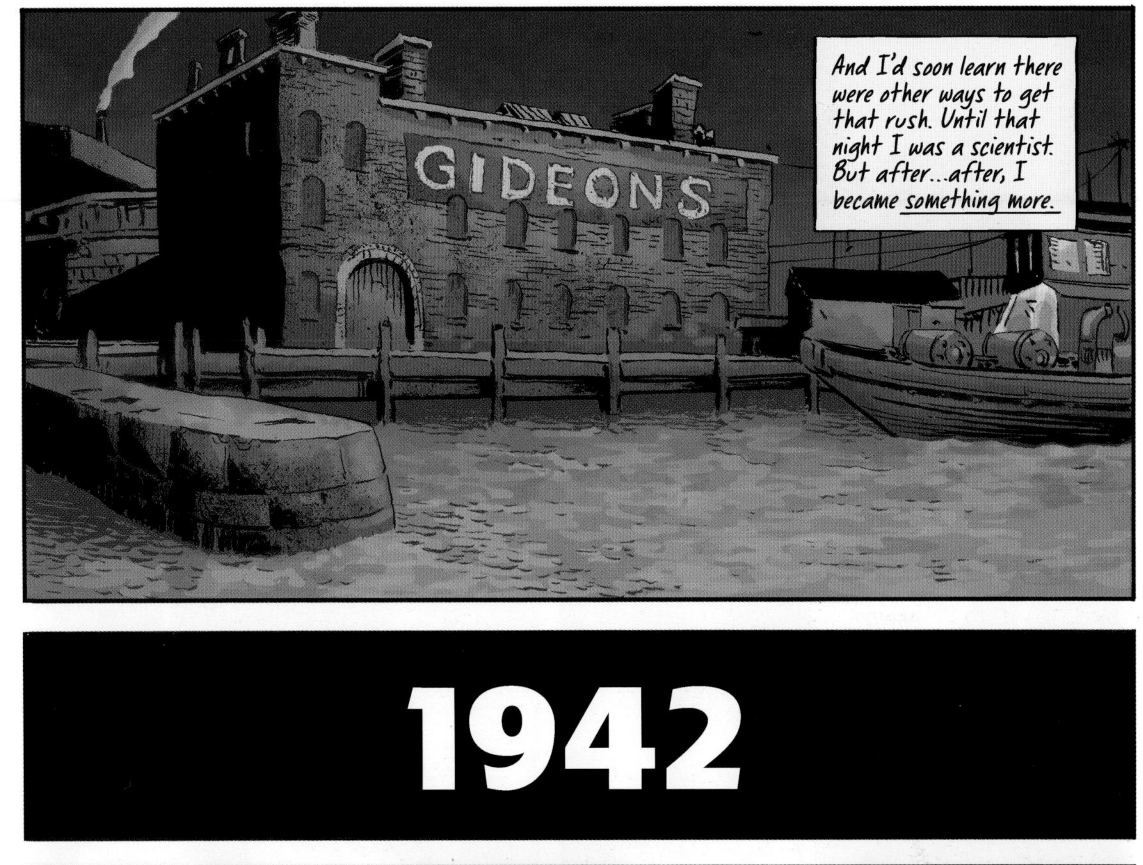
And I'd soon learn there were other ways to get that rush. Until that night I was a scientist. But after...after, I became something more.
GIDEONS

1942

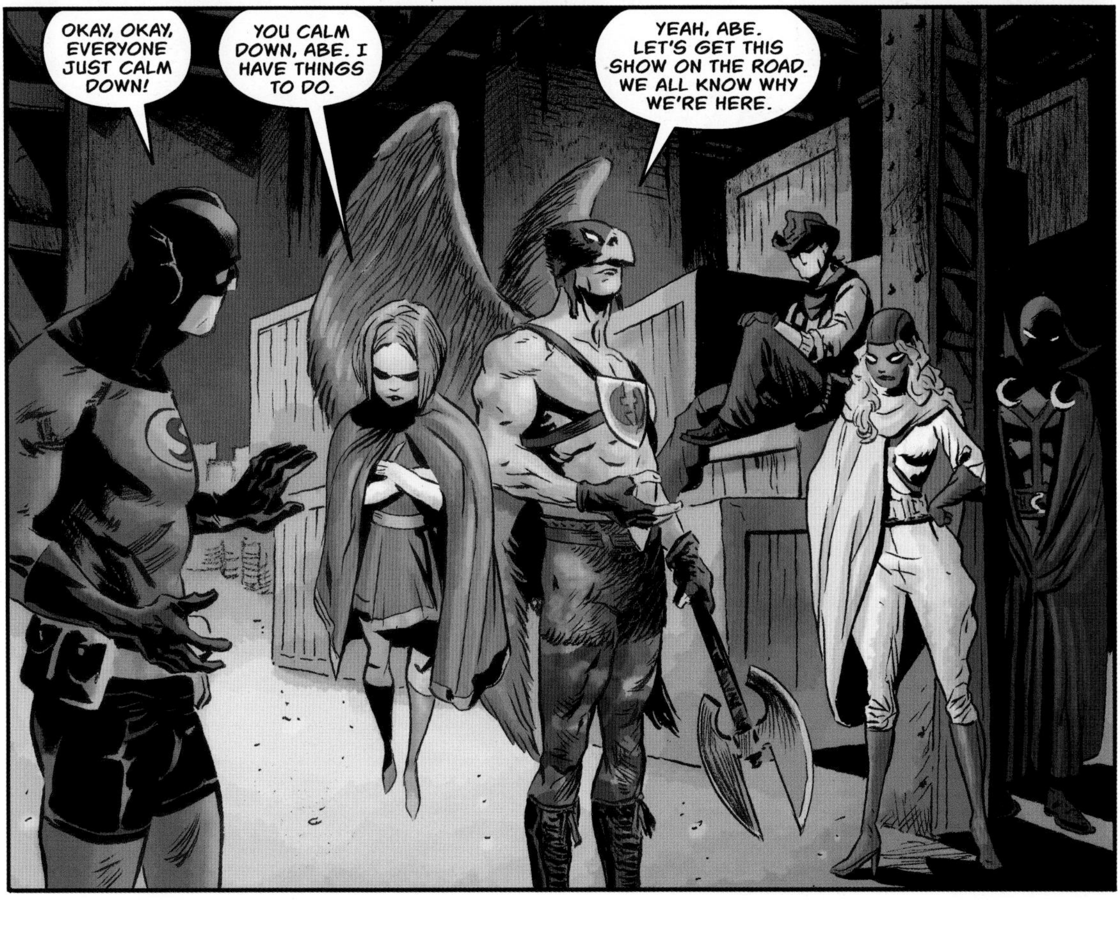
OKAY, OKAY, EVERYONE JUST CALM DOWN!
YOU CALM DOWN, ABE. I HAVE THINGS TO DO.
YEAH, ABE. LET'S GET THIS SHOW ON THE ROAD. WE ALL KNOW WHY WE'RE HERE.

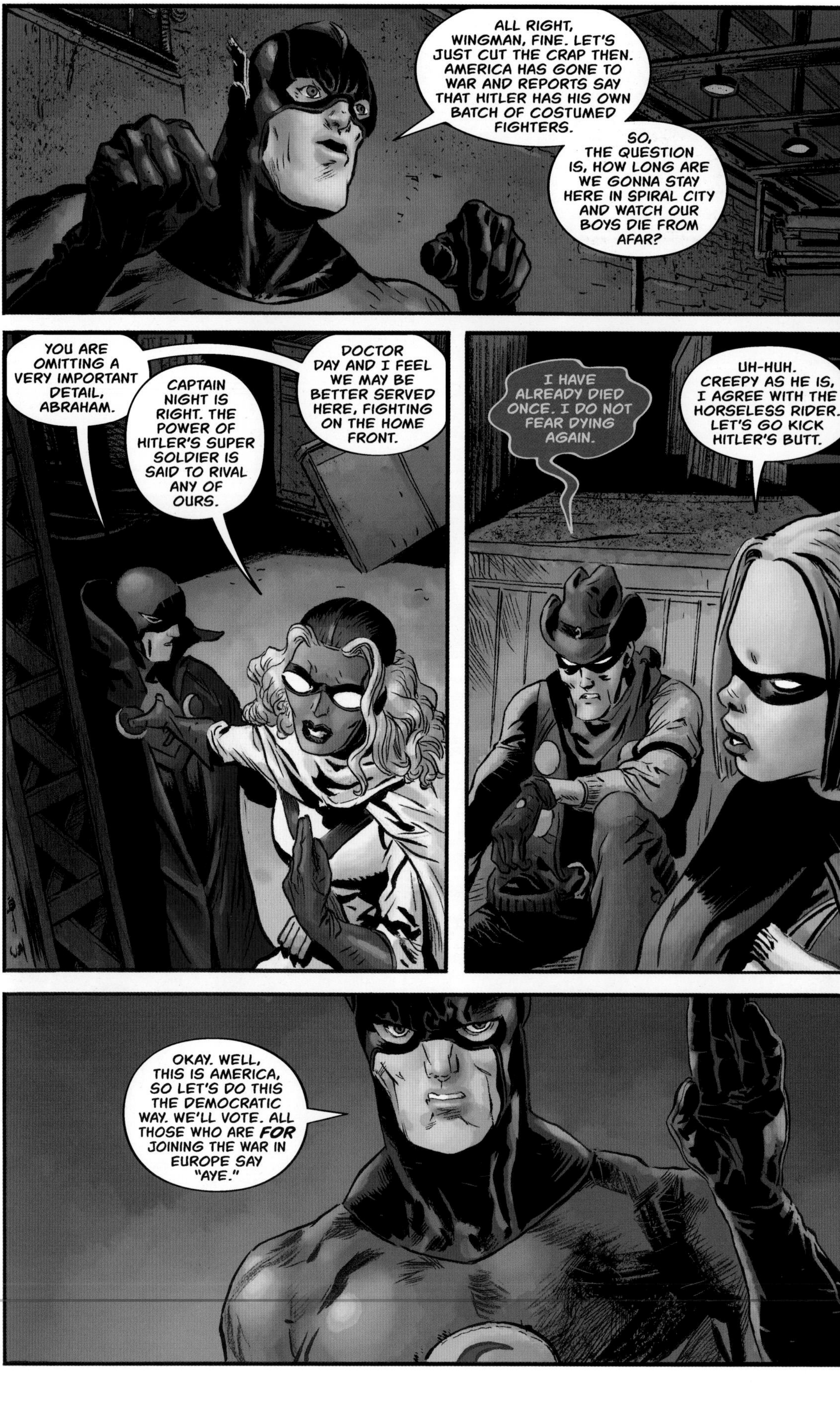
ALL RIGHT, WINGMAN, FINE. LET'S JUST CUT THE CRAP THEN. AMERICA HAS GONE TO WAR AND REPORTS SAY THAT HITLER HAS HIS OWN BATCH OF COSTUMED FIGHTERS.
SO, THE QUESTION IS, HOW LONG ARE WE GONNA STAY HERE IN SPIRAL CITY AND WATCH OUR BOYS DIE FROM AFAR?
YOU ARE OMITTING A VERY IMPORTANT DETAIL, ABRAHAM.
CAPTAIN NIGHT IS RIGHT. THE POWER OF HITLER'S SUPER SOLDIER IS SAID TO RIVAL ANY OF OURS.
DOCTOR DAY AND I FEEL WE MAY BE BETTER SERVED HERE, FIGHTING ON THE HOME FRONT.
I HAVE ALREADY DIED ONCE. I DO NOT FEAR DYING AGAIN.
UH-HUH. CREEPY AS HE IS, I AGREE WITH THE HORSELESS RIDER. LET'S GO KICK HITLER'S BUTT.
OKAY. WELL, THIS IS AMERICA, SO LET'S DO THIS THE DEMOCRATIC WAY. WE'LL VOTE. ALL THOSE WHO ARE FOR JOINING THE WAR IN EUROPE SAY "AYE."

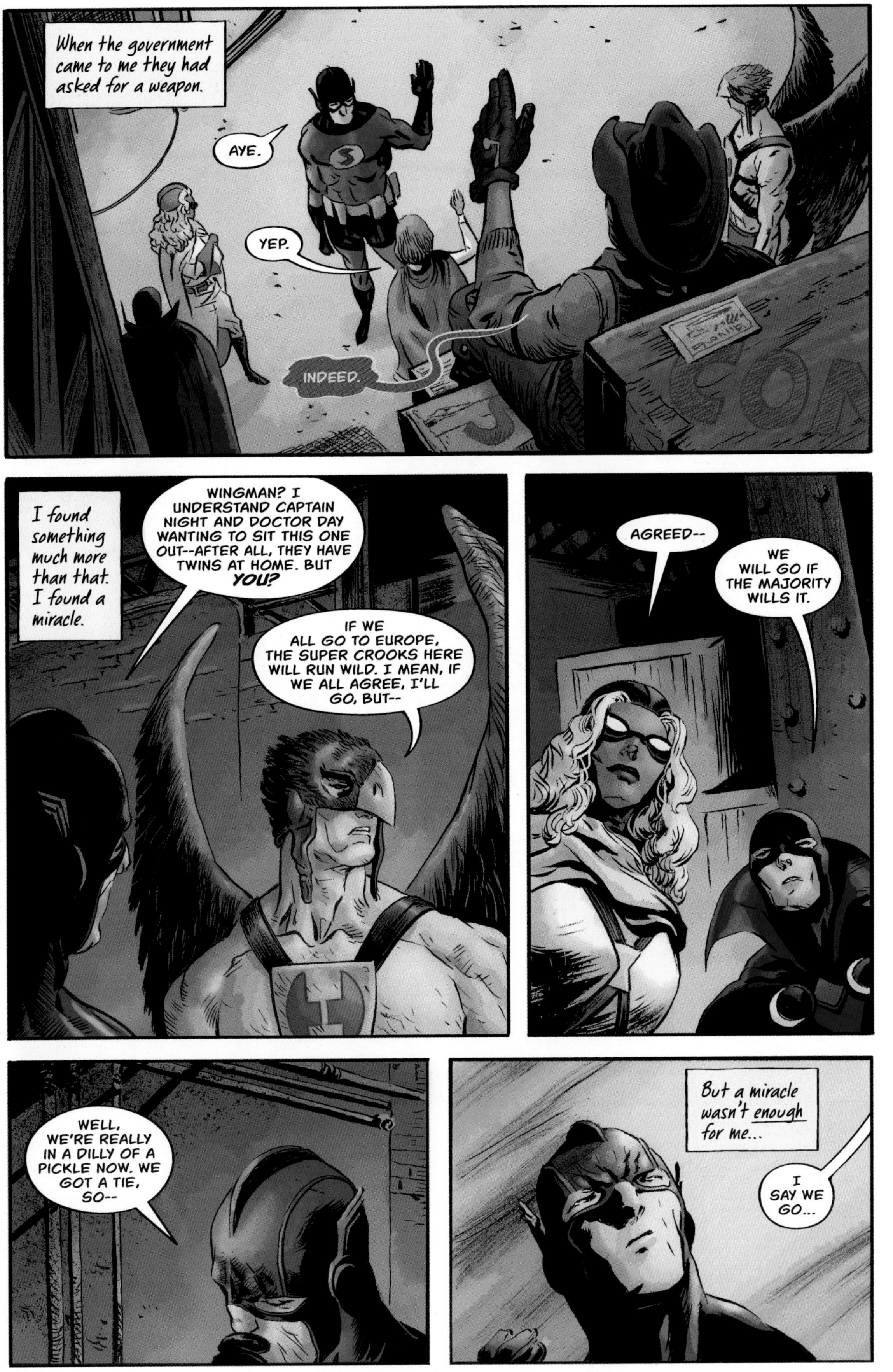
When the government came to me they had asked for a weapon.
AYE.
YEP.
INDEED.
I found something much more than that. I found a miracle.
WINGMAN? I UNDERSTAND CAPTAIN NIGHT AND DOCTOR DAY WANTING TO SIT THIS ONE OUT--AFTER ALL, THEY HAVE TWINS AT HOME. BUT YOU?
IF WE ALL GO TO EUROPE, THE SUPER CROOKS HERE WILL RUN WILD. I MEAN, IF WE ALL AGREE, I'LL GO, BUT--
AGREED--
WE WILL GO IF THE MAJORITY WILLS IT.
WELL, WE'RE REALLY IN A DILLY OF A PICKLE NOW. WE GOT A TIE, SO--
But a miracle wasn't enough for me...
I SAY WE GO...

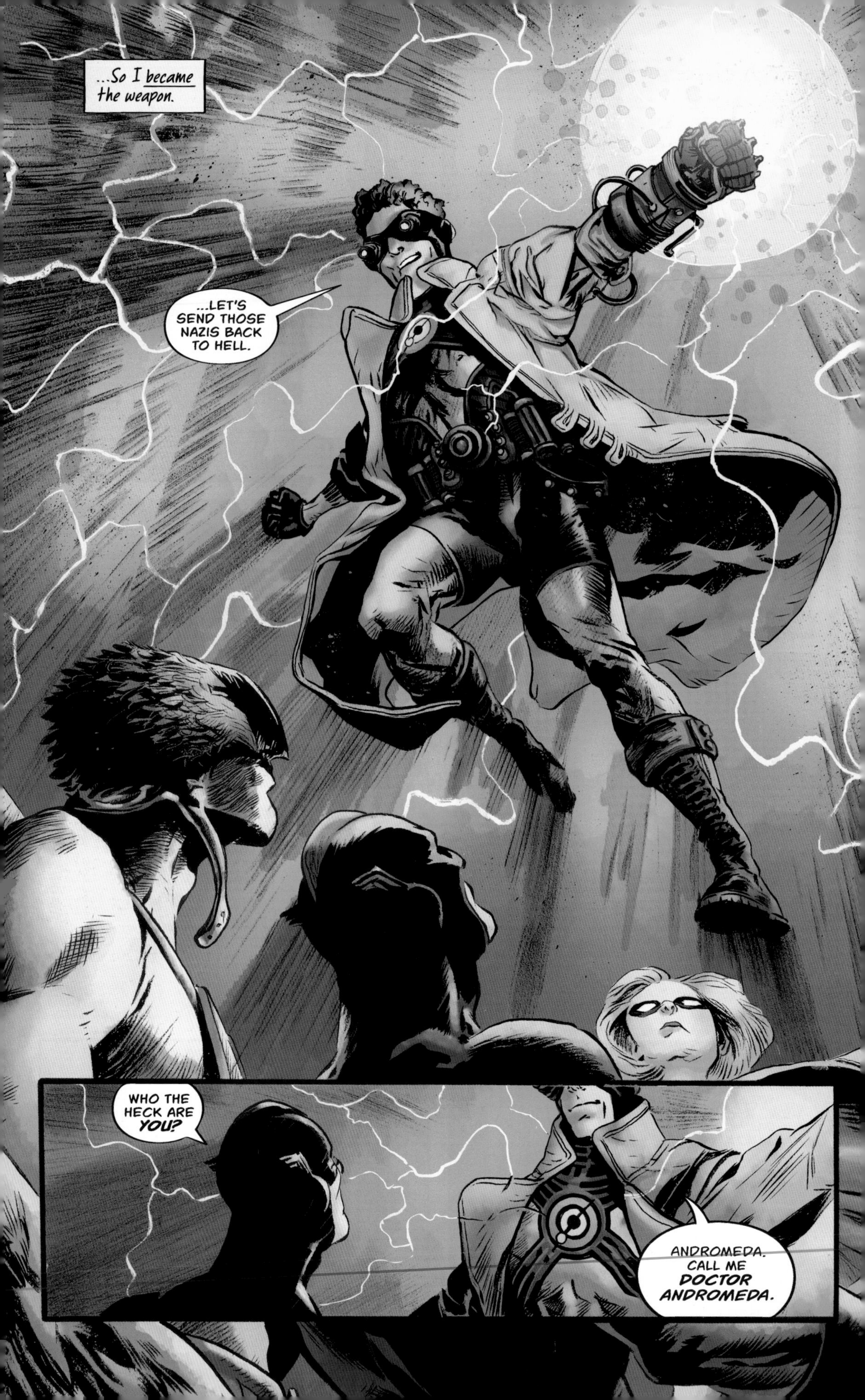
...So I became the weapon.
...LET'S SEND THOSE NAZIS BACK TO HELL.
WHO THE HECK ARE YOU?
ANDROMEDA. CALL ME DOCTOR ANDROMEDA.

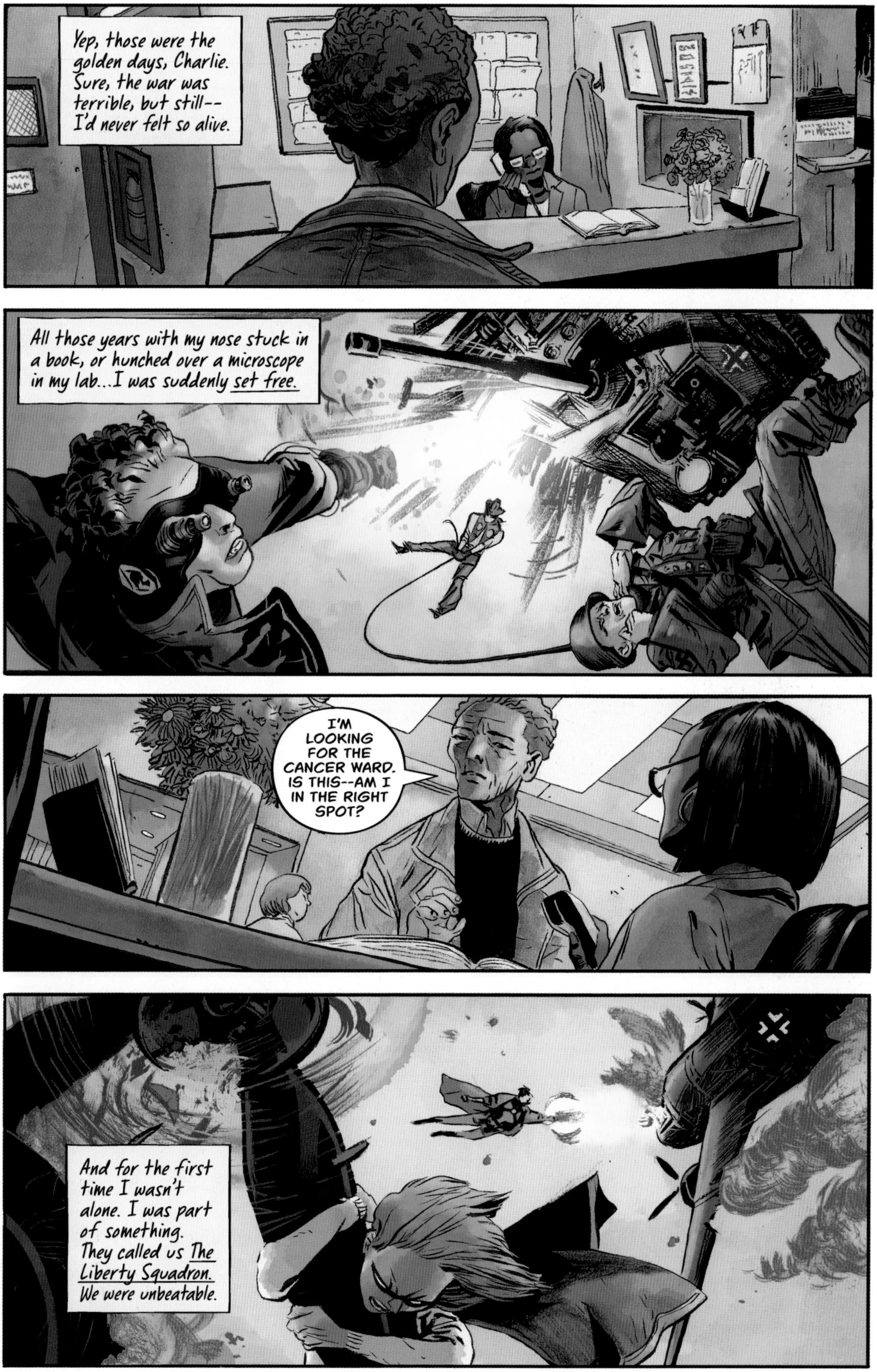

Yep, those were the golden days, Charlie. Sure, the war was terrible, but still-- I'd never felt so alive.
All those years with my nose stuck in a book, or hunched over a microscope in my lab...I was suddenly set free.
I'M LOOKING FOR THE CANCER WARD. IS THIS--AM I IN THE RIGHT SPOT?
And for the first time I wasn't alone. I was part of something. They called us The Liberty Squadron. We were unbeatable.

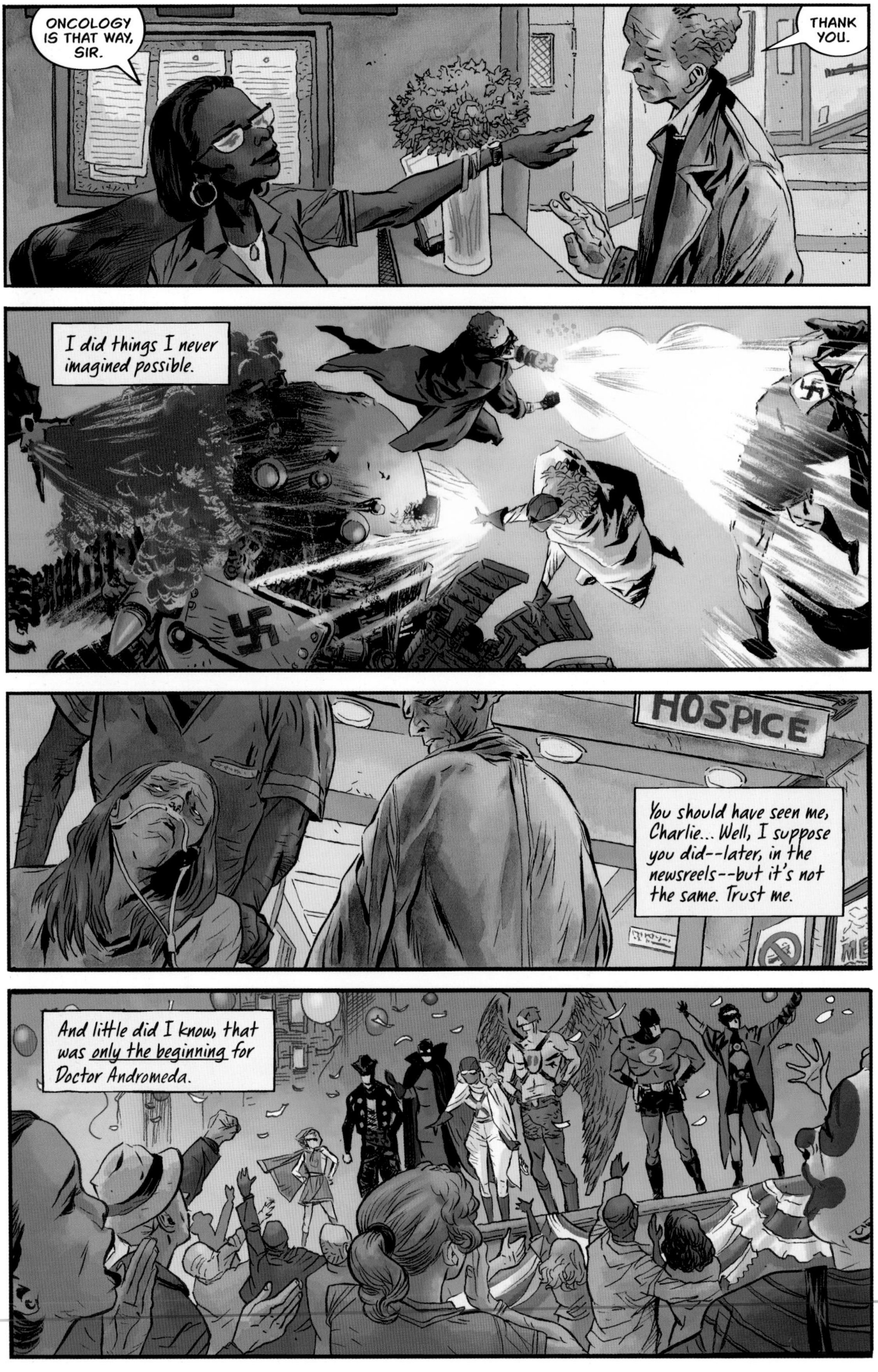
ONCOLOGY IS THAT WAY, SIR.
THANK YOU.
I did things I never imagined possible.
HOSPICE
You should have seen me, Charlie... Well, I suppose you did--later, in the newsreels--but it's not the same. Trust me.
And little did I know, that was only the beginning for Doctor Andromeda.

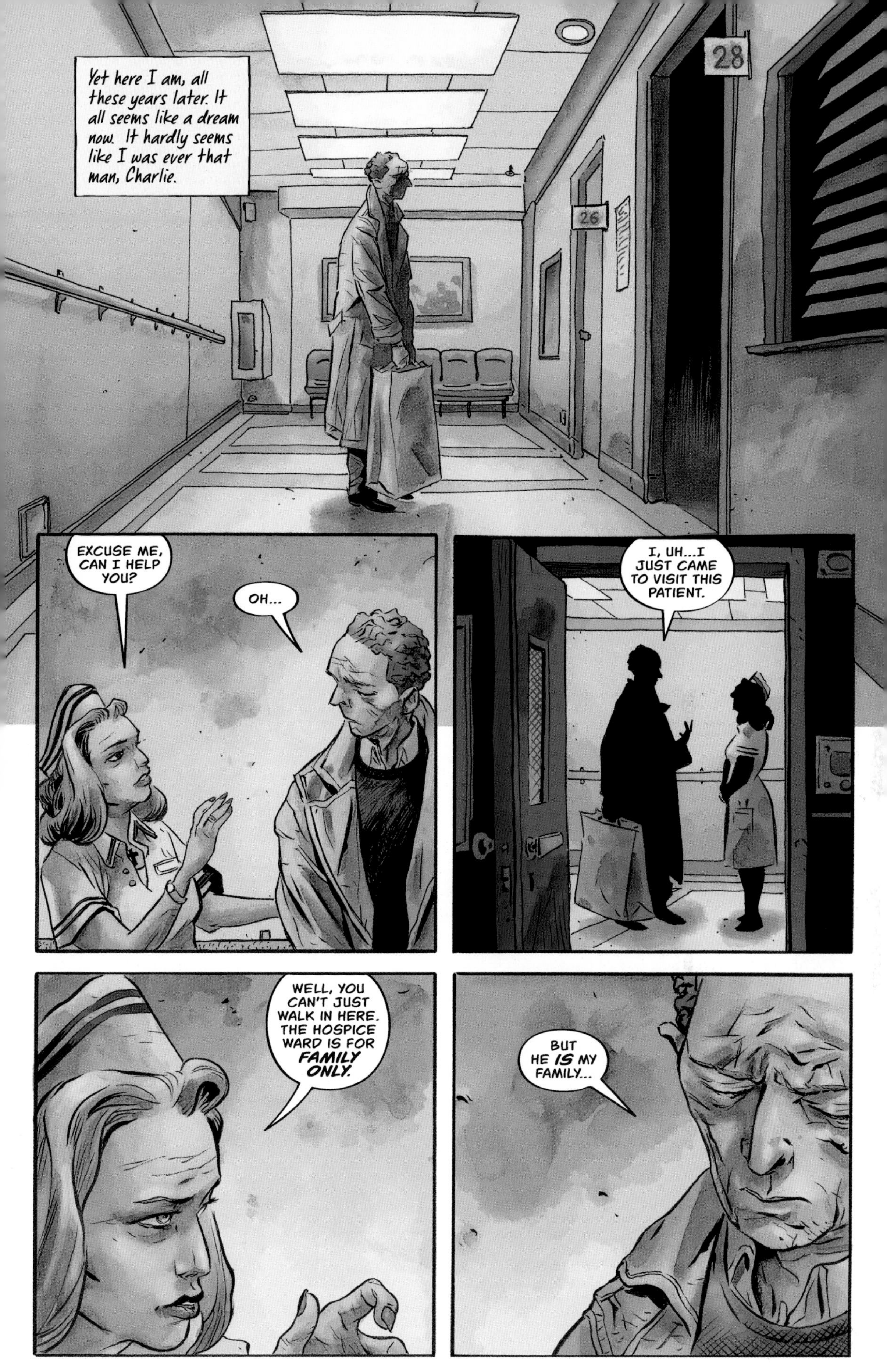
Yet here I am, all these years later. It all seems like a dream now. It hardly seems like I was ever that man, Charlie.
28
26
EXCUSE ME, CAN I HELP YOU?
OH...
I, UH...I JUST CAME TO VISIT THIS PATIENT.
WELL, YOU CAN'T JUST WALK IN HERE. THE HOSPICE WARD IS FOR FAMILY ONLY.
BUT HE IS MY FAMILY...

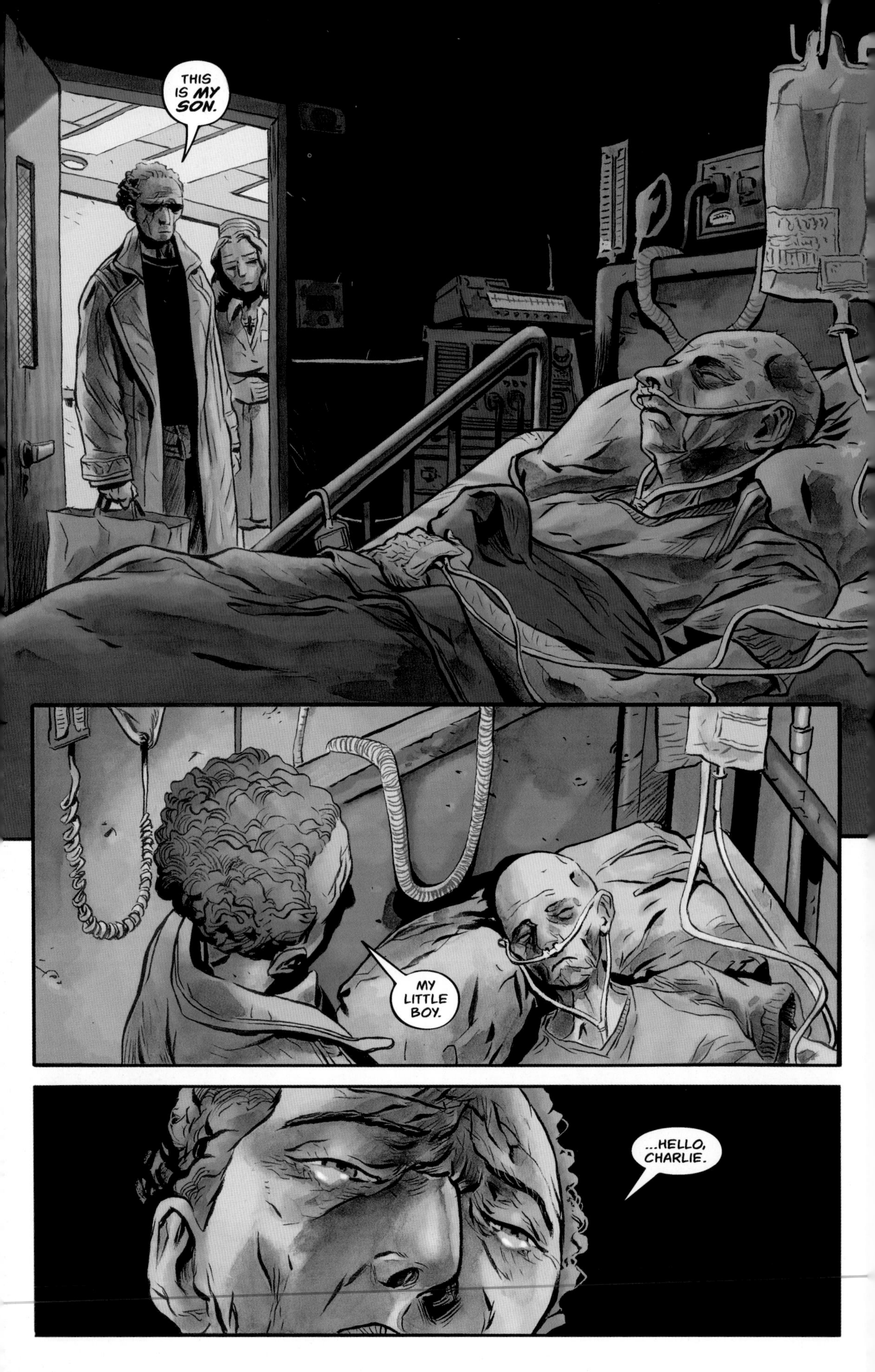
THIS IS MY SON.
MY LITTLE BOY.
...HELLO, CHARLIE.

CHAPTER TWO

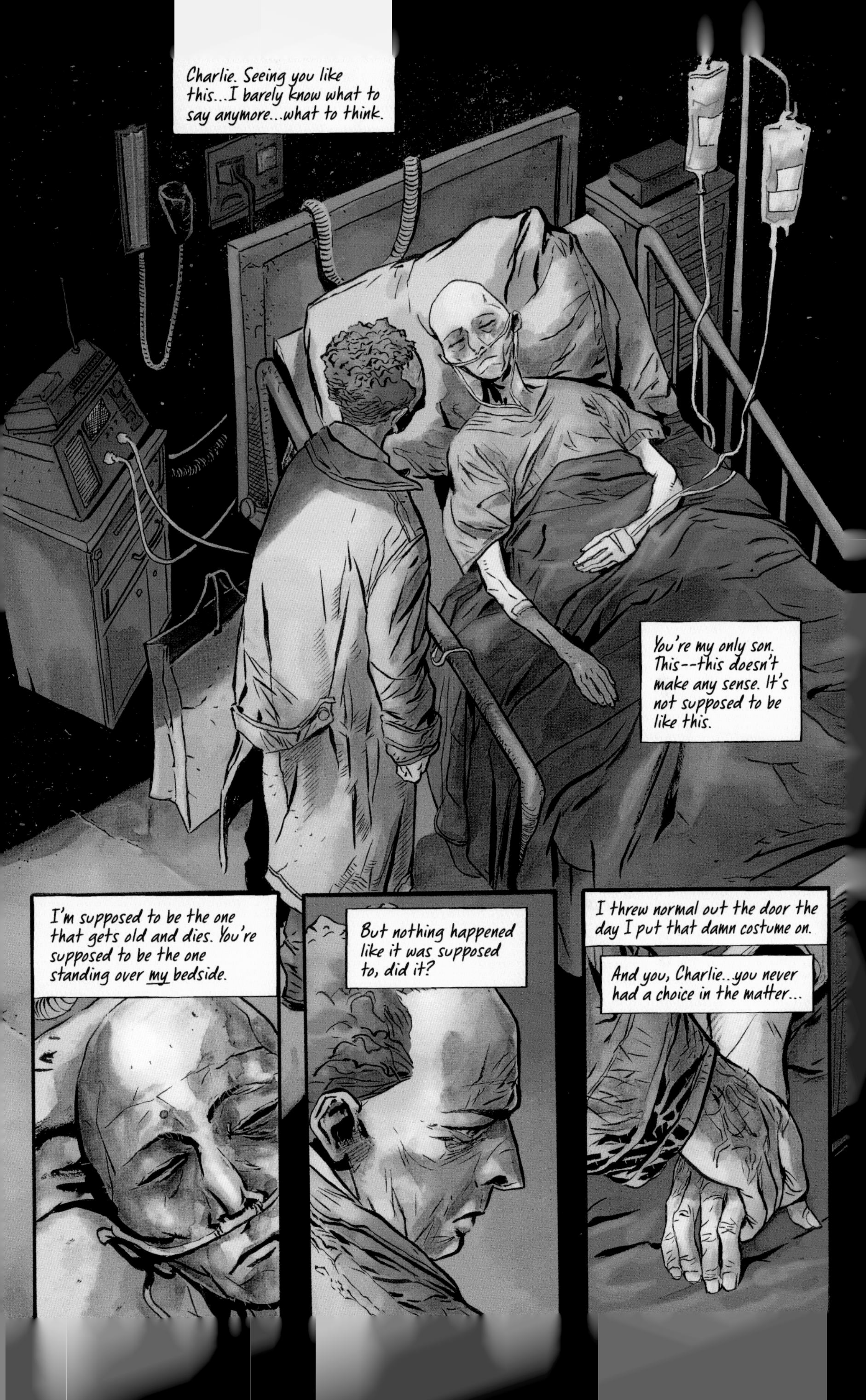
Charlie. Seeing you like this...I barely know what to say anymore...what to think.
You're my only son. This--this doesn't make any sense. It's not supposed to be like this.
I'm supposed to be the one that gets old and dies. You're supposed to be the one standing over my bedside.
But nothing happened like it was supposed to, did it?
I threw normal out the door the day I put that damn costume on.
And you, Charlie...you never had a choice in the matter...

1951

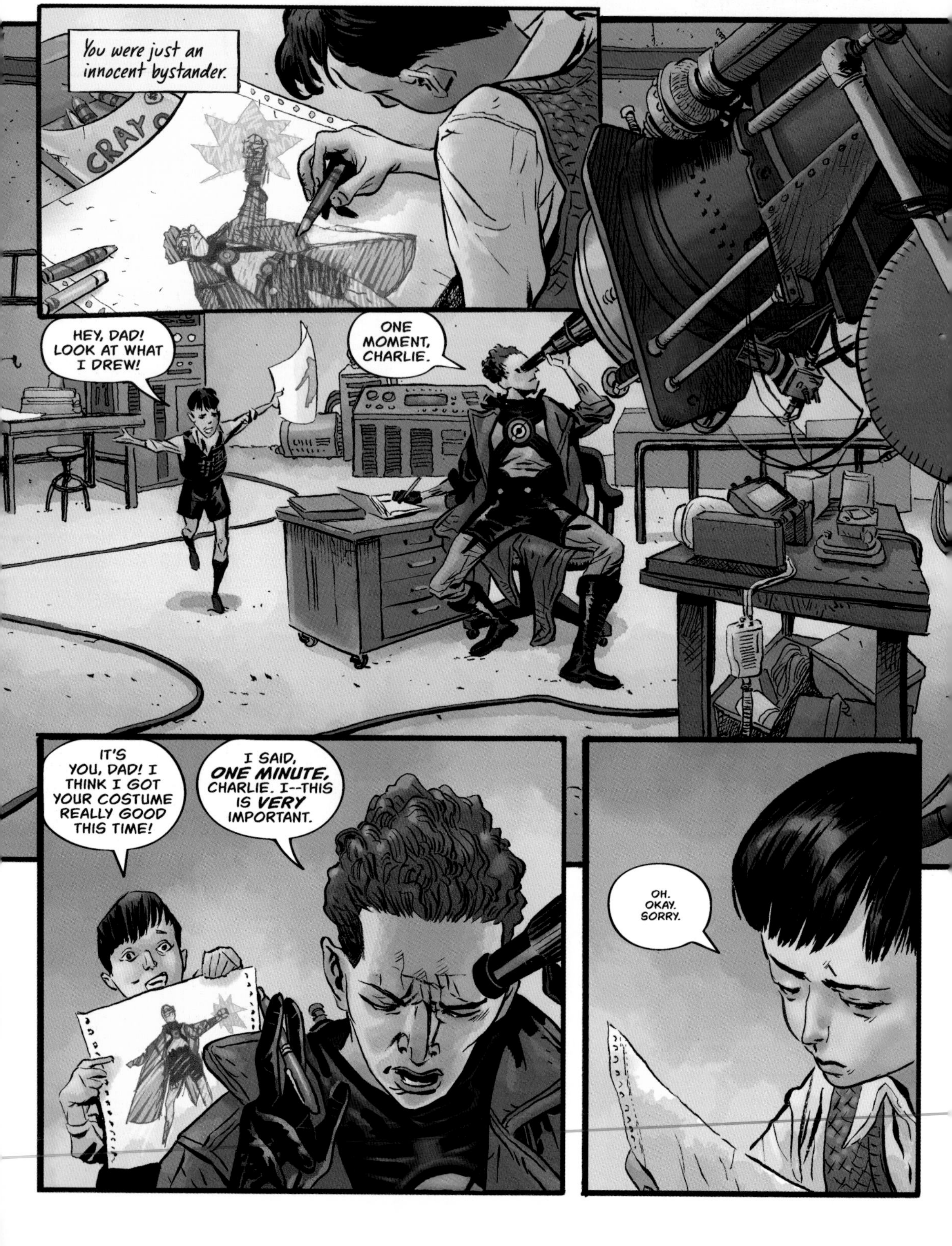
You were just an innocent bystander.
HEY, DAD! LOOK AT WHAT I DREW!
ONE MOMENT, CHARLIE.
IT'S YOU, DAD! I THINK I GOT YOUR COSTUME REALLY GOOD THIS TIME!
I SAID, ***ONE MINUTE,*** CHARLIE. I--THIS IS ***VERY*** IMPORTANT.
OH. OKAY. SORRY.

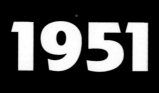

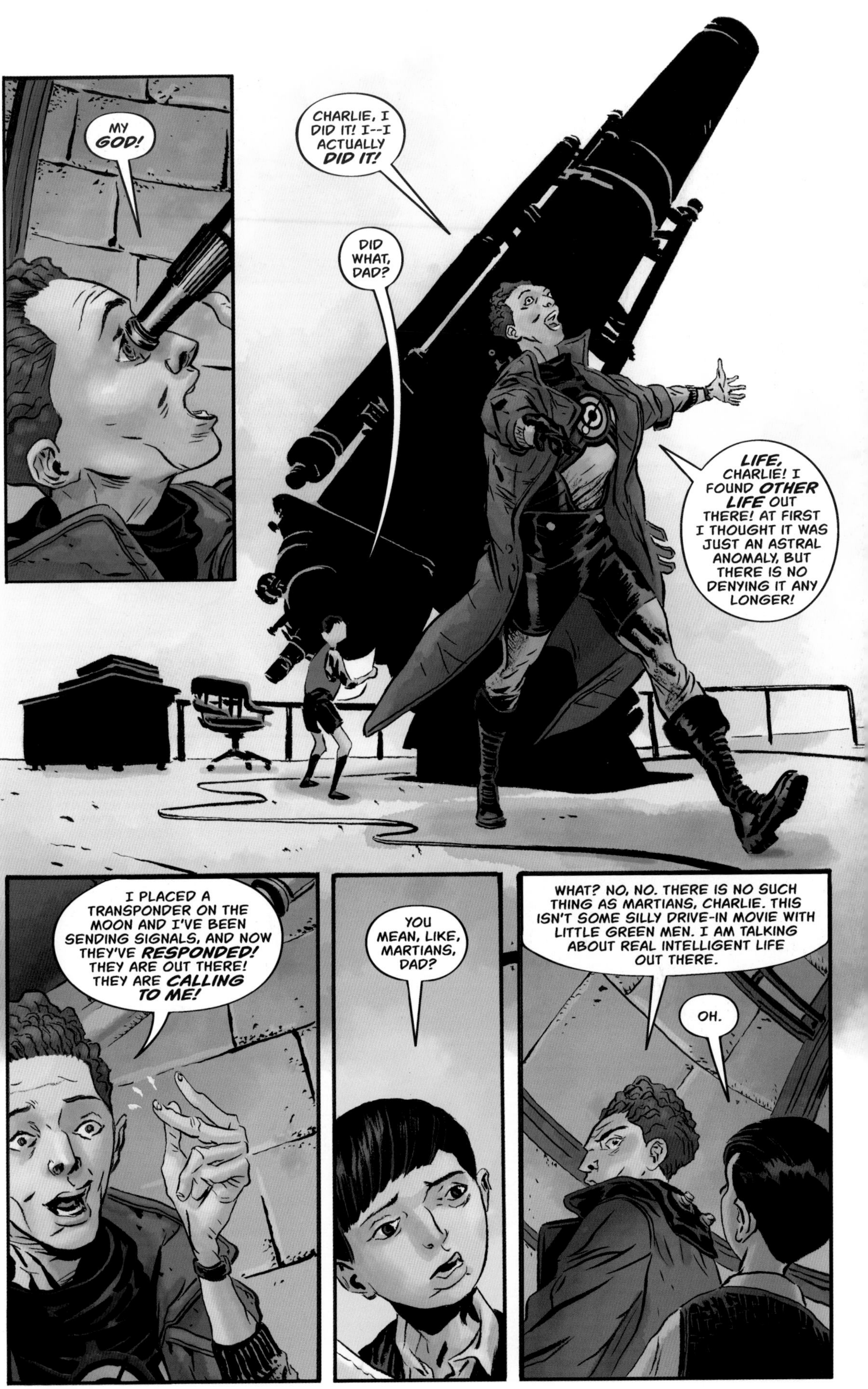
MY GOD!
CHARLIE, I DID IT! I--I ACTUALLY DID IT!
DID WHAT, DAD?
LIFE, CHARLIE! I FOUND OTHER LIFE OUT THERE! AT FIRST I THOUGHT IT WAS JUST AN ASTRAL ANOMALY, BUT THERE IS NO DENYING IT ANY LONGER!
I PLACED A TRANSPONDER ON THE MOON AND I'VE BEEN SENDING SIGNALS, AND NOW THEY'VE RESPONDED! THEY ARE OUT THERE! THEY ARE CALLING TO ME!
YOU MEAN, LIKE, MARTIANS, DAD?
WHAT? NO, NO. THERE IS NO SUCH THING AS MARTIANS, CHARLIE. THIS ISN'T SOME SILLY DRIVE-IN MOVIE WITH LITTLE GREEN MEN. I AM TALKING ABOUT REAL INTELLIGENT LIFE OUT THERE.
OH.

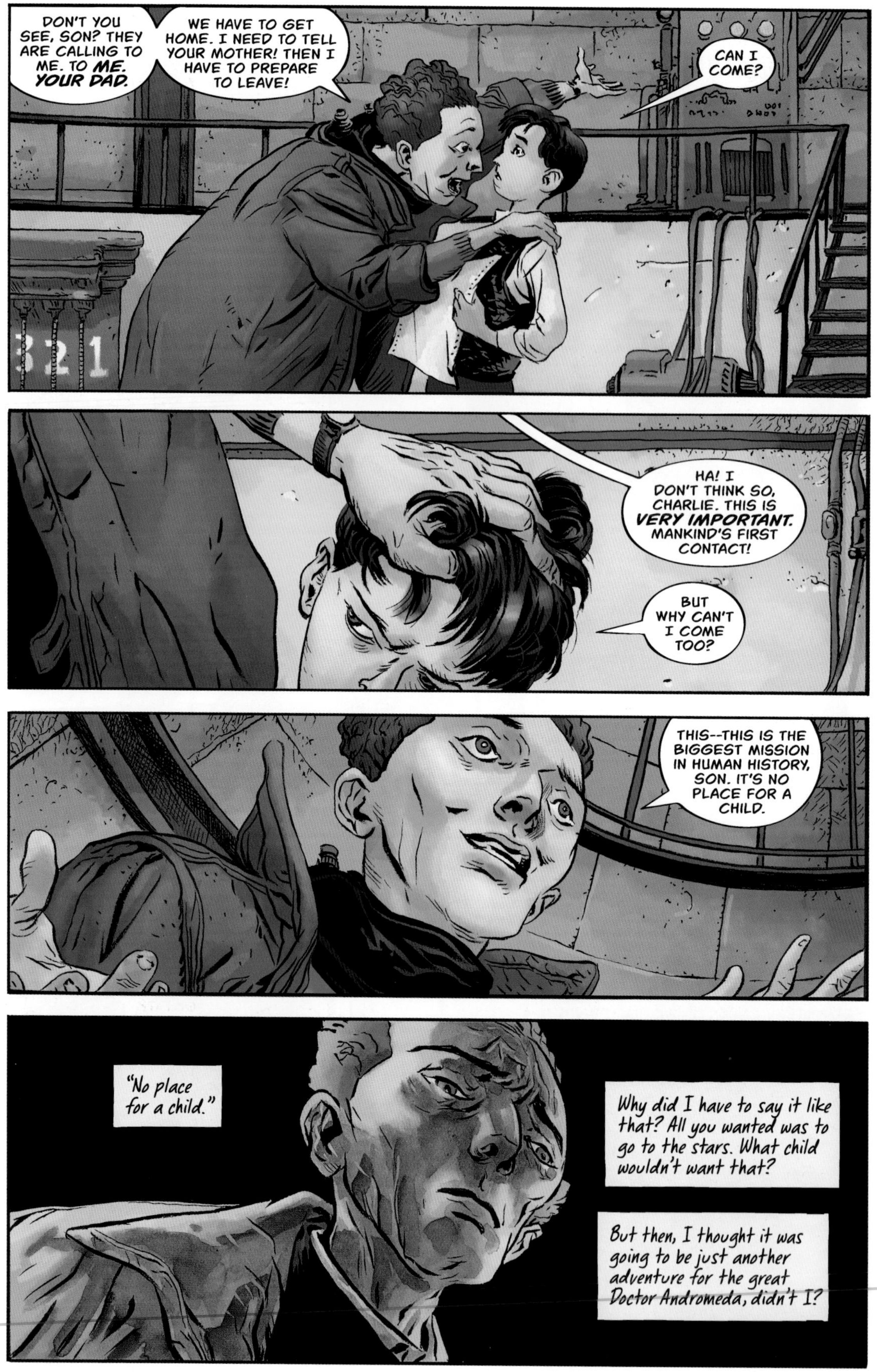
DON'T YOU SEE, SON? THEY ARE CALLING TO ME. TO **ME. YOUR DAD.**
WE HAVE TO GET HOME. I NEED TO TELL YOUR MOTHER! THEN I HAVE TO PREPARE TO LEAVE!
CAN I COME?
321
HA! I DON'T THINK SO, CHARLIE. THIS IS **VERY IMPORTANT.** MANKIND'S FIRST CONTACT!
BUT WHY CAN'T I COME TOO?
THIS--THIS IS THE BIGGEST MISSION IN HUMAN HISTORY, SON. IT'S NO PLACE FOR A CHILD.
"No place for a child."
Why did I have to say it like that? All you wanted was to go to the stars. What child wouldn't want that?
But then, I thought it was going to be just another adventure for the great Doctor Andromeda, didn't I?

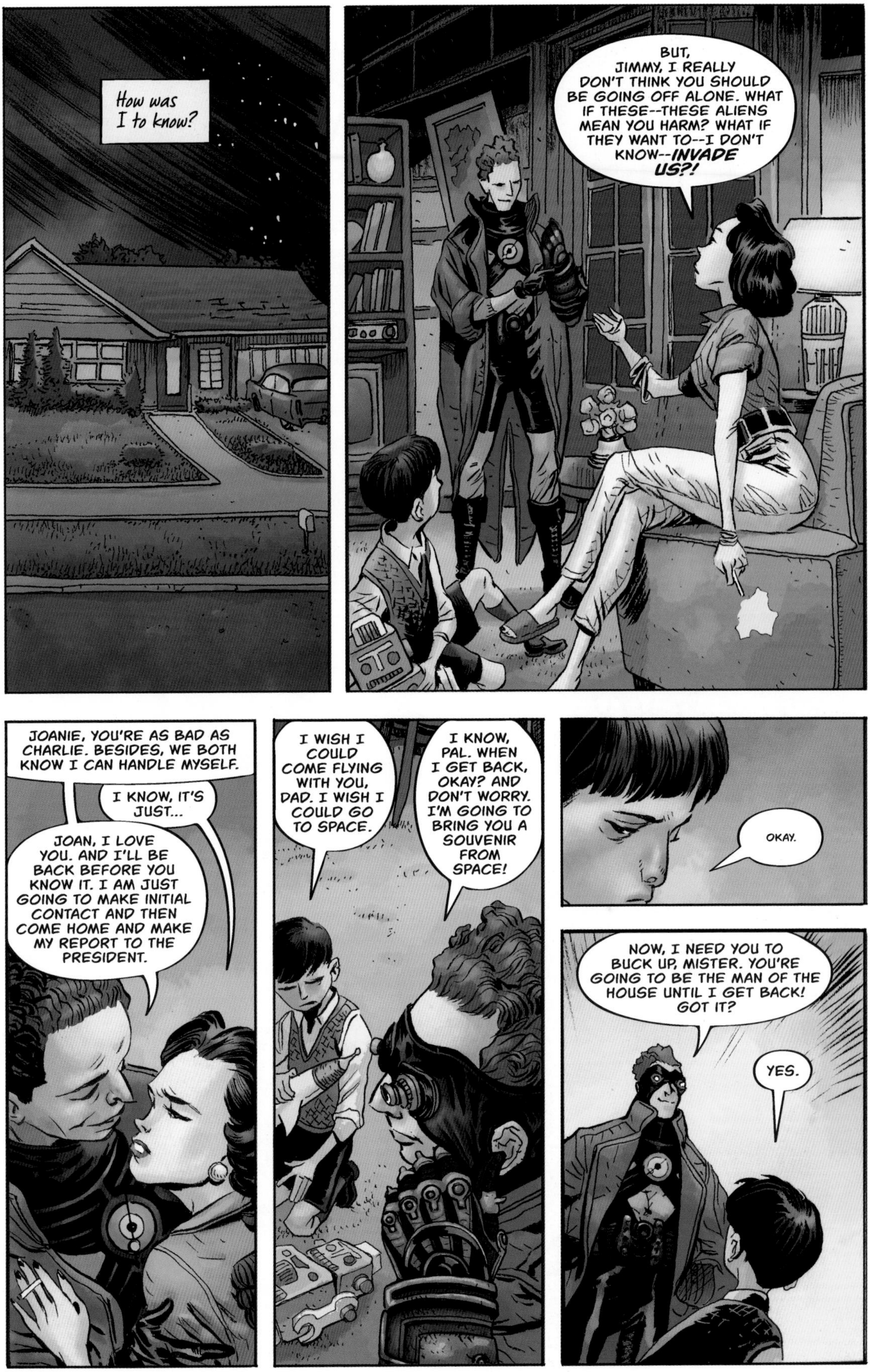
How was I to know?
BUT, JIMMY, I REALLY DON'T THINK YOU SHOULD BE GOING OFF ALONE. WHAT IF THESE--THESE ALIENS MEAN YOU HARM? WHAT IF THEY WANT TO--I DON'T KNOW--INVADE US?!
JOANIE, YOU'RE AS BAD AS CHARLIE. BESIDES, WE BOTH KNOW I CAN HANDLE MYSELF.
I KNOW, IT'S JUST...
JOAN, I LOVE YOU. AND I'LL BE BACK BEFORE YOU KNOW IT. I AM JUST GOING TO MAKE INITIAL CONTACT AND THEN COME HOME AND MAKE MY REPORT TO THE PRESIDENT.
I WISH I COULD COME FLYING WITH YOU, DAD. I WISH I COULD GO TO SPACE.
I KNOW, PAL. WHEN I GET BACK, OKAY? AND DON'T WORRY. I'M GOING TO BRING YOU A SOUVENIR FROM SPACE!
OKAY.
NOW, I NEED YOU TO BUCK UP, MISTER. YOU'RE GOING TO BE THE MAN OF THE HOUSE UNTIL I GET BACK! GOT IT?
YES.

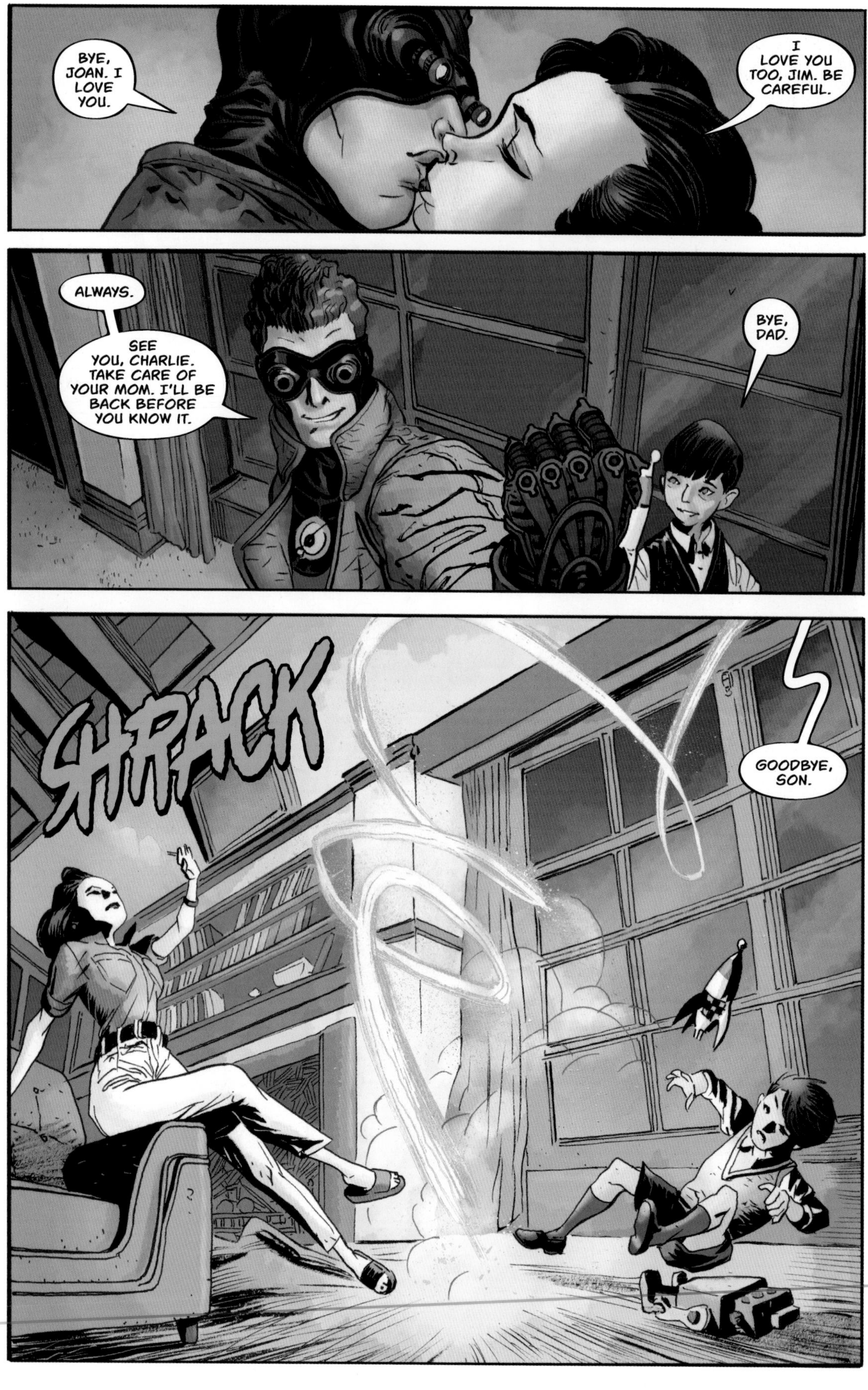
BYE, JOAN. I LOVE YOU.
I LOVE YOU TOO, JIM. BE CAREFUL.
ALWAYS.
SEE YOU, CHARLIE. TAKE CARE OF YOUR MOM. I'LL BE BACK BEFORE YOU KNOW IT.
BYE, DAD.
SHRACK
GOODBYE, SON.

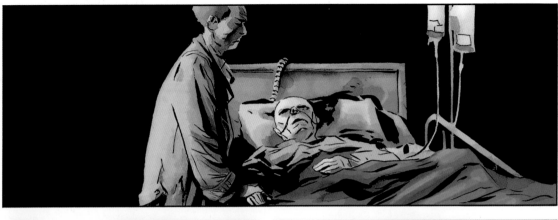

WHAT ARE YOU DOING IN HERE?

I, UH...

GET OUT!

OKAY, OKAY. I'M SORRY. I'LL GO.

NOW.

I AM. I JUST--FORGOT SOMETHING.

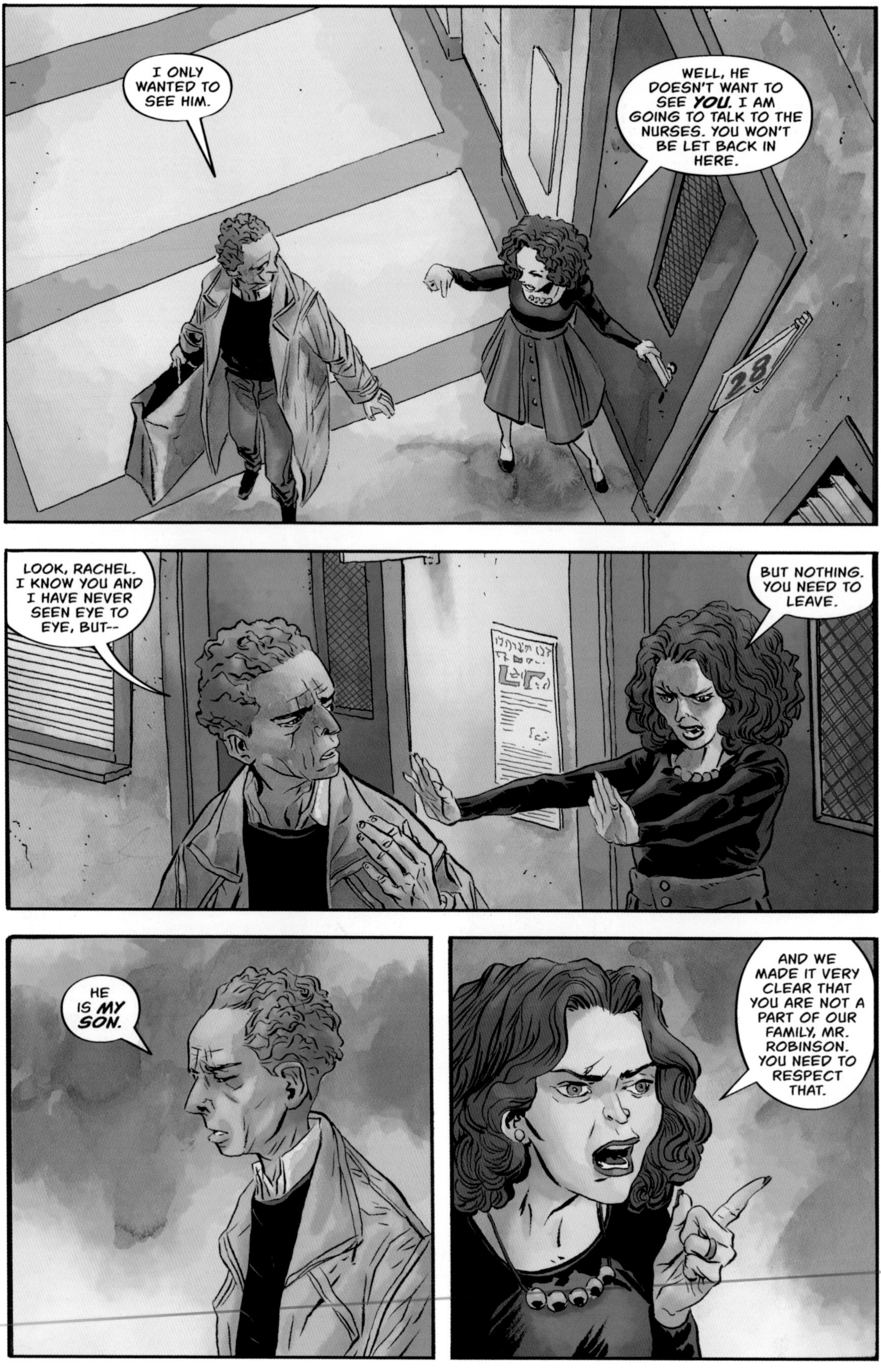
I ONLY WANTED TO SEE HIM.
WELL, HE DOESN'T WANT TO SEE YOU. I AM GOING TO TALK TO THE NURSES. YOU WON'T BE LET BACK IN HERE.
28
LOOK, RACHEL. I KNOW YOU AND I HAVE NEVER SEEN EYE TO EYE, BUT--
BUT NOTHING. YOU NEED TO LEAVE.
HE IS MY SON.
AND WE MADE IT VERY CLEAR THAT YOU ARE NOT A PART OF OUR FAMILY, MR. ROBINSON. YOU NEED TO RESPECT THAT.

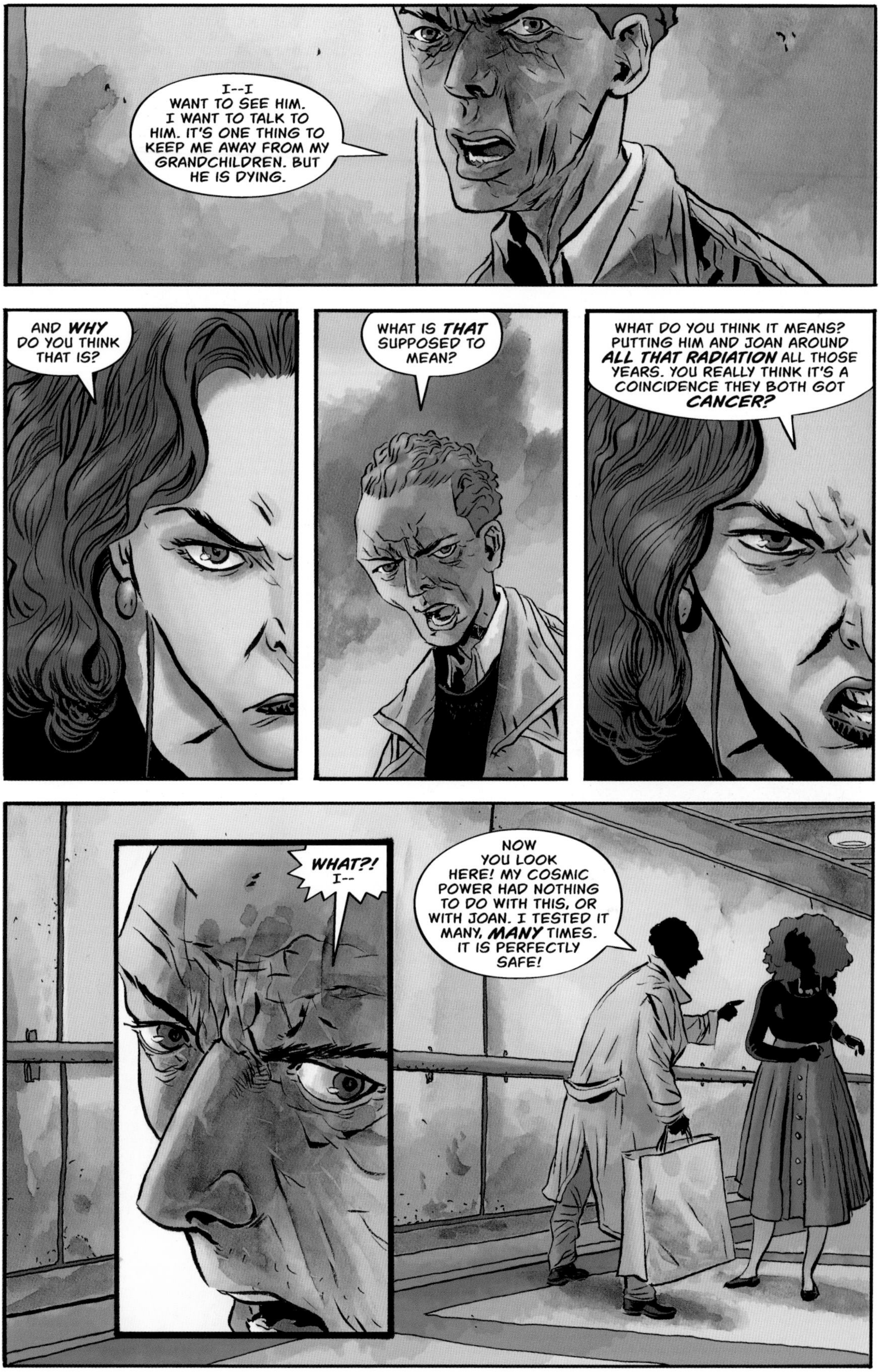
I--I WANT TO SEE HIM. I WANT TO TALK TO HIM. IT'S ONE THING TO KEEP ME AWAY FROM MY GRANDCHILDREN. BUT HE IS DYING.
AND ***WHY*** DO YOU THINK THAT IS?
WHAT IS ***THAT*** SUPPOSED TO MEAN?
WHAT DO YOU THINK IT MEANS? PUTTING HIM AND JOAN AROUND ***ALL THAT RADIATION*** ALL THOSE YEARS. YOU REALLY THINK IT'S A COINCIDENCE THEY BOTH GOT ***CANCER?***
WHAT?! I--
NOW YOU LOOK HERE! MY COSMIC POWER HAD NOTHING TO DO WITH THIS, OR WITH JOAN. I TESTED IT MANY, ***MANY*** TIMES. IT IS PERFECTLY SAFE!

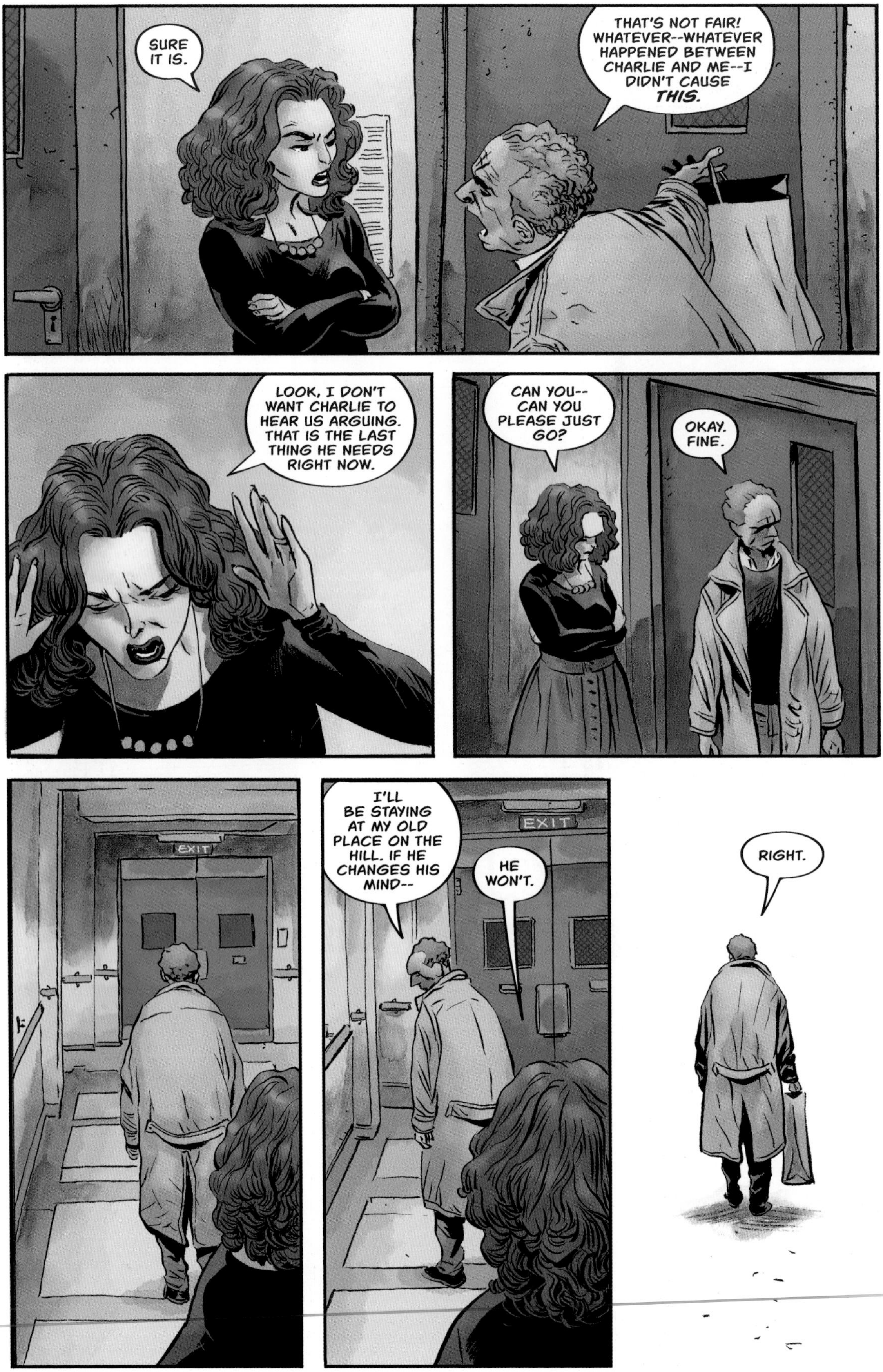
SURE IT IS.
THAT'S NOT FAIR! WHATEVER--WHATEVER HAPPENED BETWEEN CHARLIE AND ME--I DIDN'T CAUSE THIS.
LOOK, I DON'T WANT CHARLIE TO HEAR US ARGUING. THAT IS THE LAST THING HE NEEDS RIGHT NOW.
CAN YOU--CAN YOU PLEASE JUST GO?
OKAY. FINE.
EXIT
EXIT
I'LL BE STAYING AT MY OLD PLACE ON THE HILL. IF HE CHANGES HIS MIND--
HE WON'T.
RIGHT.

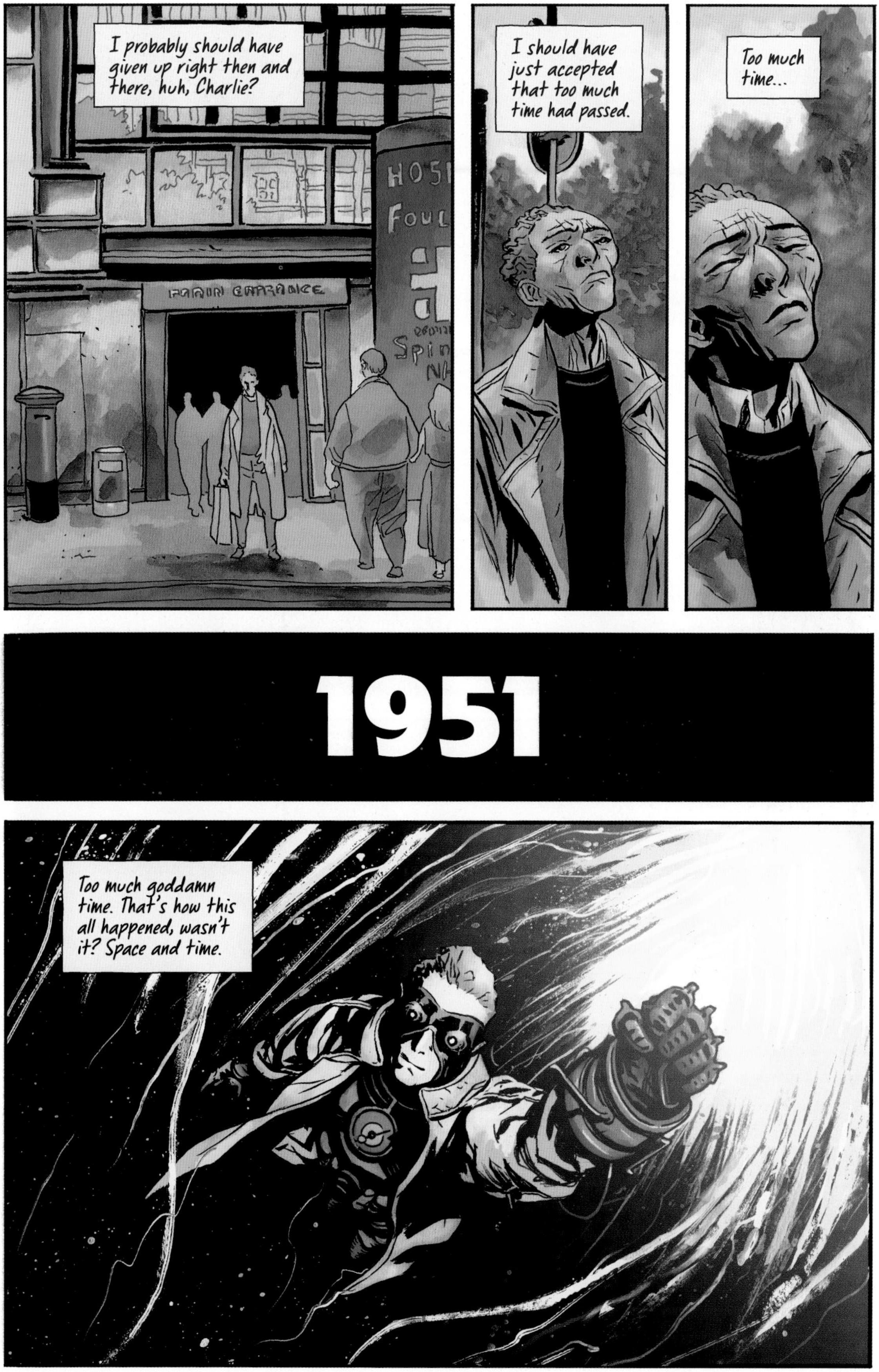
I probably should have given up right then and there, huh, Charlie?
I should have just accepted that too much time had passed.
Too much time...
1951
Too much goddamn time. That's how this all happened, wasn't it? Space and time.

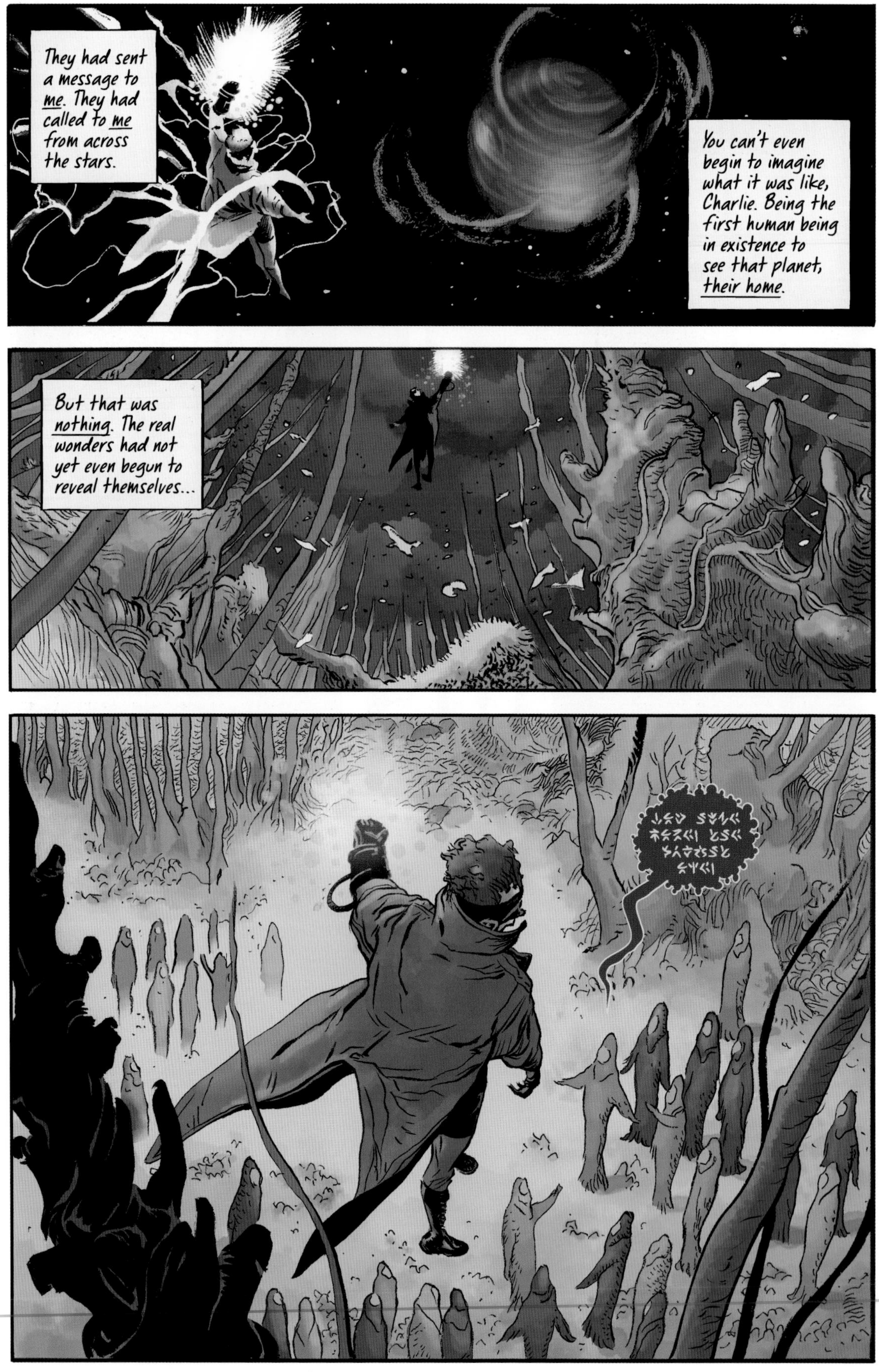
They had sent a message to me. They had called to me from across the stars.
You can't even begin to imagine what it was like, Charlie. Being the first human being in existence to see that planet, their home.
But that was nothing. The real wonders had not yet even begun to reveal themselves...

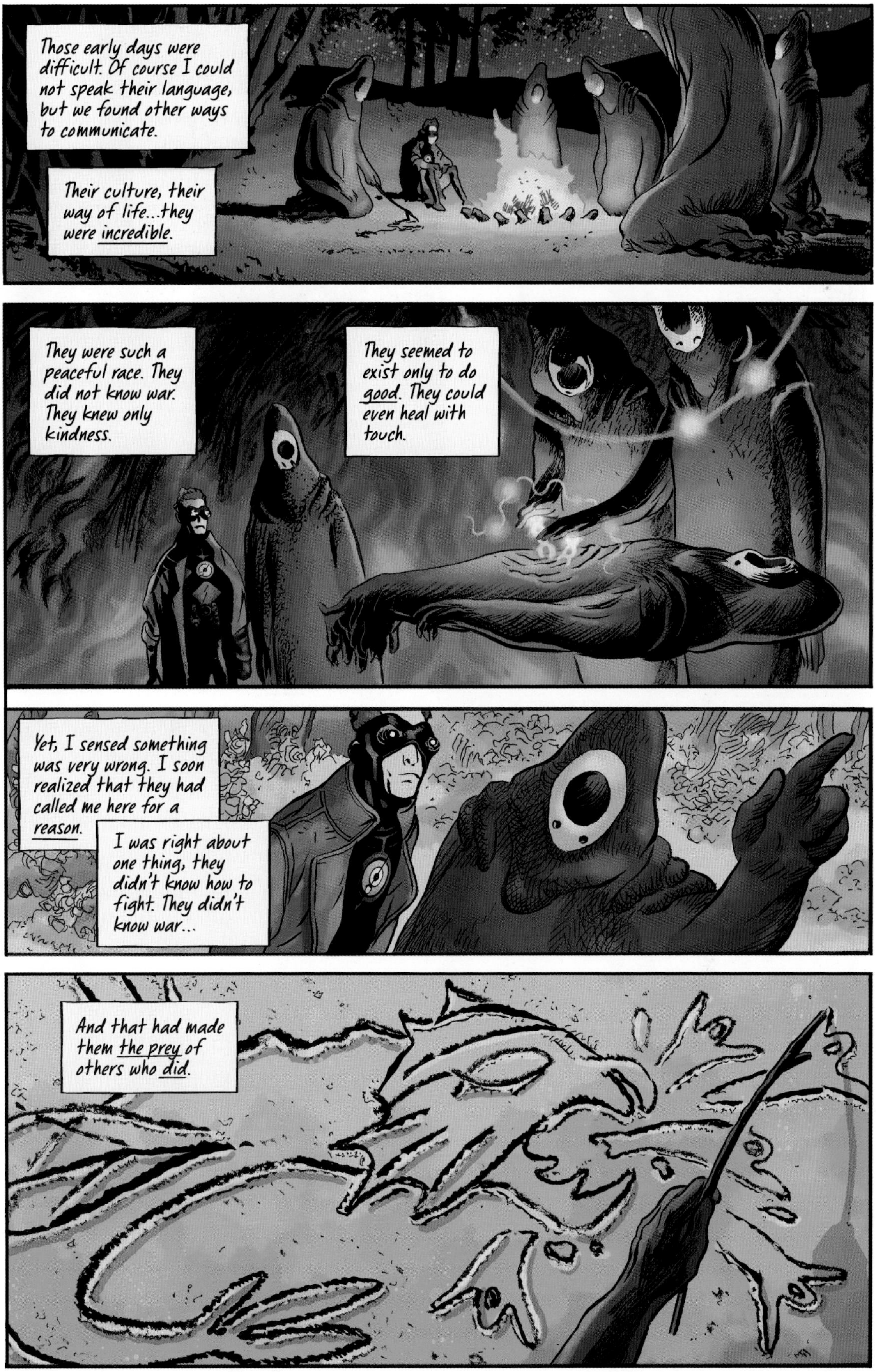
Those early days were difficult. Of course I could not speak their language, but we found other ways to communicate.
Their culture, their way of life...they were incredible.
They were such a peaceful race. They did not know war. They knew only kindness.
They seemed to exist only to do good. They could even heal with touch.
Yet, I sensed something was very wrong. I soon realized that they had called me here for a reason.
I was right about one thing, they didn't know how to fight. They didn't know war...
And that had made them the prey of others who did.

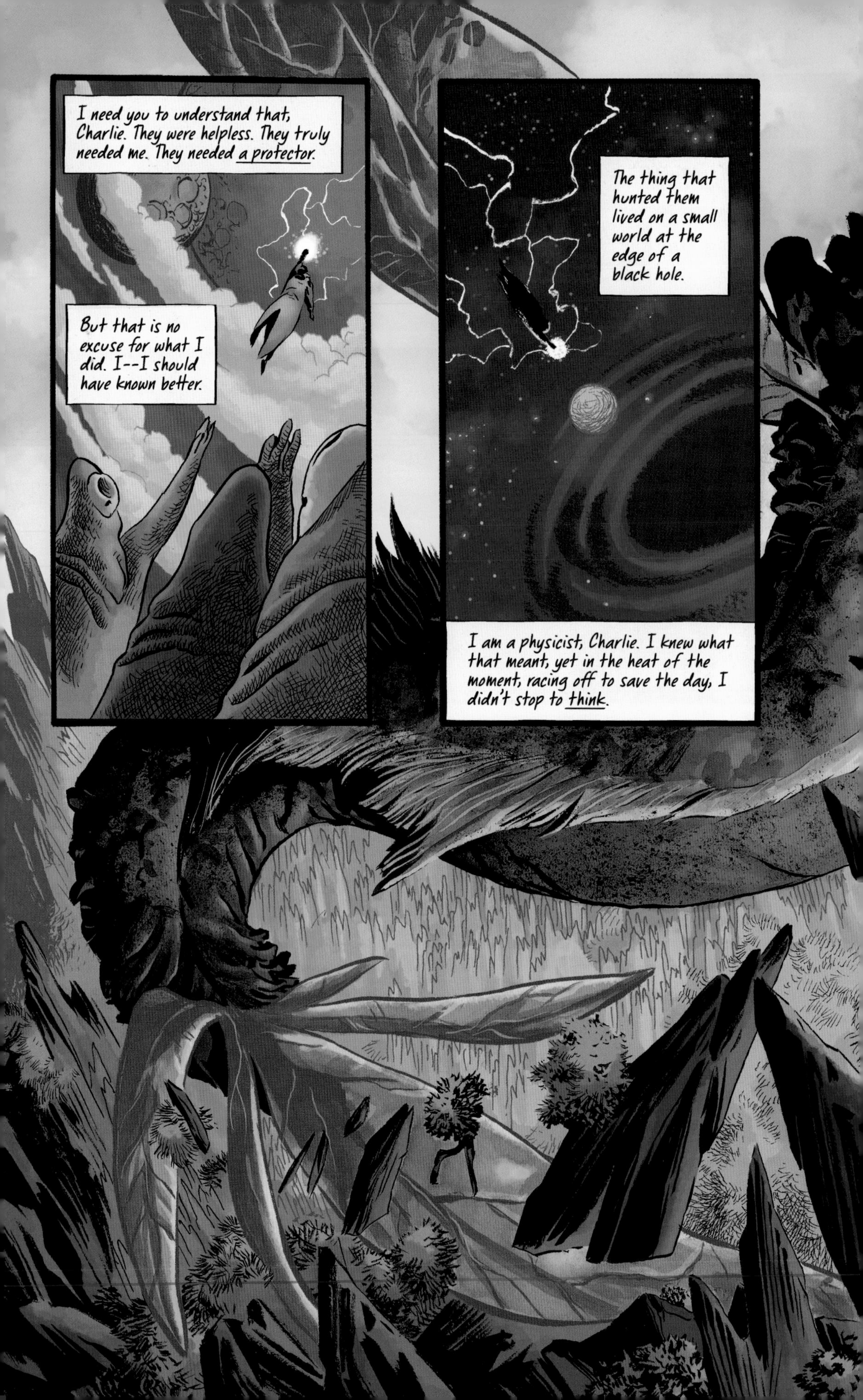
I need you to understand that, Charlie. They were helpless. They truly needed me. They needed a protector.
But that is no excuse for what I did. I--I should have known better.
The thing that hunted them lived on a small world at the edge of a black hole.
I am a physicist, Charlie. I knew what that meant, yet in the heat of the moment, racing off to save the day, I didn't stop to think.

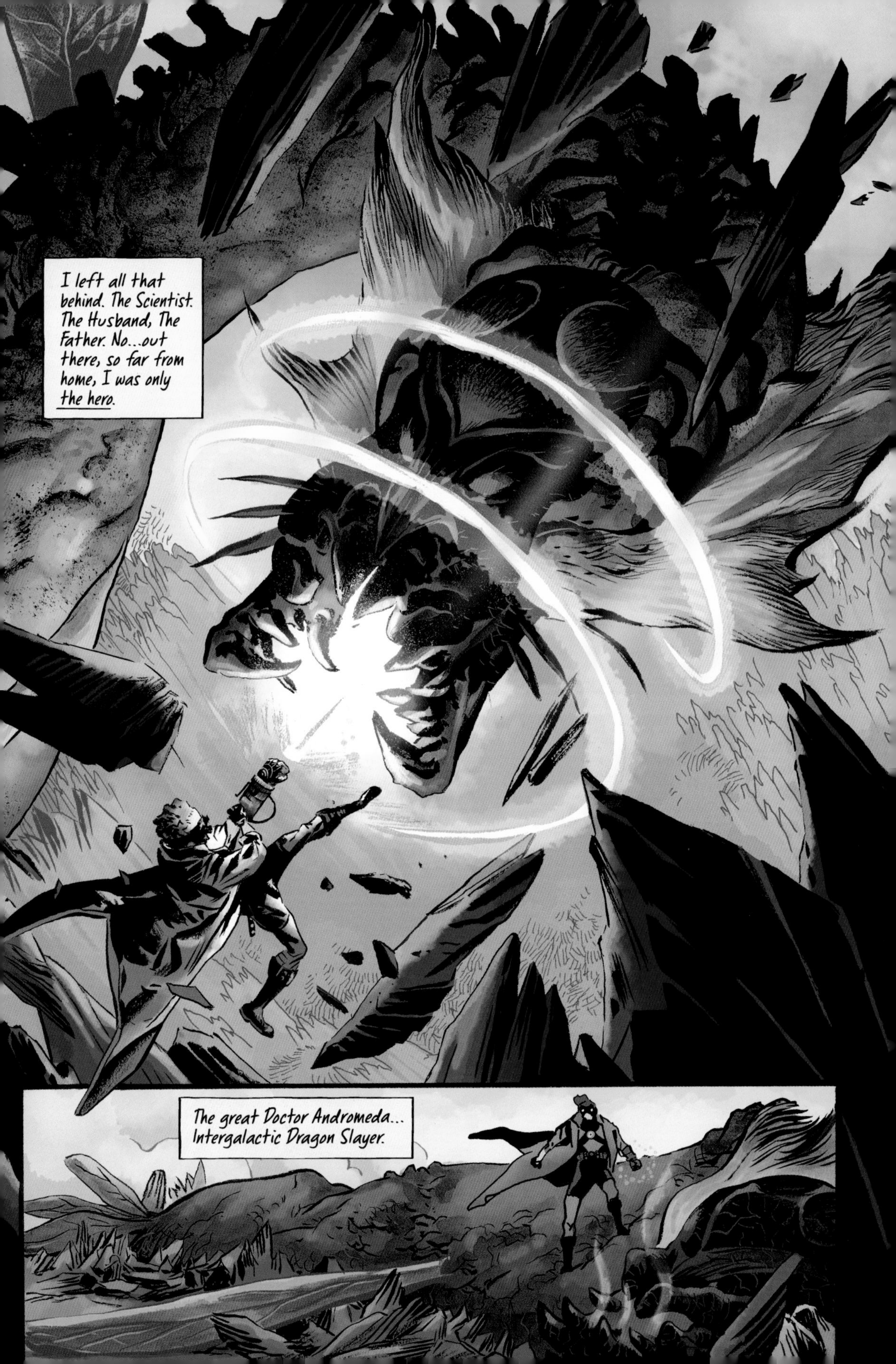
I left all that behind. The Scientist. The Husband, The Father. No...out there, so far from home, I was only the hero.
The great Doctor Andromeda... Intergalactic Dragon Slayer.

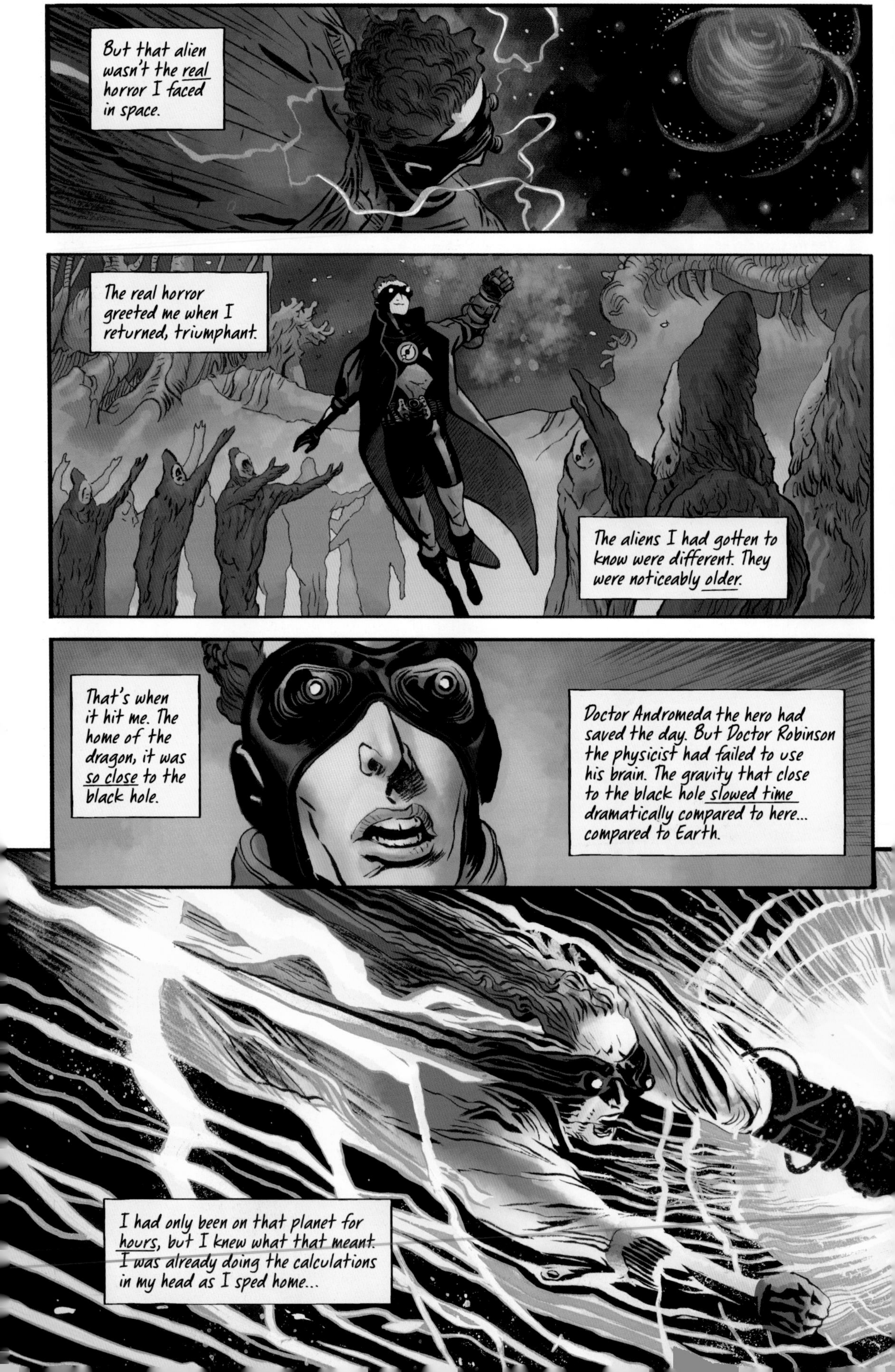

But that alien wasn't the real horror I faced in space.
The real horror greeted me when I returned, triumphant.
The aliens I had gotten to know were different. They were noticeably older.
That's when it hit me. The home of the dragon, it was so close to the black hole.
Doctor Andromeda the hero had saved the day. But Doctor Robinson the physicist had failed to use his brain. The gravity that close to the black hole slowed time dramatically compared to here... compared to Earth.
I had only been on that planet for hours, but I knew what that meant. I was already doing the calculations in my head as I sped home...

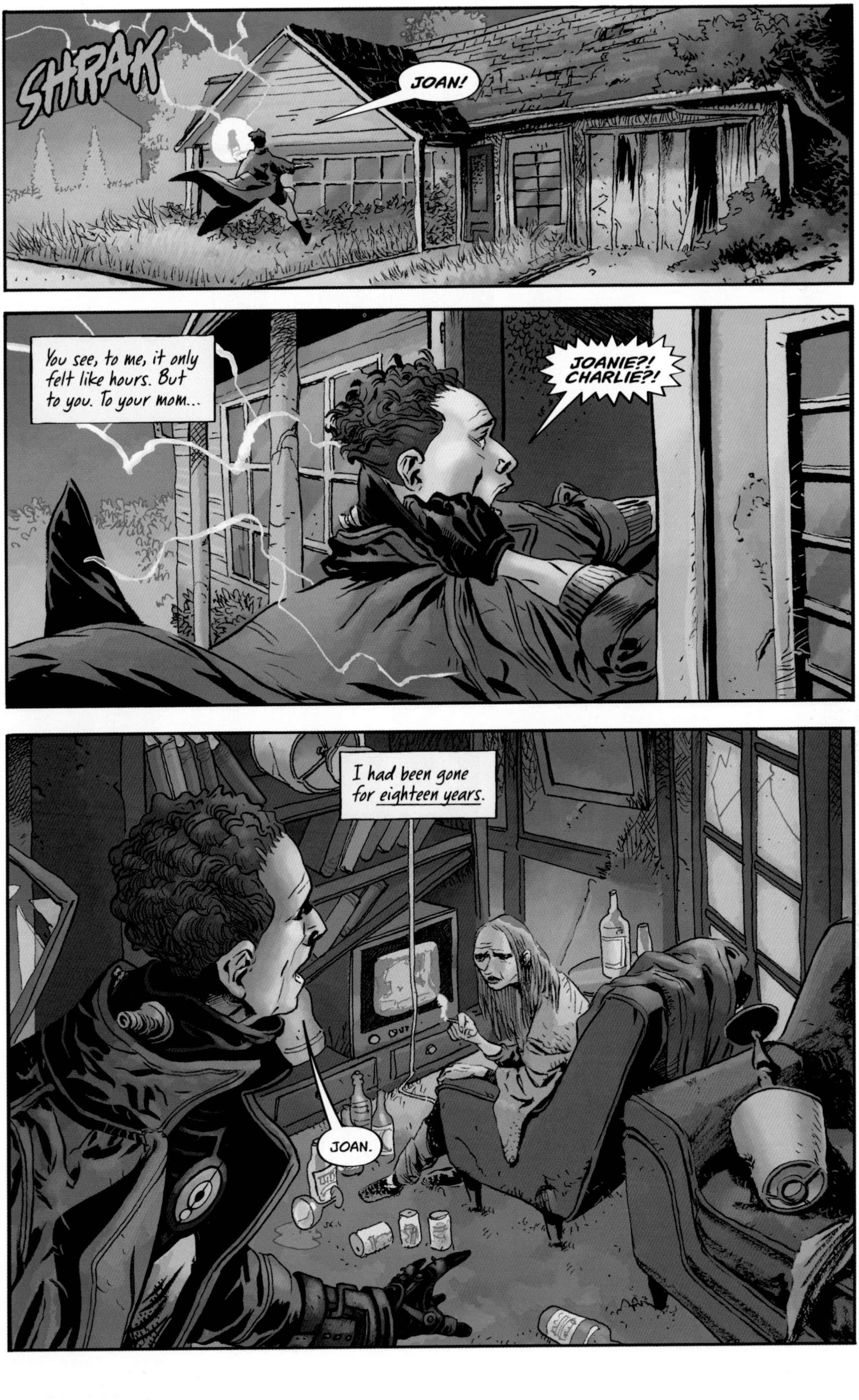
SHRAK
JOAN!
You see, to me, it only felt like hours. But to you. To your mom...
JOANIE?! CHARLIE?!
I had been gone for eighteen years.
JOAN.

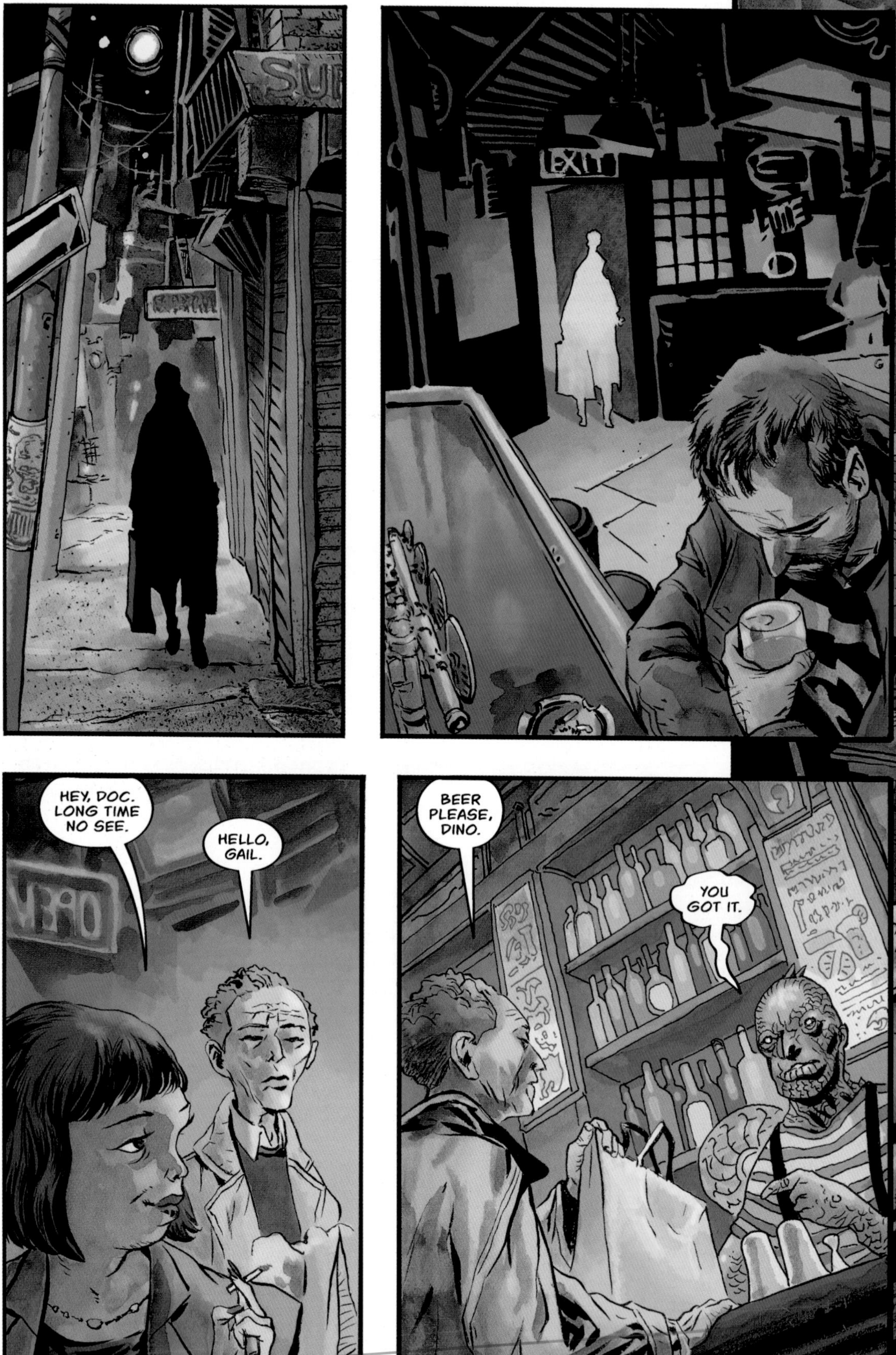
EXIT
HEY, DOC. LONG TIME NO SEE.
HELLO, GAIL.
BEER PLEASE, DINO.
YOU GOT IT.

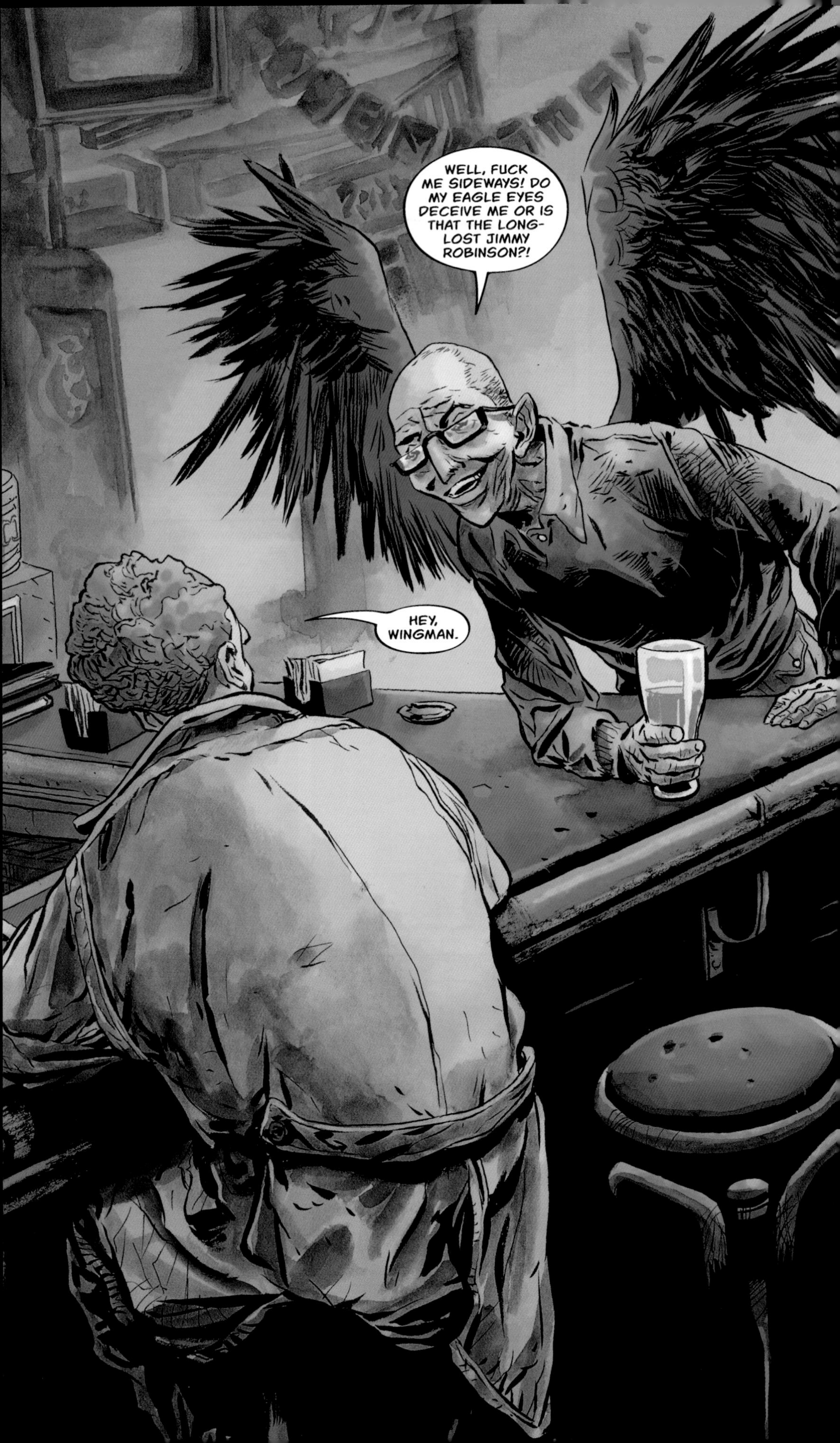
WELL, FUCK ME SIDEWAYS! DO MY EAGLE EYES DECEIVE ME OR IS THAT THE LONG-LOST JIMMY ROBINSON?!
HEY, WINGMAN.

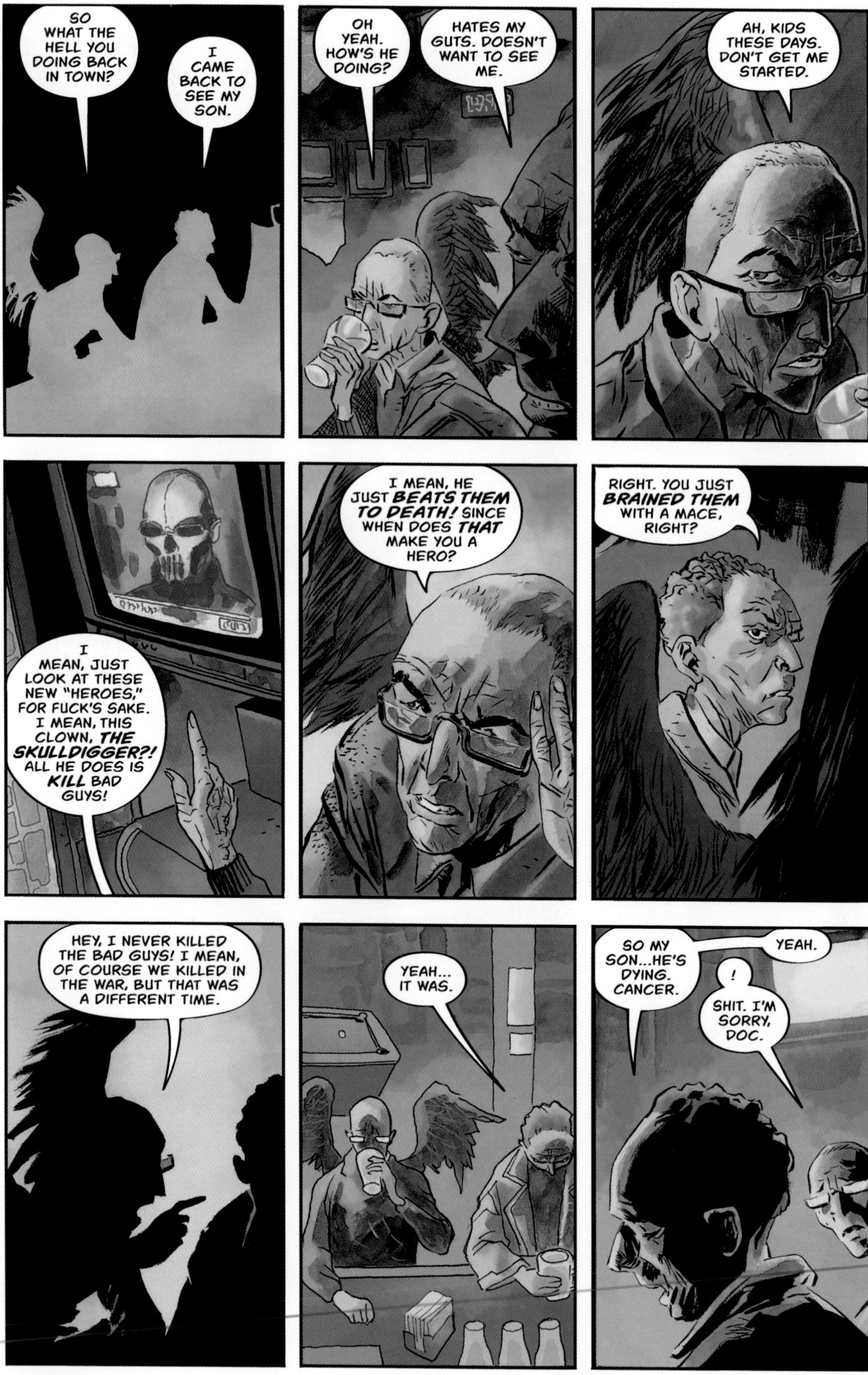
SO WHAT THE HELL YOU DOING BACK IN TOWN?
I CAME BACK TO SEE MY SON.
OH YEAH. HOW'S HE DOING?
HATES MY GUTS. DOESN'T WANT TO SEE ME.
AH, KIDS THESE DAYS. DON'T GET ME STARTED.
I MEAN, JUST LOOK AT THESE NEW "HEROES," FOR FUCK'S SAKE. I MEAN, THIS CLOWN, THE SKULLDIGGER?! ALL HE DOES IS KILL BAD GUYS!
I MEAN, HE JUST BEATS THEM TO DEATH! SINCE WHEN DOES THAT MAKE YOU A HERO?
RIGHT. YOU JUST BRAINED THEM WITH A MACE, RIGHT?
HEY, I NEVER KILLED THE BAD GUYS! I MEAN, OF COURSE WE KILLED IN THE WAR, BUT THAT WAS A DIFFERENT TIME.
YEAH... IT WAS.
SO MY SON...HE'S DYING. CANCER.
YEAH.
!
SHIT. I'M SORRY, DOC.

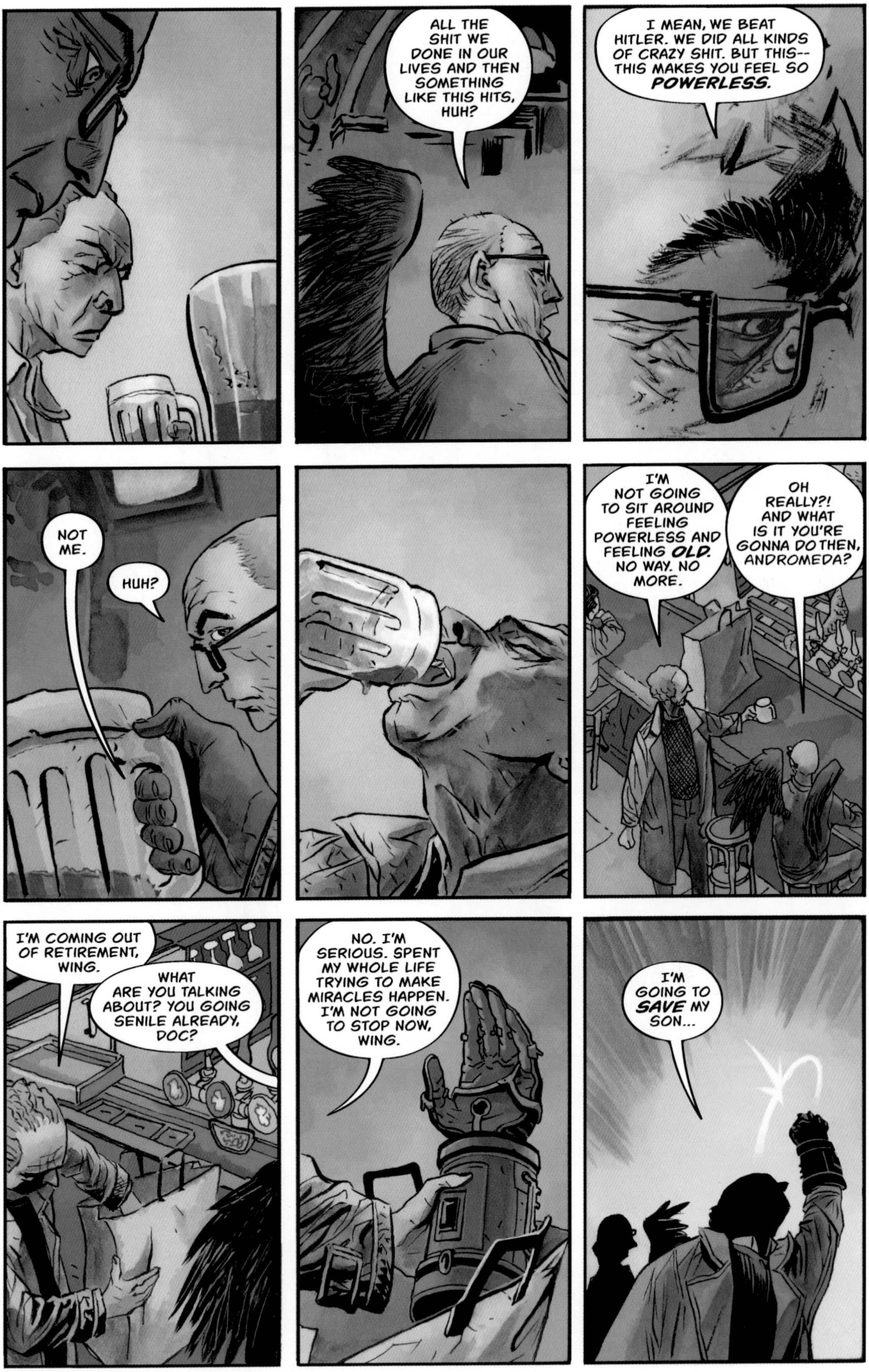
ALL THE SHIT WE DONE IN OUR LIVES AND THEN SOMETHING LIKE THIS HITS, HUH?
I MEAN, WE BEAT HITLER. WE DID ALL KINDS OF CRAZY SHIT. BUT THIS-- THIS MAKES YOU FEEL SO POWERLESS.
NOT ME.
HUH?
I'M NOT GOING TO SIT AROUND FEELING POWERLESS AND FEELING OLD. NO WAY. NO MORE.
OH REALLY?! AND WHAT IS IT YOU'RE GONNA DO THEN, ANDROMEDA?
I'M COMING OUT OF RETIREMENT, WING.
WHAT ARE YOU TALKING ABOUT? YOU GOING SENILE ALREADY, DOC?
NO. I'M SERIOUS. SPENT MY WHOLE LIFE TRYING TO MAKE MIRACLES HAPPEN. I'M NOT GOING TO STOP NOW, WING.
I'M GOING TO SAVE MY SON...

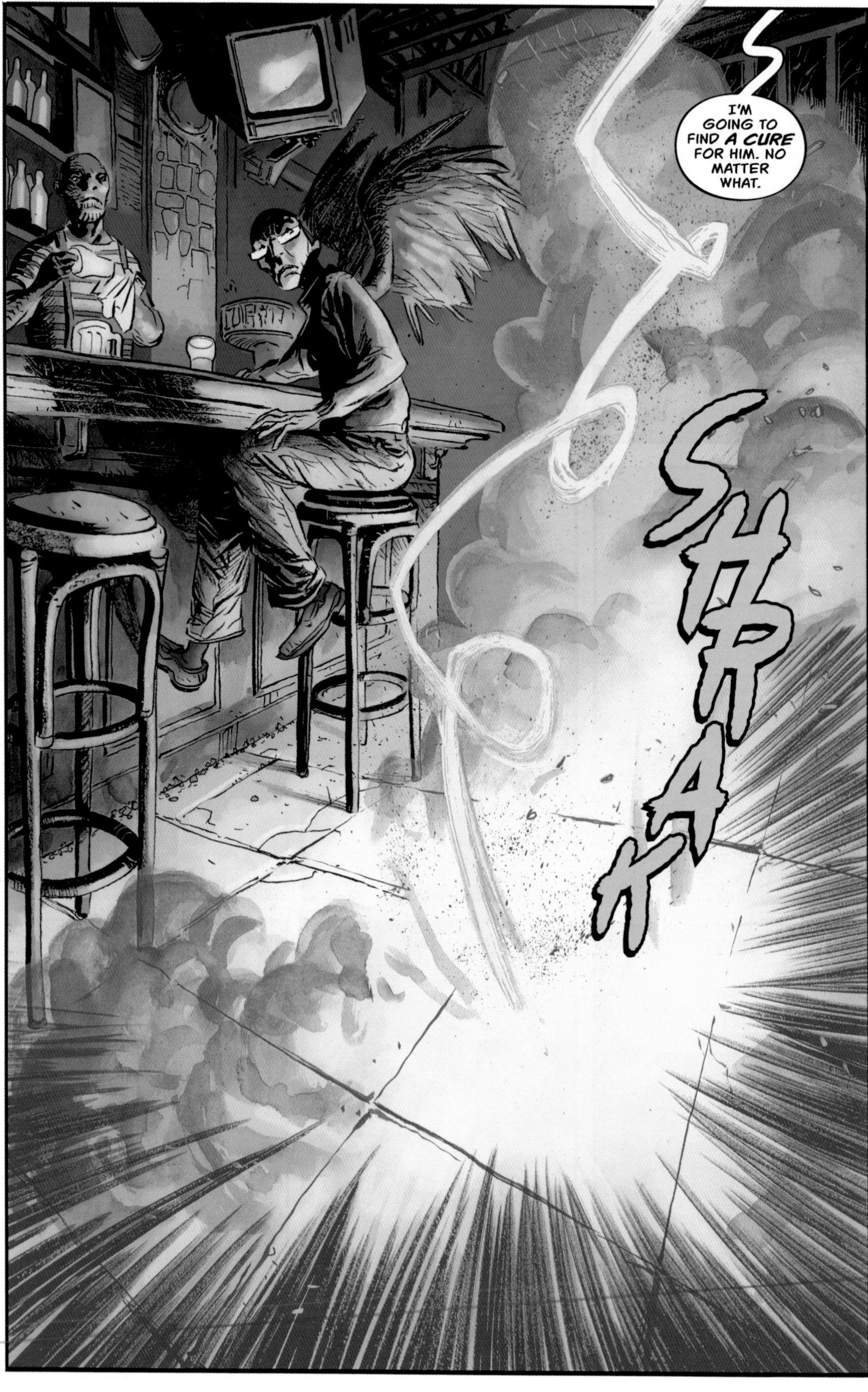
I'M GOING TO FIND A CURE FOR HIM. NO MATTER WHAT.
SHRAK

CHAPTER THREE

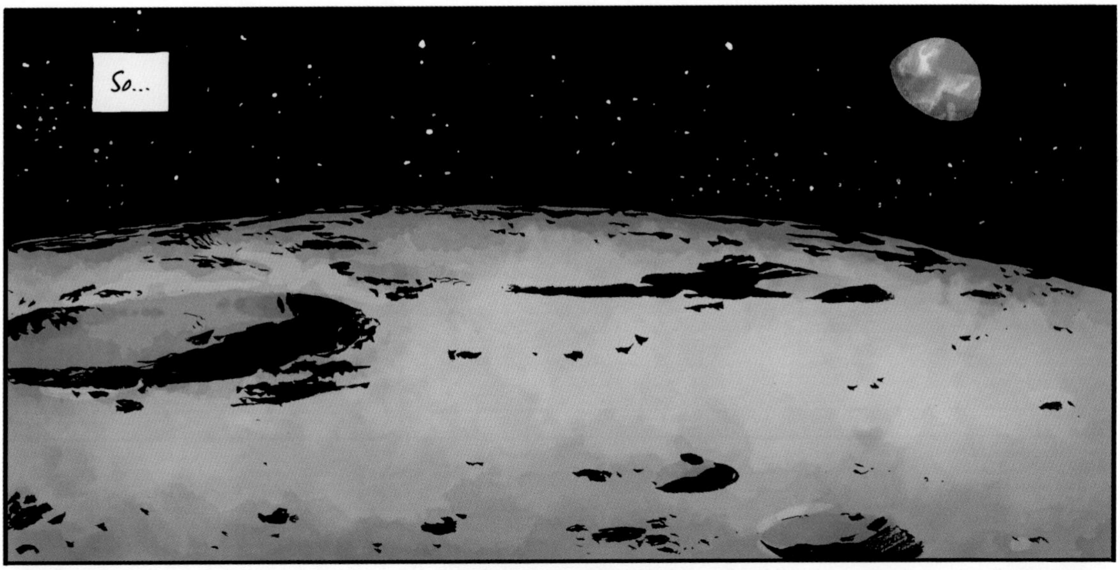
So...

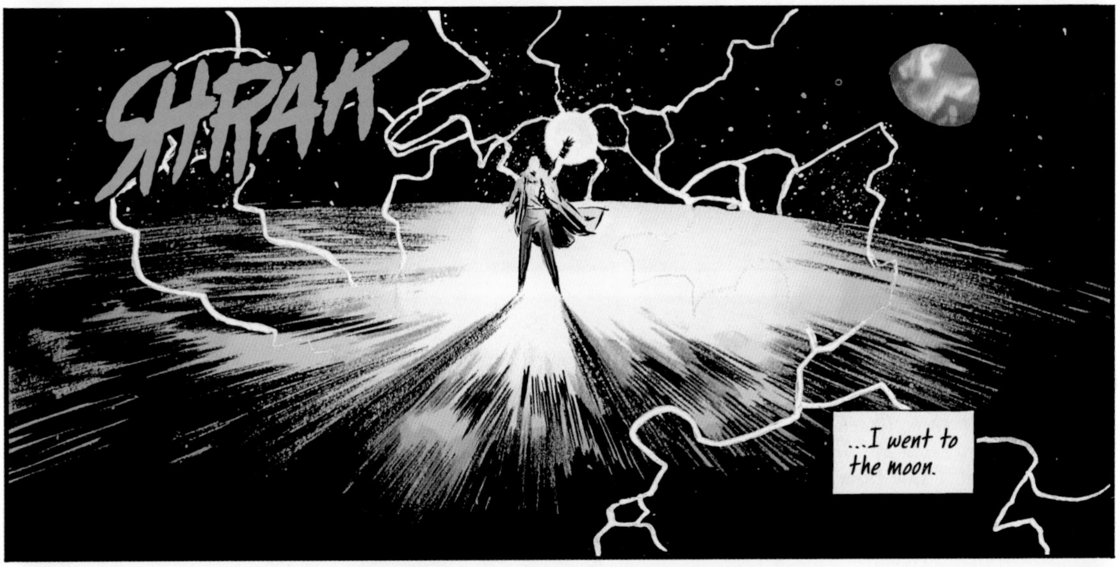
SHRAK
...I went to the moon.

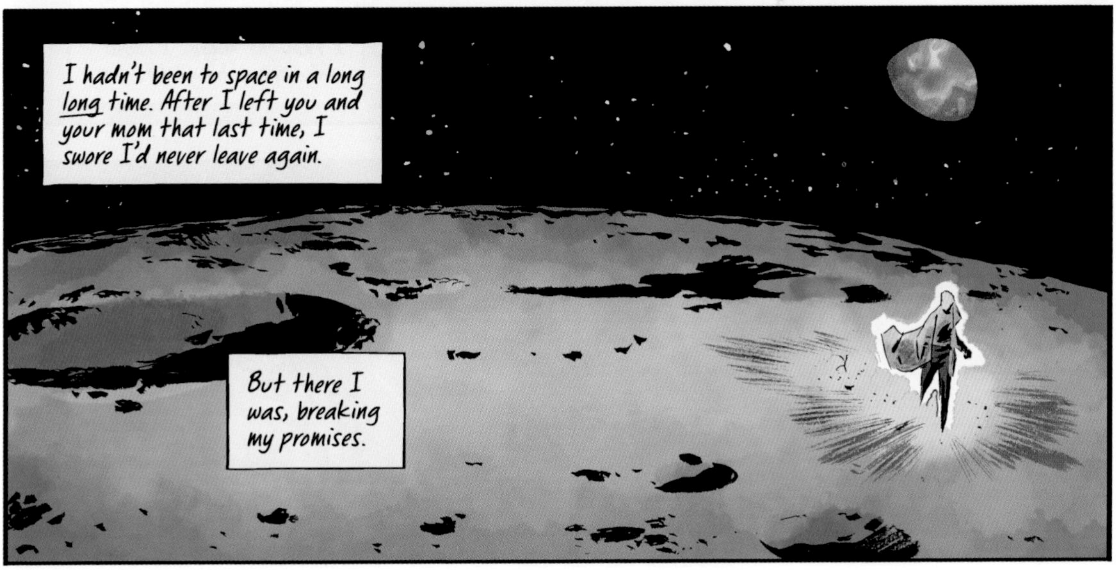
I hadn't been to space in a long long time. After I left you and your mom that last time, I swore I'd never leave again.
But there I was, breaking my promises.

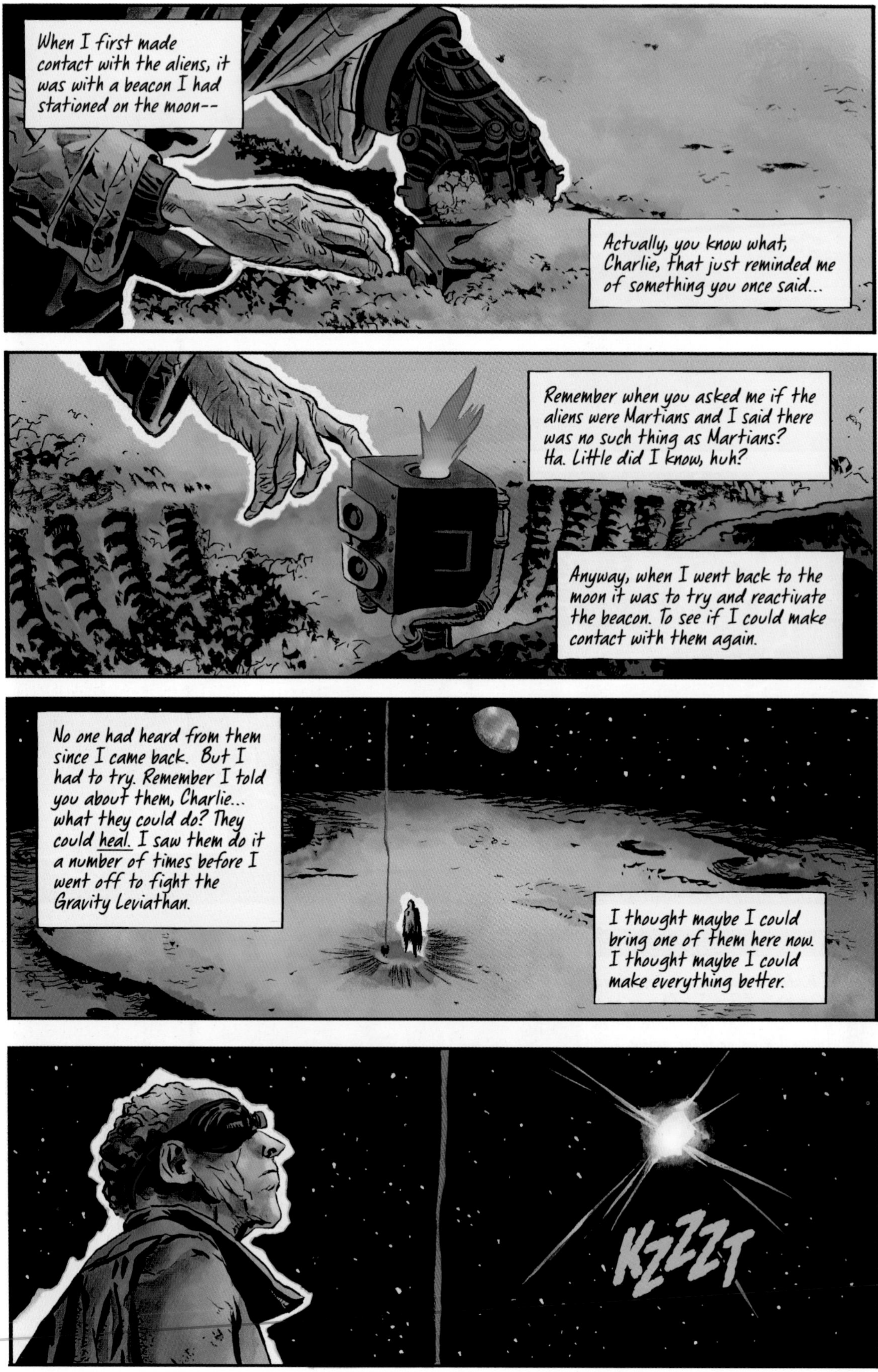
When I first made contact with the aliens, it was with a beacon I had stationed on the moon--
Actually, you know what, Charlie, that just reminded me of something you once said...
Remember when you asked me if the aliens were Martians and I said there was no such thing as Martians? Ha. Little did I know, huh?
Anyway, when I went back to the moon it was to try and reactivate the beacon. To see if I could make contact with them again.
No one had heard from them since I came back. But I had to try. Remember I told you about them, Charlie... what they could do? They could heal. I saw them do it a number of times before I went off to fight the Gravity Leviathan.
I thought maybe I could bring one of them here now. I thought maybe I could make everything better.
KZZZT

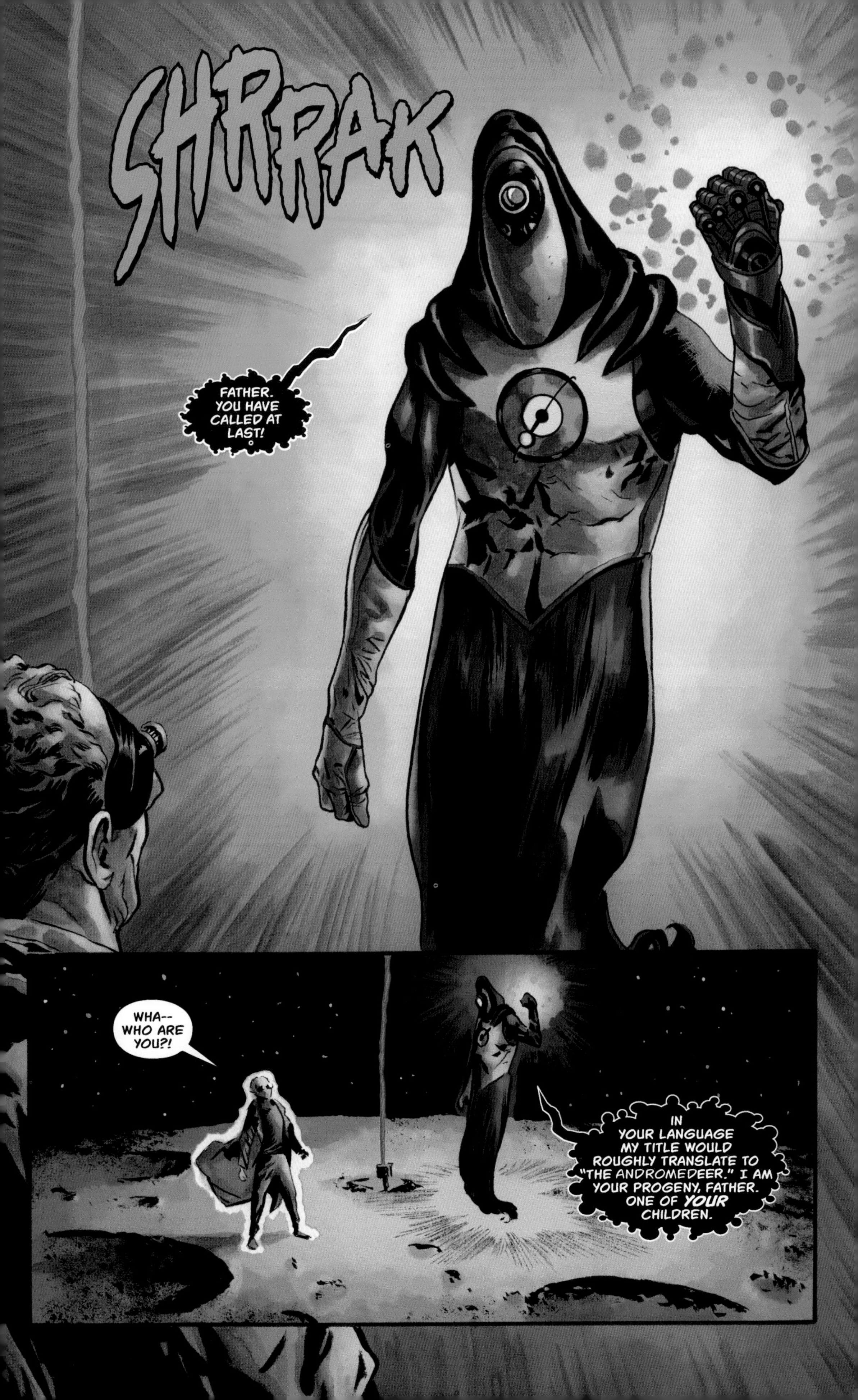
SHRRAK
FATHER. YOU HAVE CALLED AT LAST!
WHA-- WHO ARE YOU?!
IN YOUR LANGUAGE MY TITLE WOULD ROUGHLY TRANSLATE TO "THE ANDROMEDEER." I AM YOUR PROGENY, FATHER. ONE OF YOUR CHILDREN.

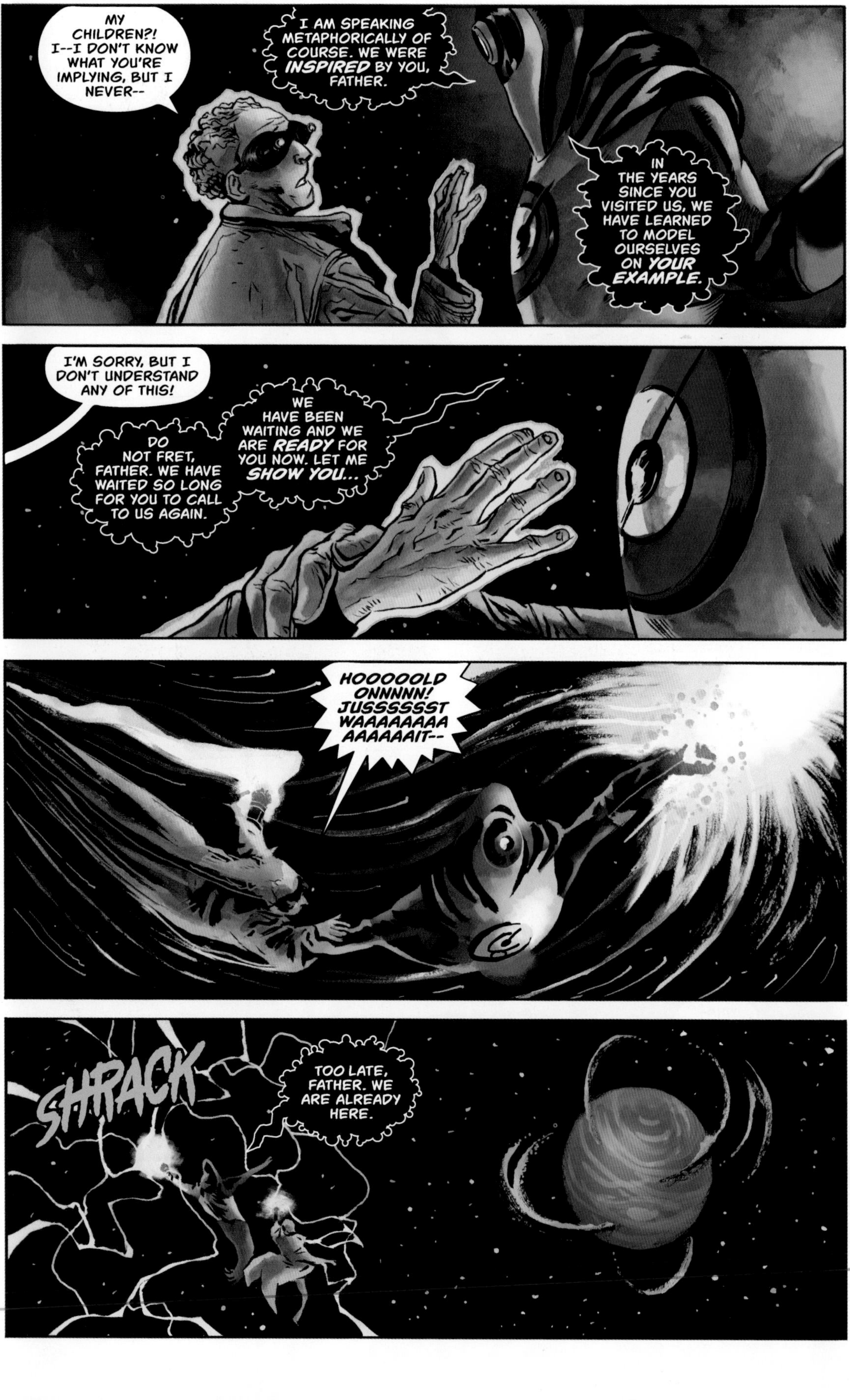
MY CHILDREN?! I--I DON'T KNOW WHAT YOU'RE IMPLYING, BUT I NEVER--
I AM SPEAKING METAPHORICALLY OF COURSE. WE WERE INSPIRED BY YOU, FATHER.
IN THE YEARS SINCE YOU VISITED US, WE HAVE LEARNED TO MODEL OURSELVES ON YOUR EXAMPLE.
I'M SORRY, BUT I DON'T UNDERSTAND ANY OF THIS!
DO NOT FRET, FATHER. WE HAVE WAITED SO LONG FOR YOU TO CALL TO US AGAIN.
WE HAVE BEEN WAITING AND WE ARE READY FOR YOU NOW. LET ME SHOW YOU...
HOOOOOLD ONNNNN! JUSSSSSST WAAAAAAAA AAAAAAIT--
SHRACK
TOO LATE, FATHER. WE ARE ALREADY HERE.

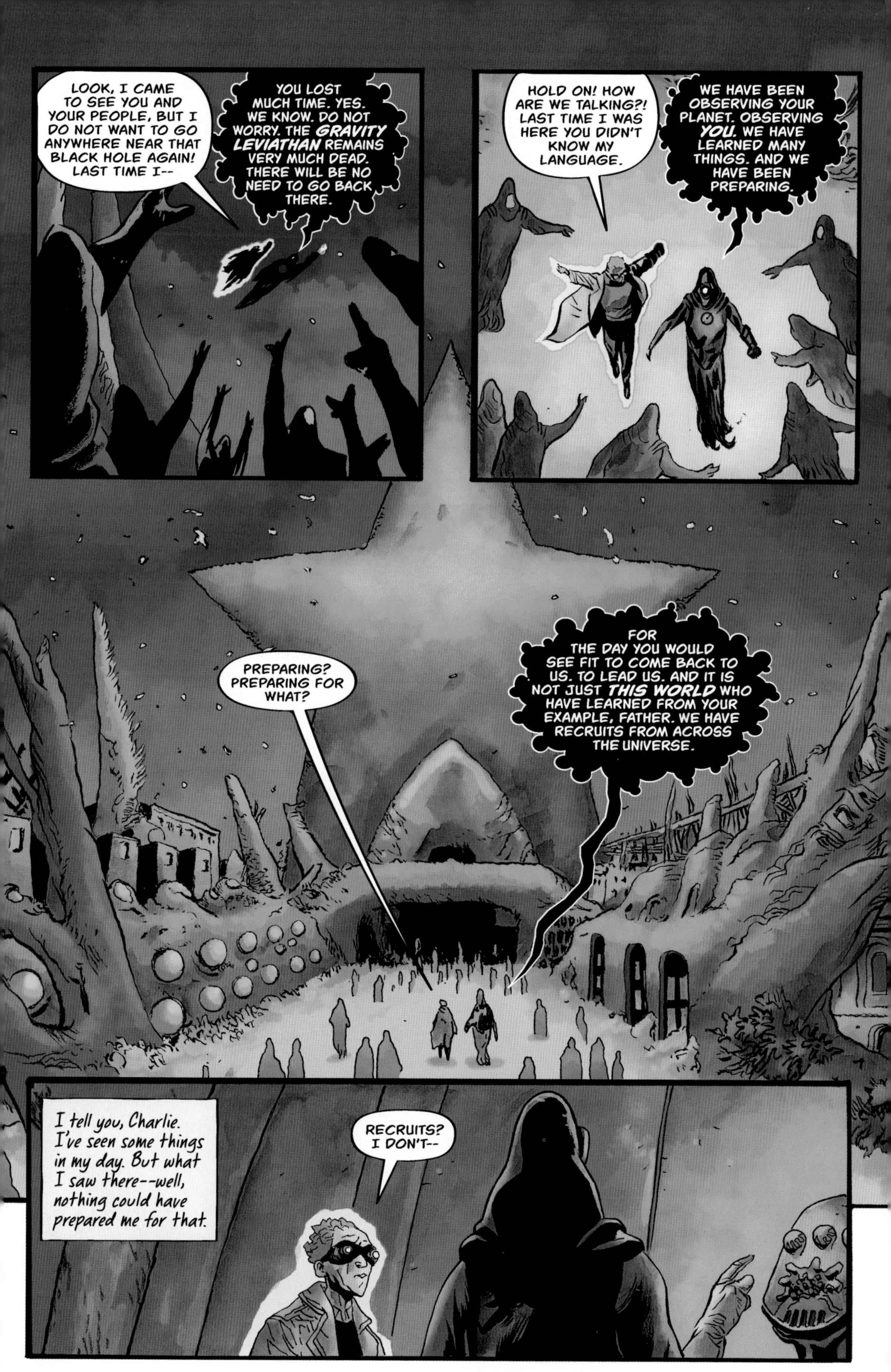
LOOK, I CAME TO SEE YOU AND YOUR PEOPLE, BUT I DO NOT WANT TO GO ANYWHERE NEAR THAT BLACK HOLE AGAIN! LAST TIME I--
YOU LOST MUCH TIME. YES. WE KNOW. DO NOT WORRY. THE GRAVITY LEVIATHAN REMAINS VERY MUCH DEAD. THERE WILL BE NO NEED TO GO BACK THERE.
HOLD ON! HOW ARE WE TALKING?! LAST TIME I WAS HERE YOU DIDN'T KNOW MY LANGUAGE.
WE HAVE BEEN OBSERVING YOUR PLANET. OBSERVING YOU. WE HAVE LEARNED MANY THINGS. AND WE HAVE BEEN PREPARING.
PREPARING? PREPARING FOR WHAT?
FOR THE DAY YOU WOULD SEE FIT TO COME BACK TO US. TO LEAD US. AND IT IS NOT JUST THIS WORLD WHO HAVE LEARNED FROM YOUR EXAMPLE, FATHER. WE HAVE RECRUITS FROM ACROSS THE UNIVERSE.
I tell you, Charlie. I've seen some things in my day. But what I saw there--well, nothing could have prepared me for that.
RECRUITS? I DON'T--

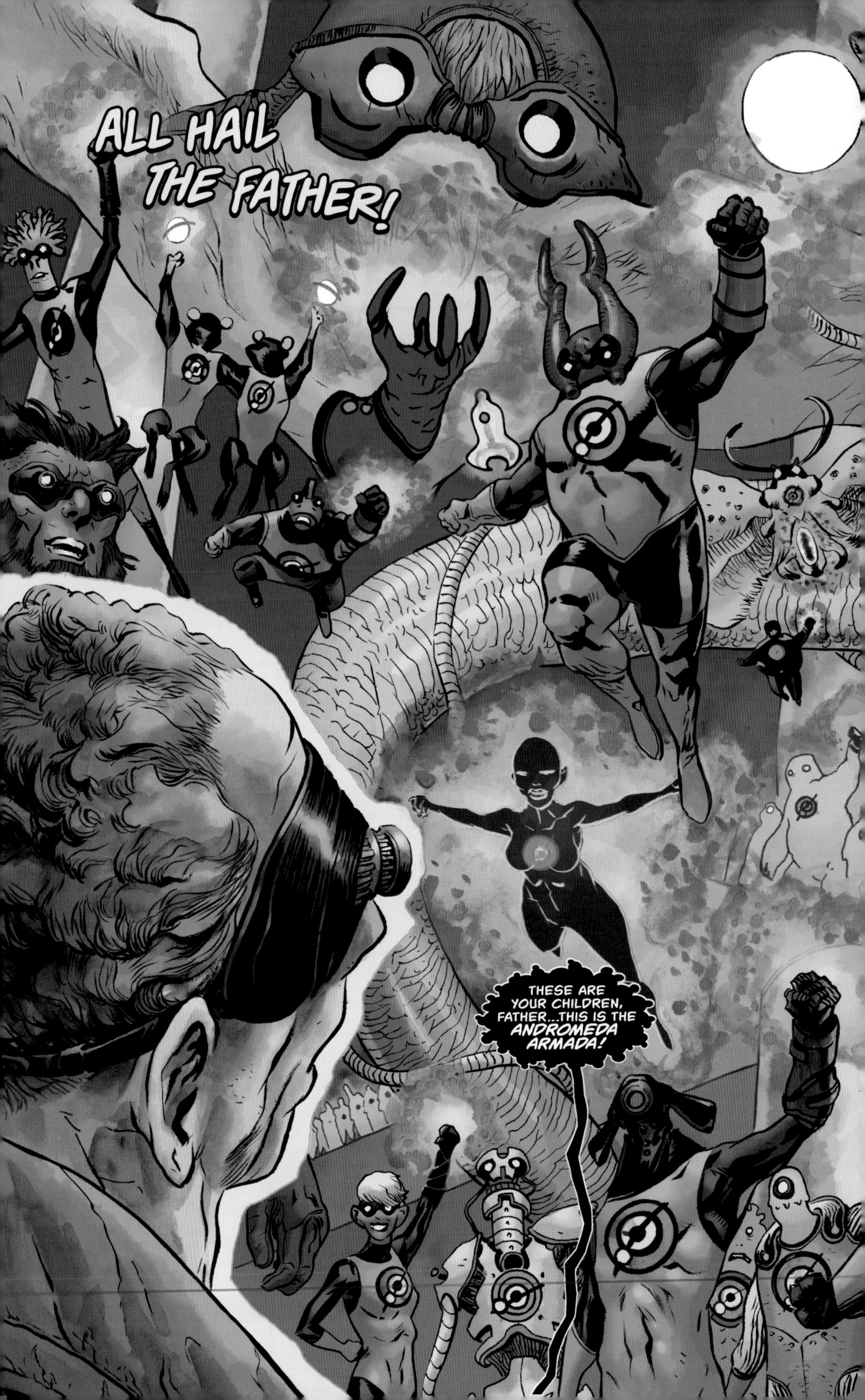
ALL HAIL THE FATHER!
THESE ARE YOUR CHILDREN, FATHER...THIS IS THE ANDROMEDA ARMADA!

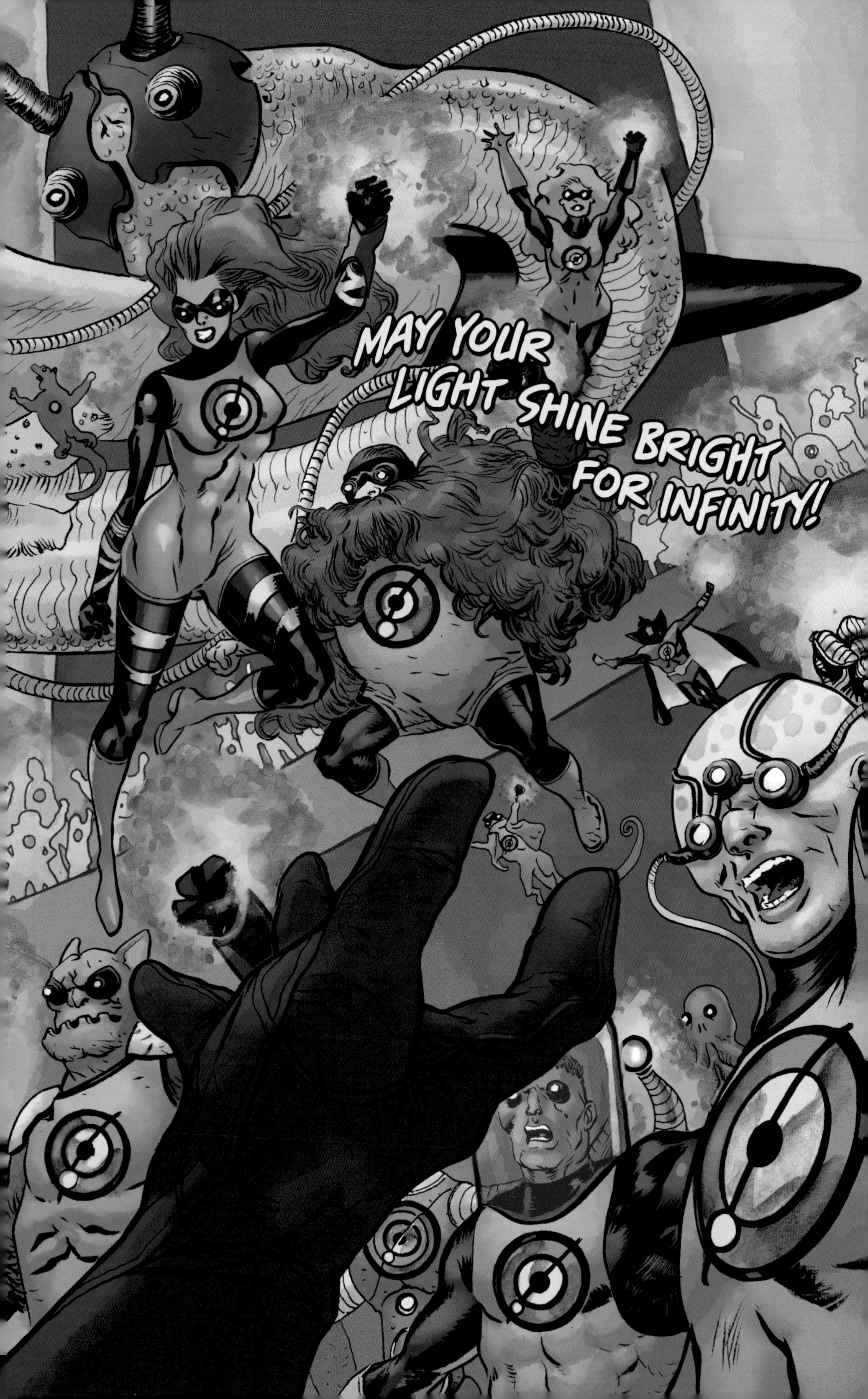
MAY YOUR LIGHT SHINE BRIGHT FOR INFINITY!

1969

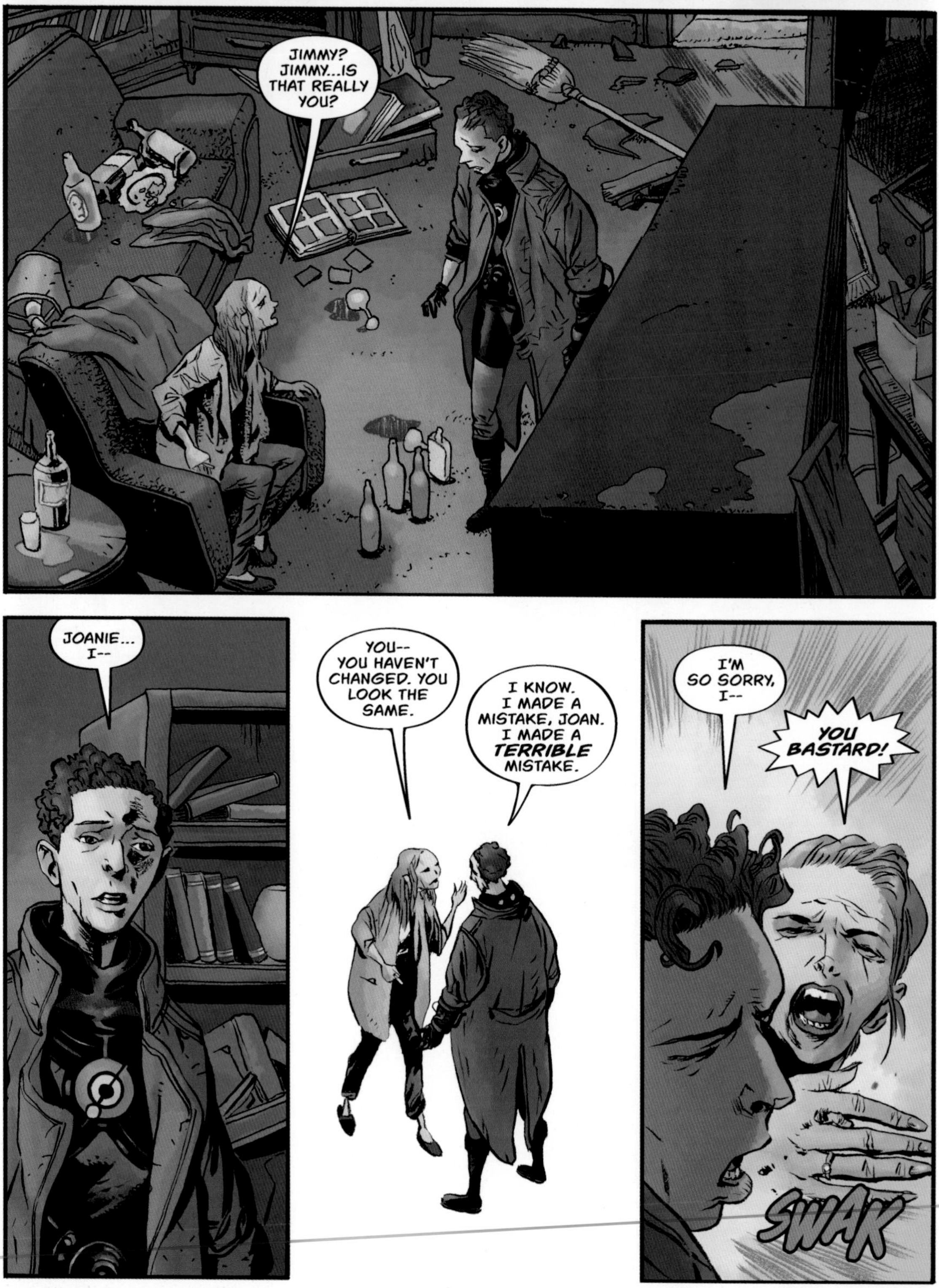
JIMMY? JIMMY...IS THAT REALLY YOU?
JOANIE... I--
YOU-- YOU HAVEN'T CHANGED. YOU LOOK THE SAME.
I KNOW. I MADE A MISTAKE, JOAN. I MADE A TERRIBLE MISTAKE.
I'M SO SORRY, I--
YOU BASTARD!
SWAK

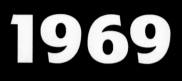

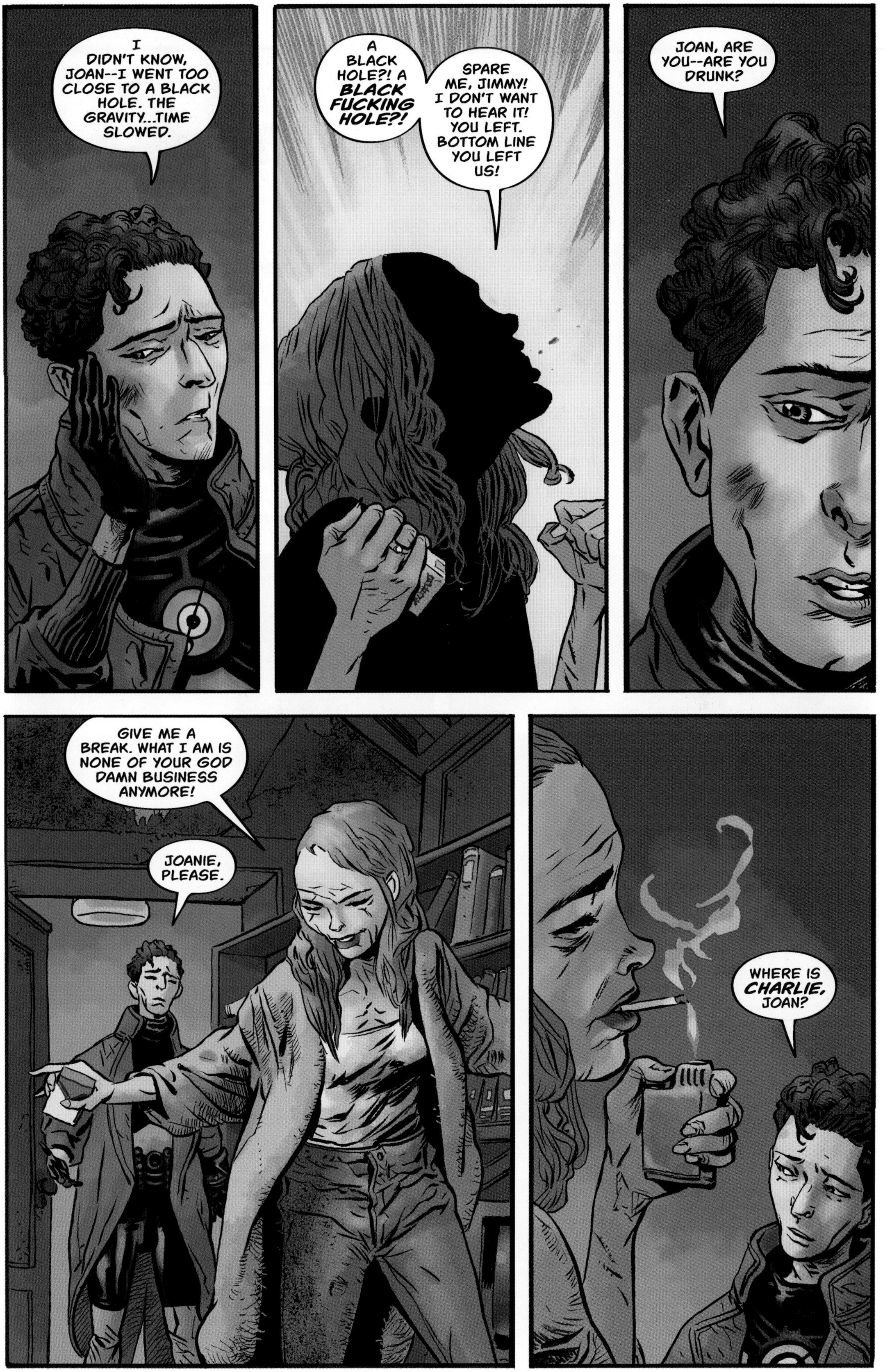
I DIDN'T KNOW, JOAN--I WENT TOO CLOSE TO A BLACK HOLE. THE GRAVITY...TIME SLOWED.
A BLACK HOLE?! A *BLACK FUCKING HOLE?!*
SPARE ME, JIMMY! I DON'T WANT TO HEAR IT! YOU LEFT. BOTTOM LINE YOU LEFT US!
JOAN, ARE YOU--ARE YOU DRUNK?
GIVE ME A BREAK. WHAT I AM IS NONE OF YOUR GOD DAMN BUSINESS ANYMORE!
JOANIE, PLEASE.
WHERE IS *CHARLIE,* JOAN?

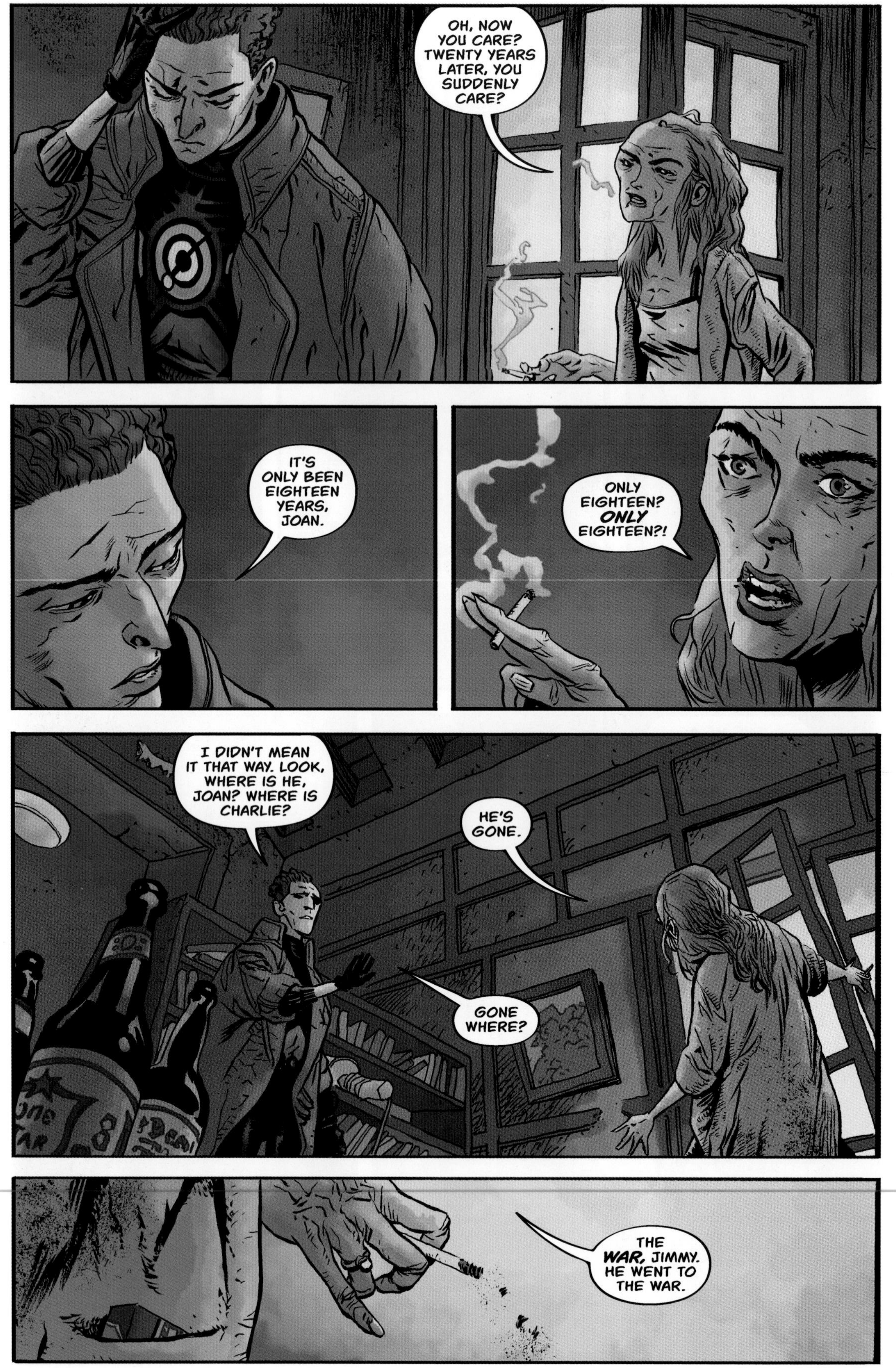
OH, NOW YOU CARE? TWENTY YEARS LATER, YOU SUDDENLY CARE?
IT'S ONLY BEEN EIGHTEEN YEARS, JOAN.
ONLY EIGHTEEN? ONLY EIGHTEEN?!
I DIDN'T MEAN IT THAT WAY. LOOK, WHERE IS HE, JOAN? WHERE IS CHARLIE?
HE'S GONE.
GONE WHERE?
THE WAR, JIMMY. HE WENT TO THE WAR.

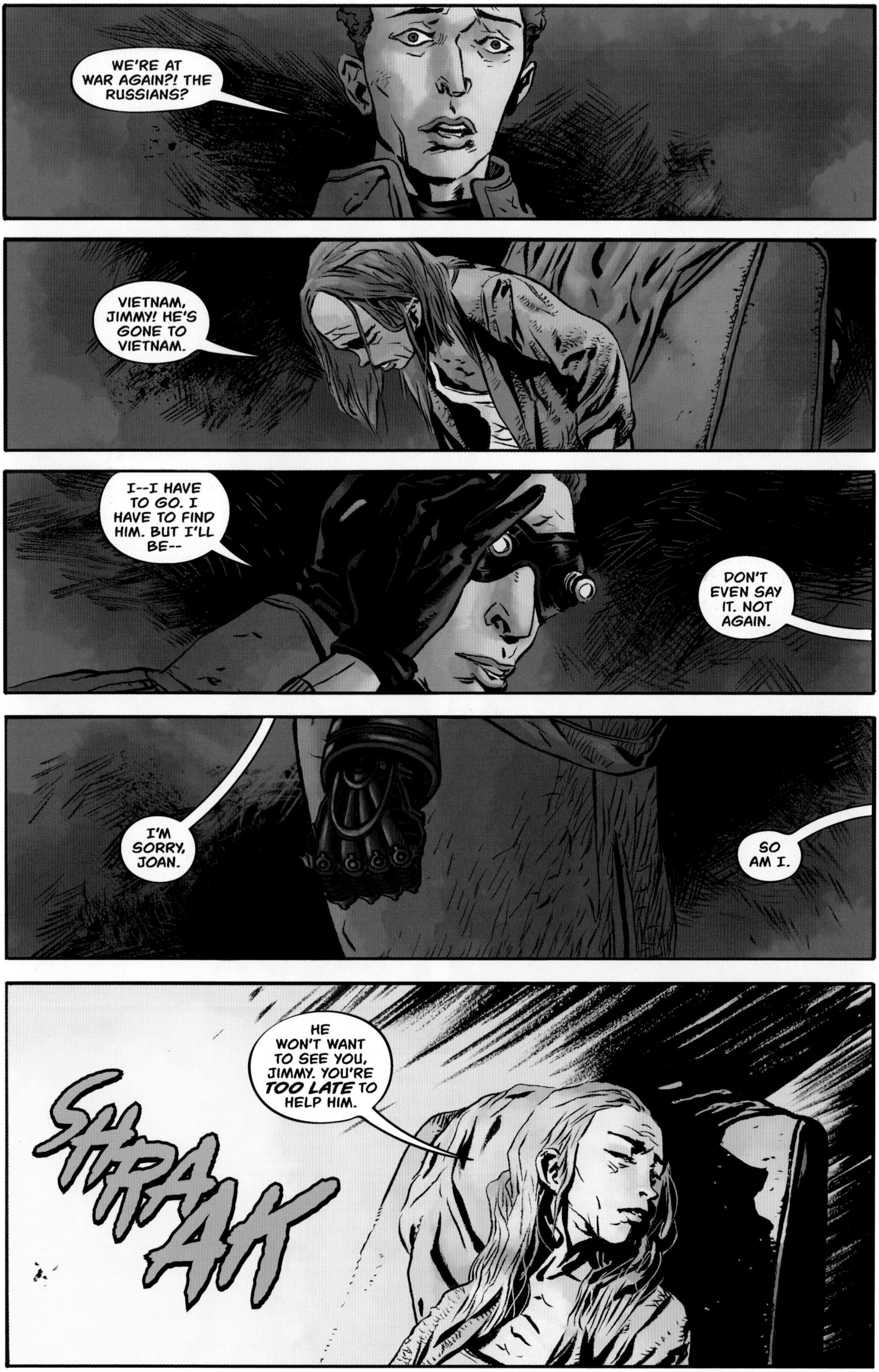
WE'RE AT WAR AGAIN?! THE RUSSIANS?
VIETNAM, JIMMY! HE'S GONE TO VIETNAM.
I--I HAVE TO GO. I HAVE TO FIND HIM. BUT I'LL BE--
DON'T EVEN SAY IT. NOT AGAIN.
I'M SORRY, JOAN.
SO AM I.
SHRAAK
HE WON'T WANT TO SEE YOU, JIMMY. YOU'RE TOO LATE TO HELP HIM.

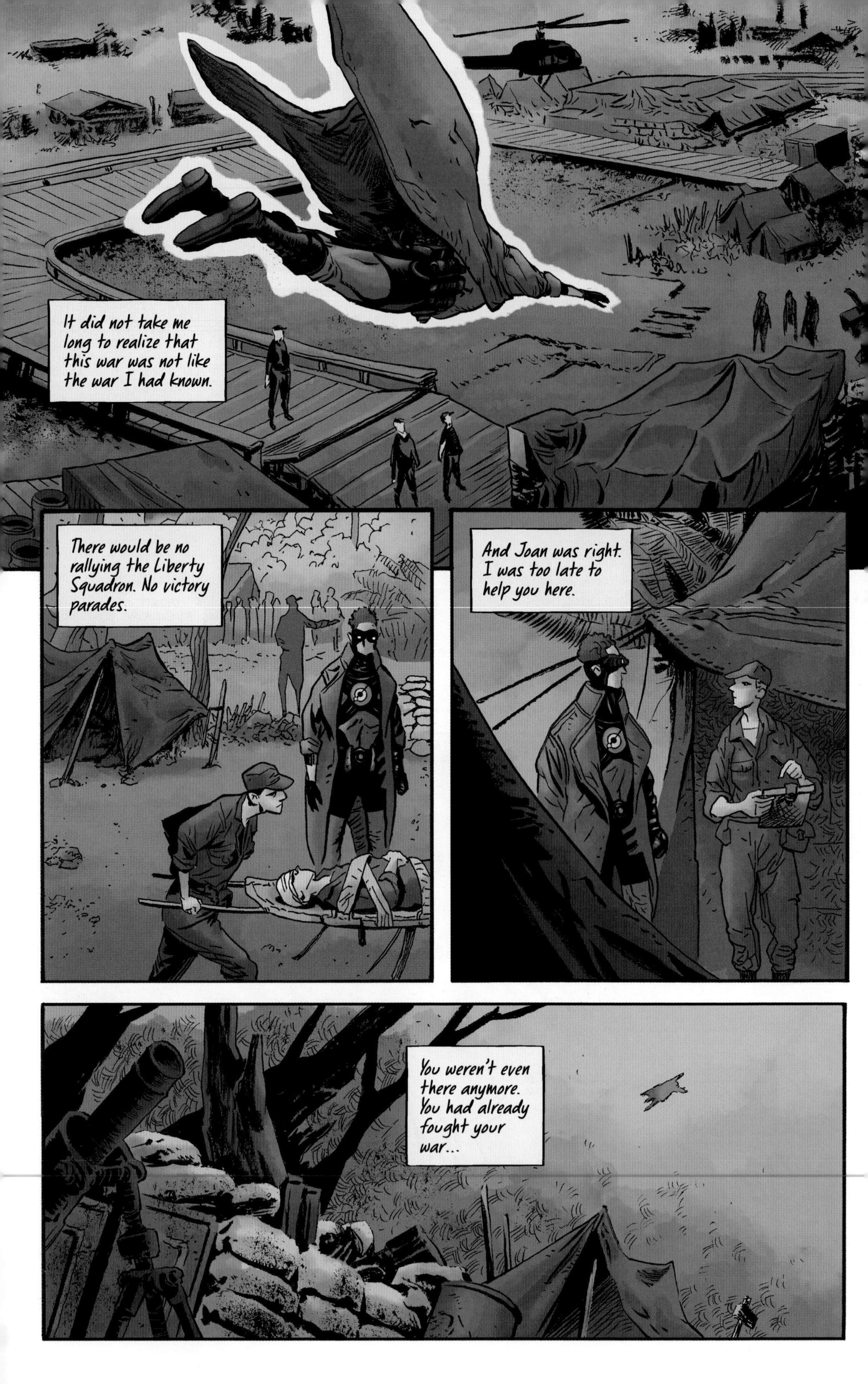
It did not take me long to realize that this war was not like the war I had known.
There would be no rallying the Liberty Squadron. No victory parades.
And Joan was right. I was too late to help you here.
You weren't even there anymore. You had already fought your war...

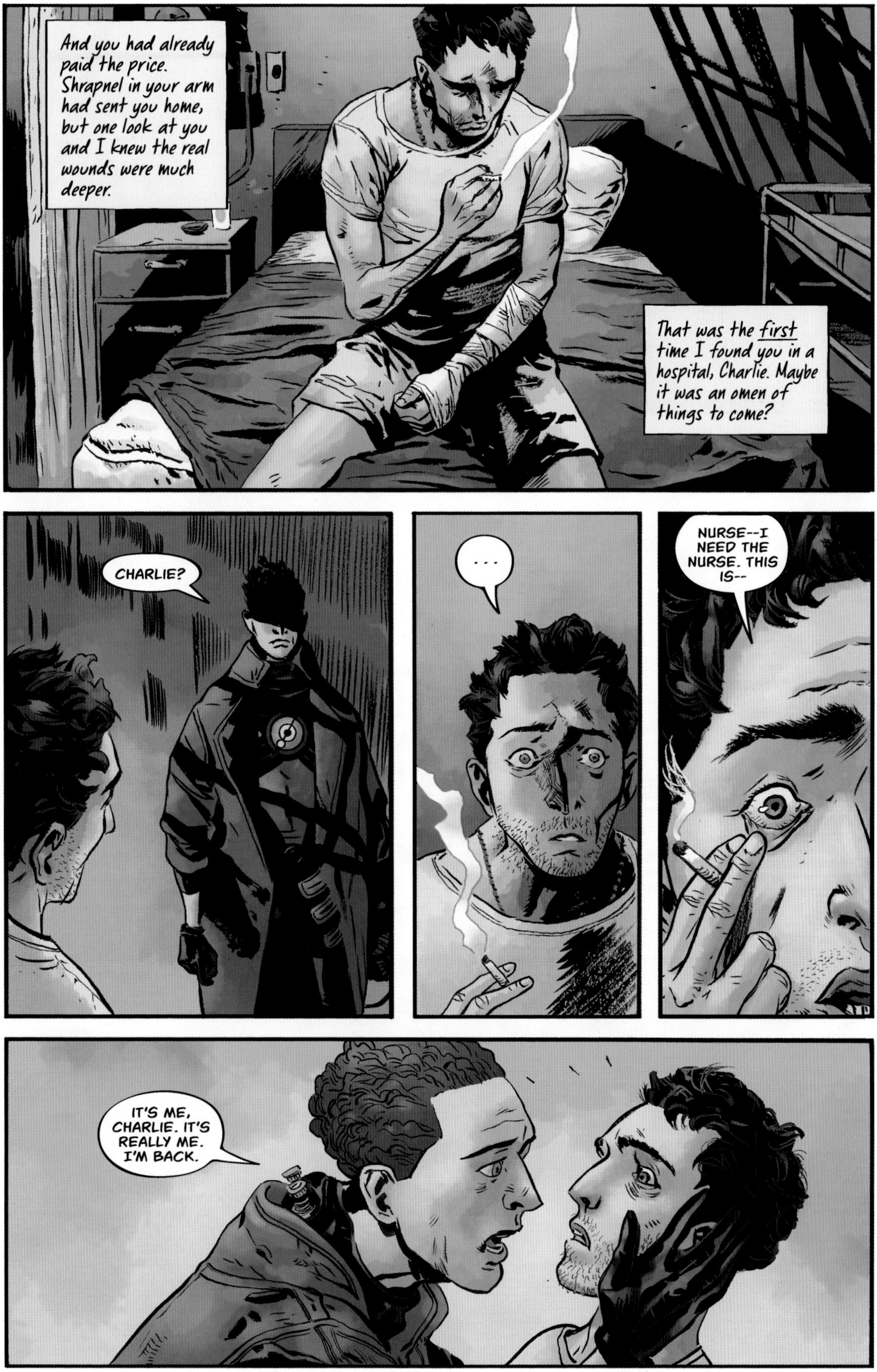

And you had already paid the price. Shrapnel in your arm had sent you home, but one look at you and I knew the real wounds were much deeper.
That was the first time I found you in a hospital, Charlie. Maybe it was an omen of things to come?
CHARLIE?
. . .
NURSE--I NEED THE NURSE. THIS IS--
IT'S ME, CHARLIE. IT'S REALLY ME. I'M BACK.

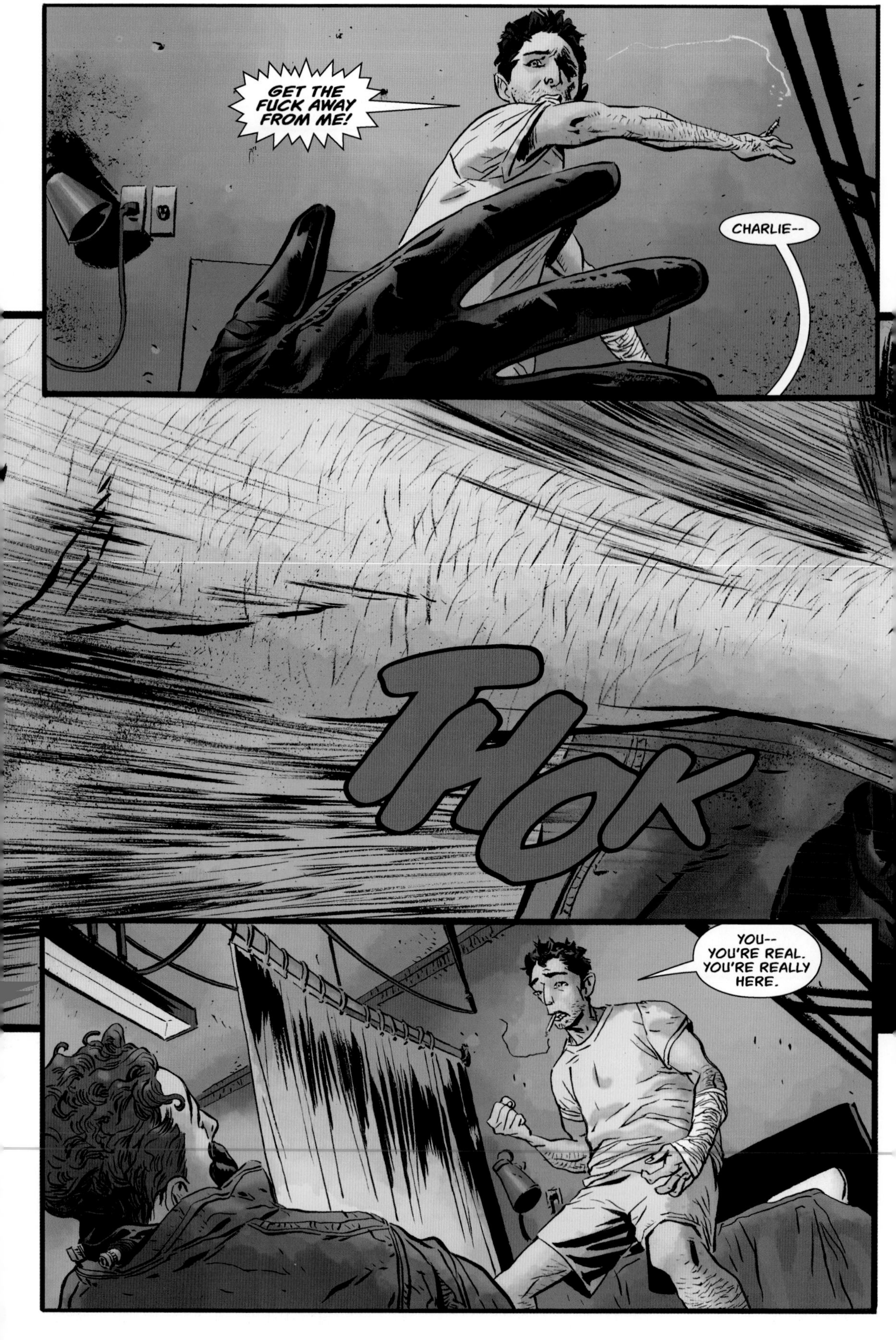
GET THE FUCK AWAY FROM ME!
CHARLIE--
THOK
YOU-- YOU'RE REAL. YOU'RE REALLY HERE.

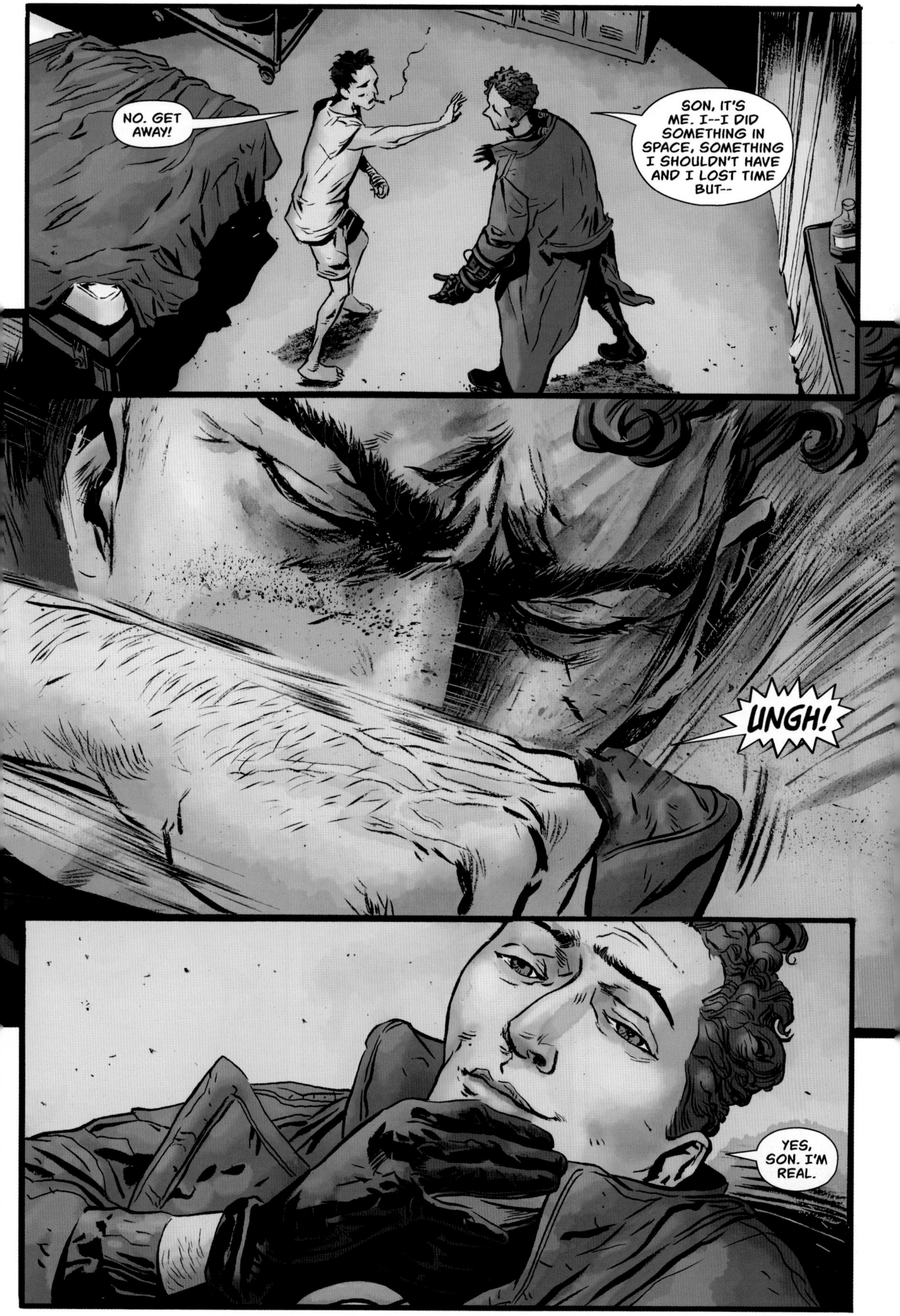
NO. GET AWAY!
SON, IT'S ME. I--I DID SOMETHING IN SPACE, SOMETHING I SHOULDN'T HAVE AND I LOST TIME BUT--
UNGH!
YES, SON. I'M REAL.

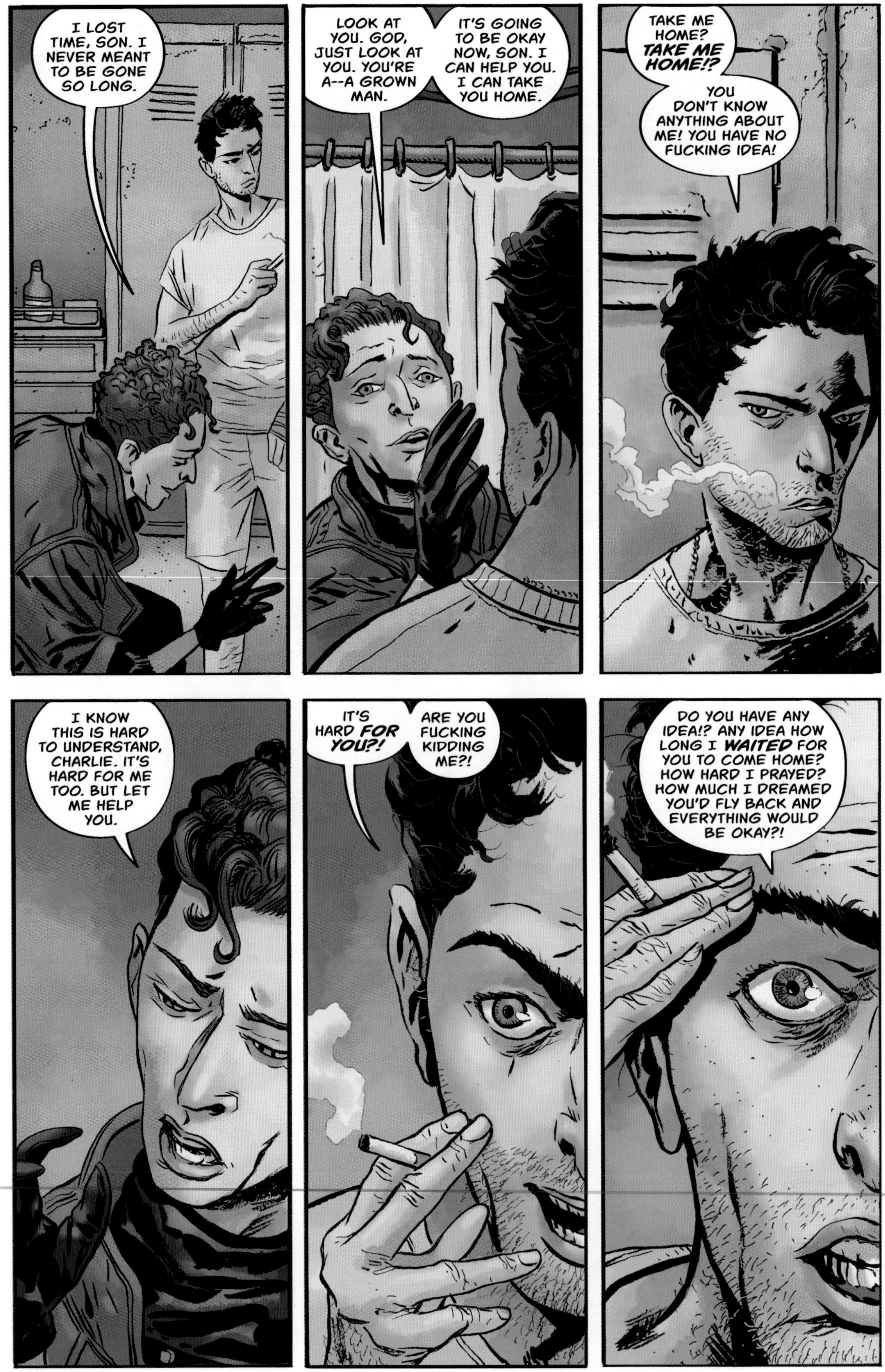
I LOST TIME, SON. I NEVER MEANT TO BE GONE SO LONG.
LOOK AT YOU. GOD, JUST LOOK AT YOU. YOU'RE A--A GROWN MAN.
IT'S GOING TO BE OKAY NOW, SON. I CAN HELP YOU. I CAN TAKE YOU HOME.
TAKE ME HOME? TAKE ME HOME!?
YOU DON'T KNOW ANYTHING ABOUT ME! YOU HAVE NO FUCKING IDEA!
I KNOW THIS IS HARD TO UNDERSTAND, CHARLIE. IT'S HARD FOR ME TOO. BUT LET ME HELP YOU.
IT'S HARD FOR YOU?!
ARE YOU FUCKING KIDDING ME?!
DO YOU HAVE ANY IDEA!? ANY IDEA HOW LONG I WAITED FOR YOU TO COME HOME? HOW HARD I PRAYED? HOW MUCH I DREAMED YOU'D FLY BACK AND EVERYTHING WOULD BE OKAY?!

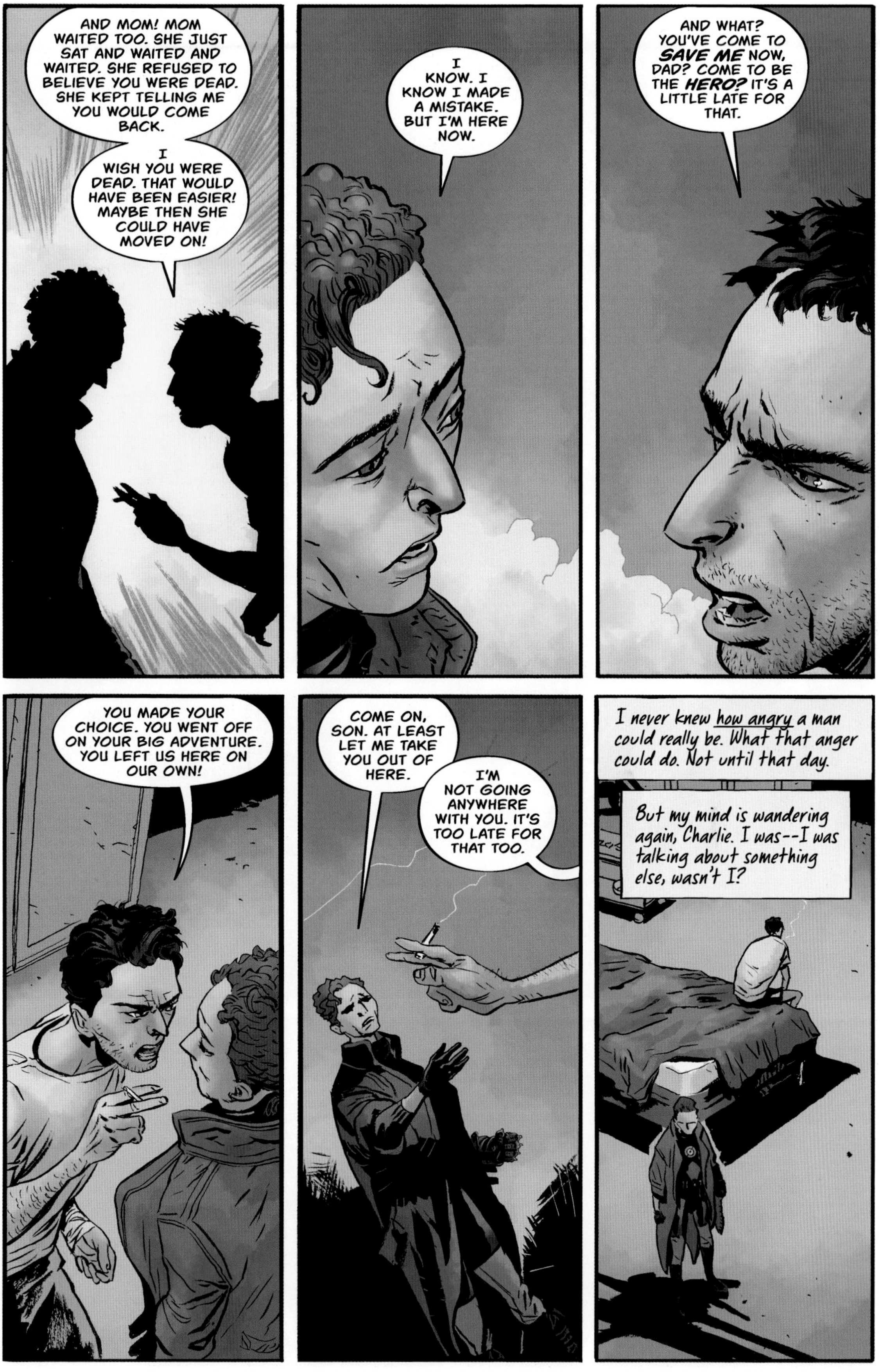

AND MOM! MOM WAITED TOO. SHE JUST SAT AND WAITED AND WAITED. SHE REFUSED TO BELIEVE YOU WERE DEAD. SHE KEPT TELLING ME YOU WOULD COME BACK.
I WISH YOU WERE DEAD. THAT WOULD HAVE BEEN EASIER! MAYBE THEN SHE COULD HAVE MOVED ON!
I KNOW. I KNOW I MADE A MISTAKE. BUT I'M HERE NOW.
AND WHAT? YOU'VE COME TO SAVE ME NOW, DAD? COME TO BE THE HERO? IT'S A LITTLE LATE FOR THAT.
YOU MADE YOUR CHOICE. YOU WENT OFF ON YOUR BIG ADVENTURE. YOU LEFT US HERE ON OUR OWN!
COME ON, SON. AT LEAST LET ME TAKE YOU OUT OF HERE.
I'M NOT GOING ANYWHERE WITH YOU. IT'S TOO LATE FOR THAT TOO.
I never knew how angry a man could really be. What that anger could do. Not until that day.
But my mind is wandering again, Charlie. I was--I was talking about something else, wasn't I?

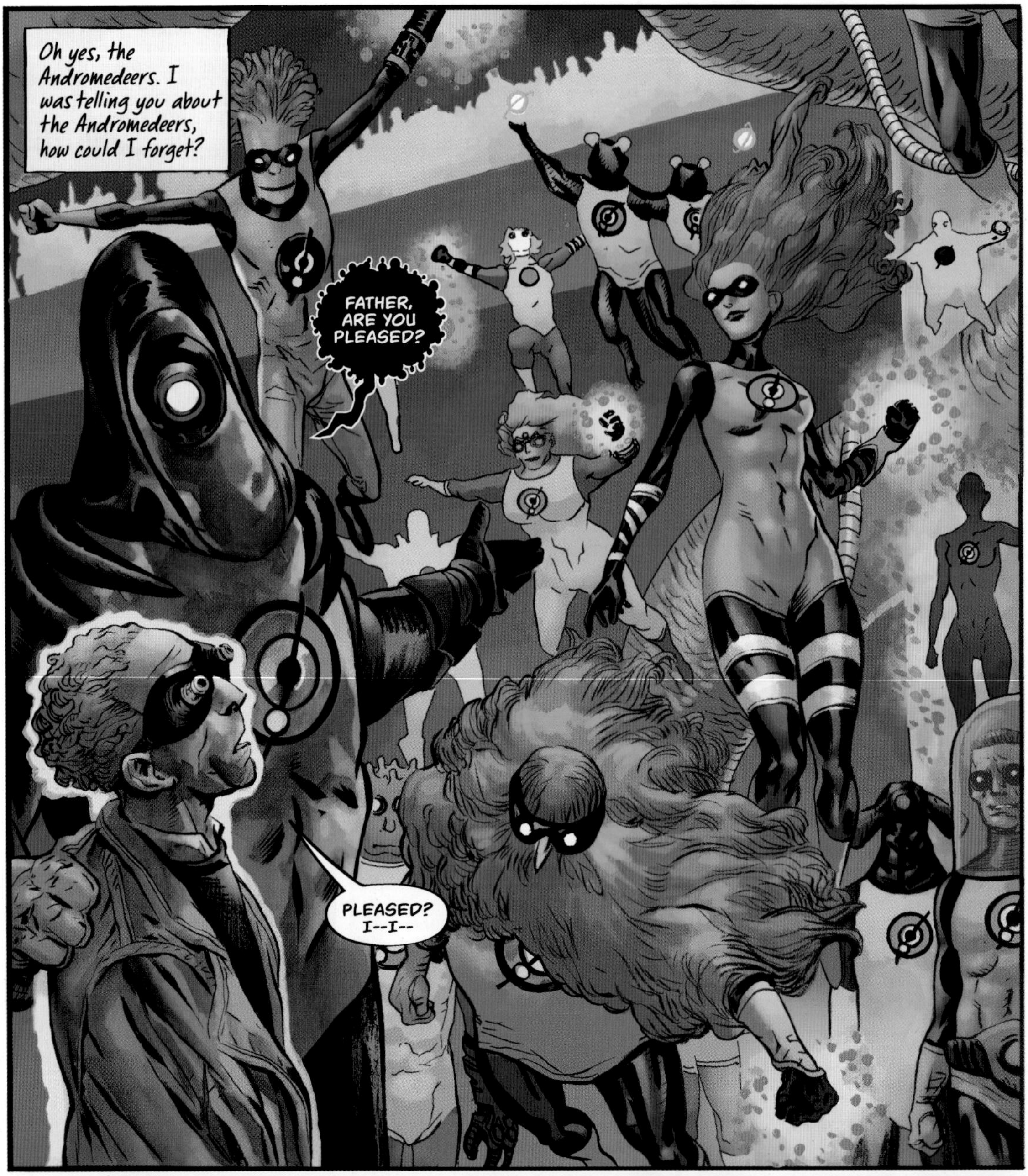
Oh yes, the Andromedeers. I was telling you about the Andromedeers, how could I forget?
FATHER, ARE YOU PLEASED?
PLEASED? I--I--

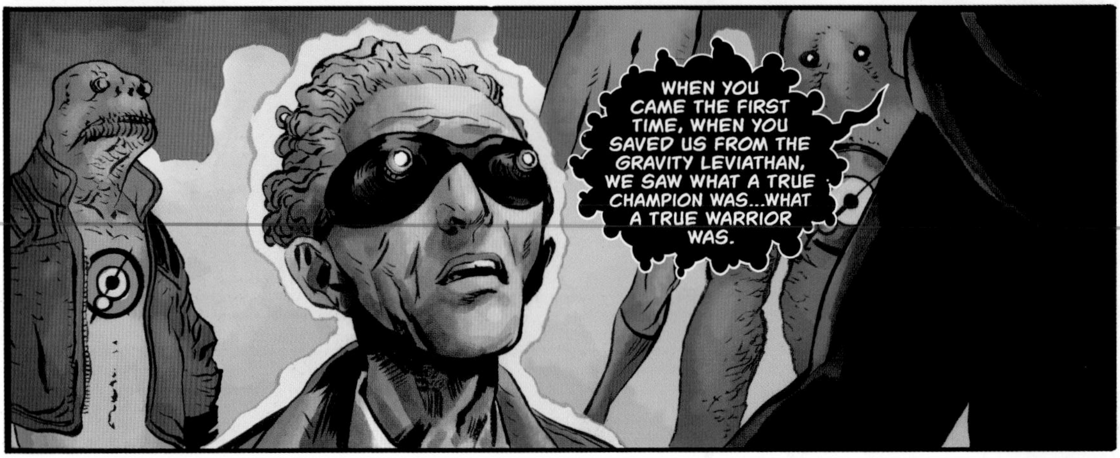
WHEN YOU CAME THE FIRST TIME, WHEN YOU SAVED US FROM THE GRAVITY LEVIATHAN, WE SAW WHAT A TRUE CHAMPION WAS...WHAT A TRUE WARRIOR WAS.

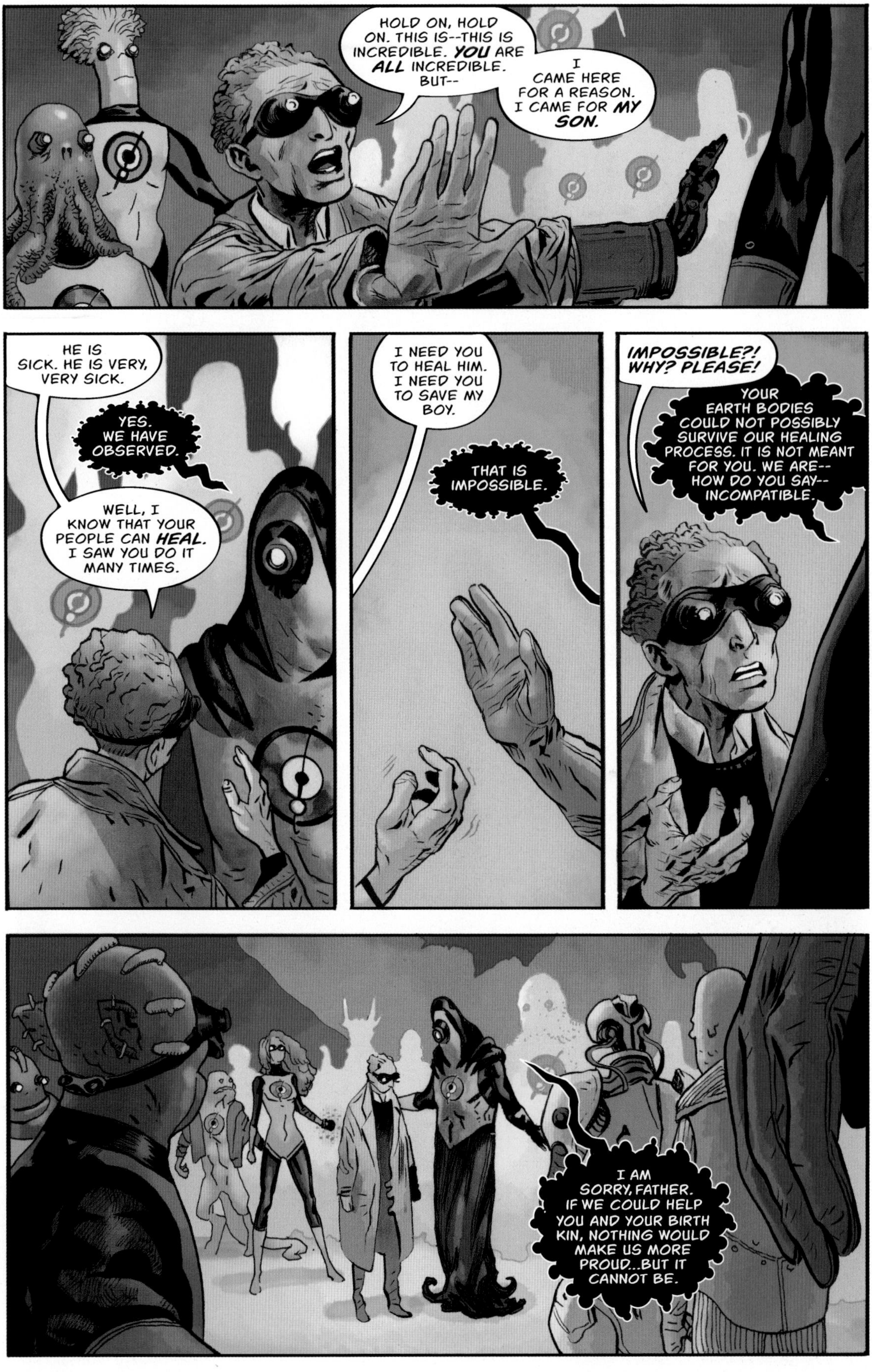
HOLD ON, HOLD ON. THIS IS--THIS IS INCREDIBLE. YOU ARE ALL INCREDIBLE. BUT--
I CAME HERE FOR A REASON. I CAME FOR MY SON.
HE IS SICK. HE IS VERY, VERY SICK.
YES. WE HAVE OBSERVED.
WELL, I KNOW THAT YOUR PEOPLE CAN HEAL. I SAW YOU DO IT MANY TIMES.
I NEED YOU TO HEAL HIM. I NEED YOU TO SAVE MY BOY.
THAT IS IMPOSSIBLE.
IMPOSSIBLE?! WHY? PLEASE!
YOUR EARTH BODIES COULD NOT POSSIBLY SURVIVE OUR HEALING PROCESS. IT IS NOT MEANT FOR YOU. WE ARE--HOW DO YOU SAY--INCOMPATIBLE.
I AM SORRY, FATHER. IF WE COULD HELP YOU AND YOUR BIRTH KIN, NOTHING WOULD MAKE US MORE PROUD...BUT IT CANNOT BE.

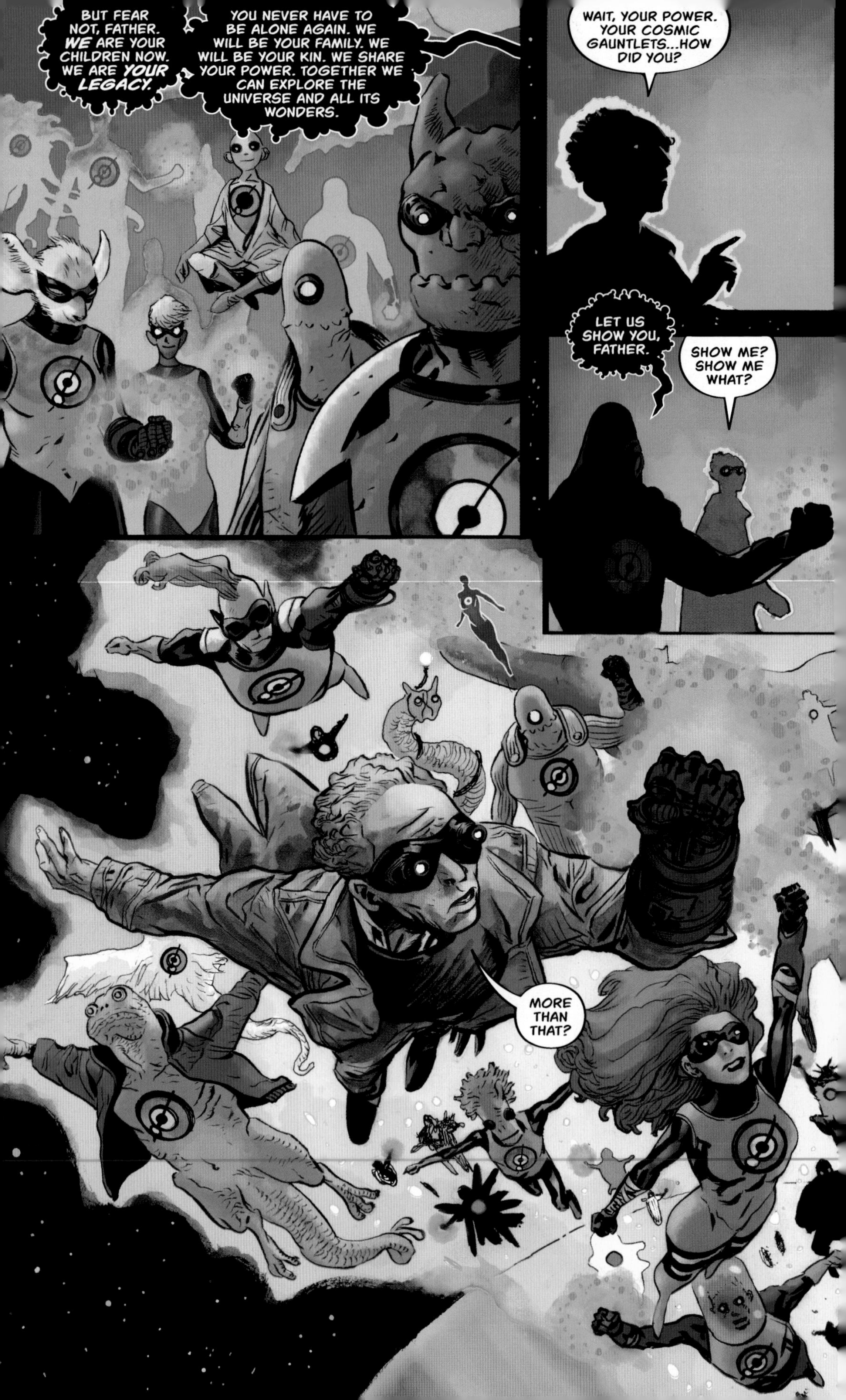
BUT FEAR NOT, FATHER. WE ARE YOUR CHILDREN NOW. WE ARE YOUR LEGACY.
YOU NEVER HAVE TO BE ALONE AGAIN. WE WILL BE YOUR FAMILY. WE WILL BE YOUR KIN. WE SHARE YOUR POWER. TOGETHER WE CAN EXPLORE THE UNIVERSE AND ALL ITS WONDERS.
WAIT, YOUR POWER. YOUR COSMIC GAUNTLETS...HOW DID YOU?
LET US SHOW YOU, FATHER.
SHOW ME? SHOW ME WHAT?
MORE THAN THAT?

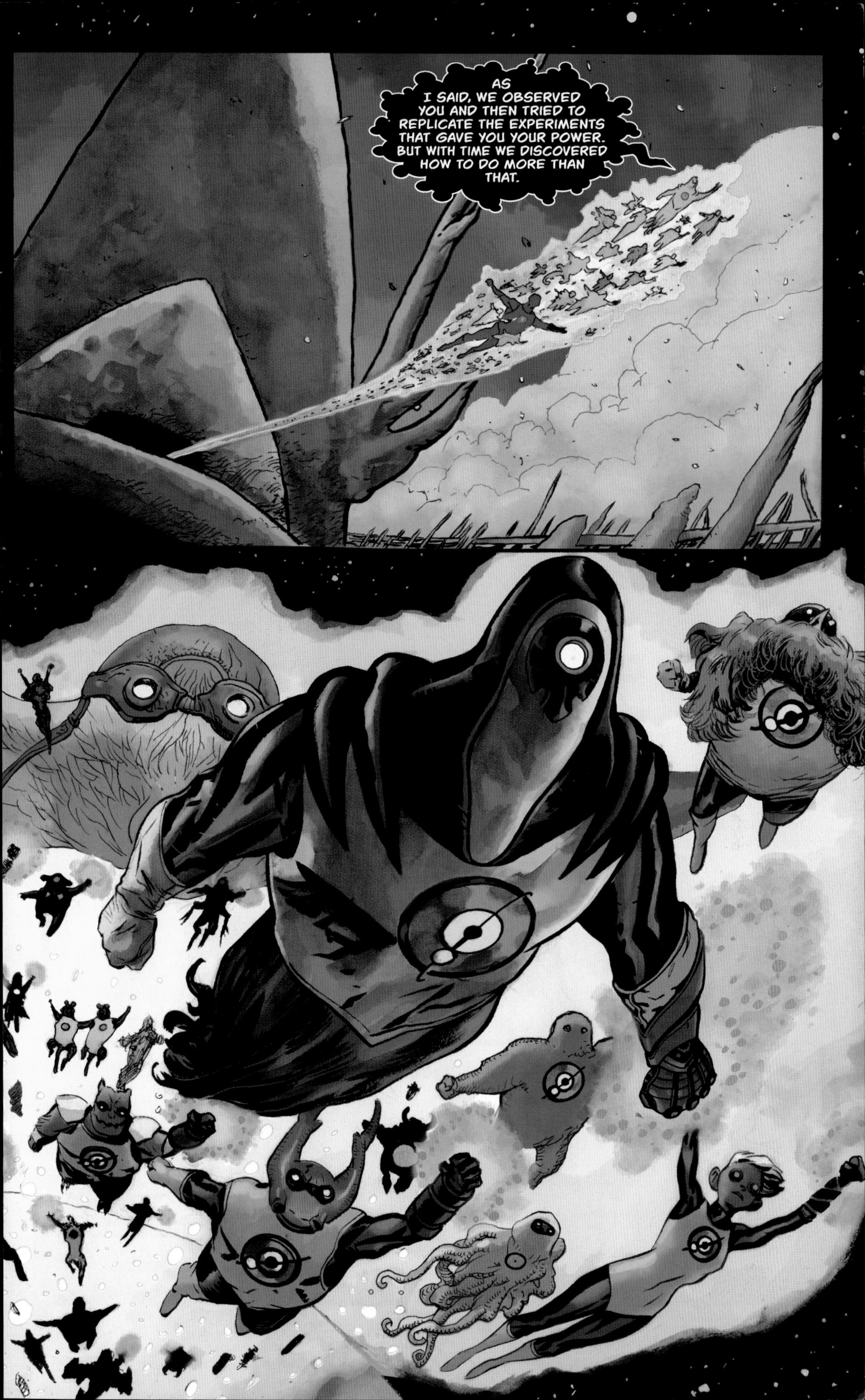
AS I SAID, WE OBSERVED YOU AND THEN TRIED TO REPLICATE THE EXPERIMENTS THAT GAVE YOU YOUR POWER. BUT WITH TIME WE DISCOVERED HOW TO DO MORE THAN THAT.

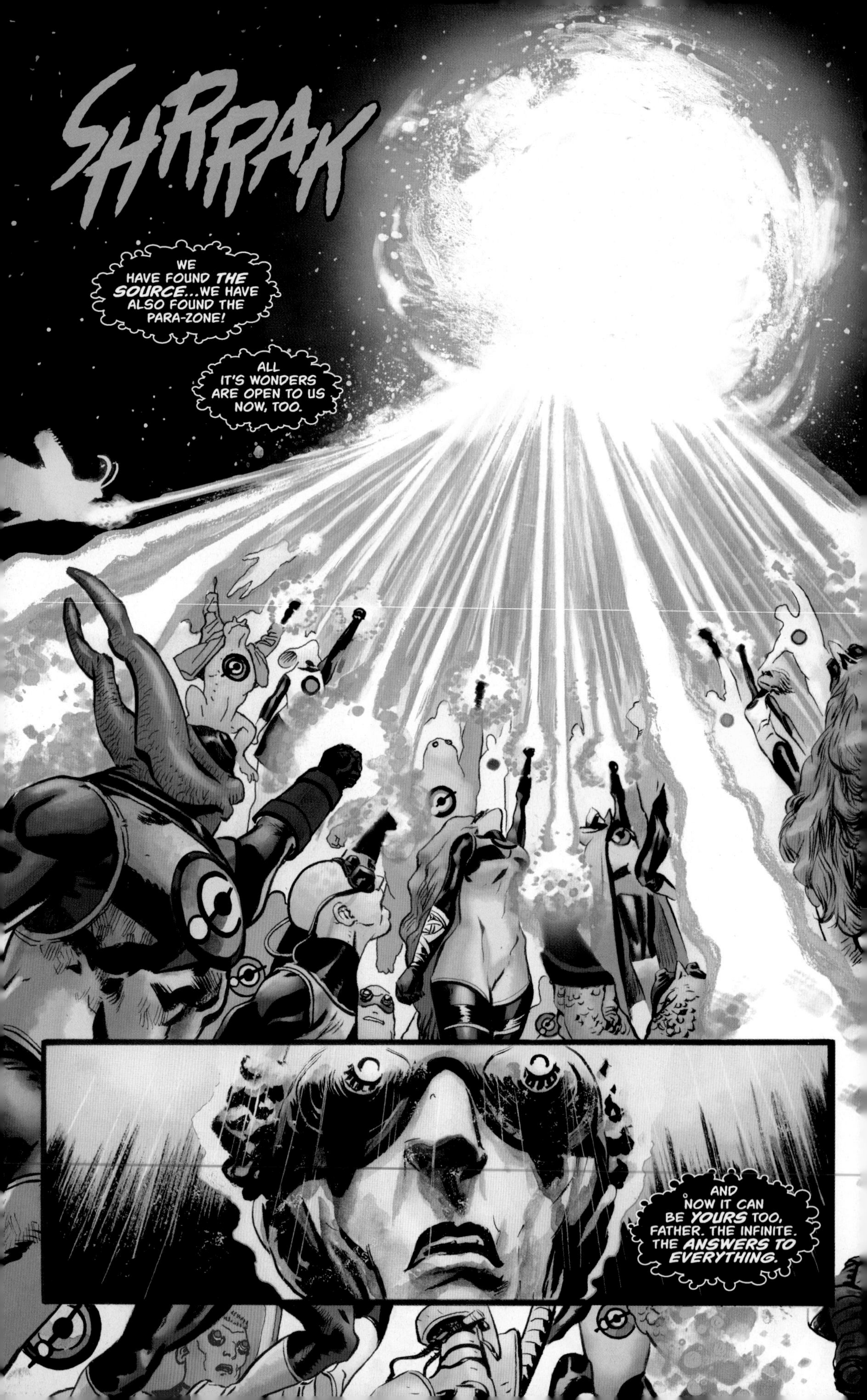
SHRRAK
WE HAVE FOUND THE SOURCE...WE HAVE ALSO FOUND THE PARA-ZONE!
ALL IT'S WONDERS ARE OPEN TO US NOW, TOO.
AND NOW IT CAN BE YOURS TOO, FATHER. THE INFINITE. THE ANSWERS TO EVERYTHING.

CHAPTER FOUR

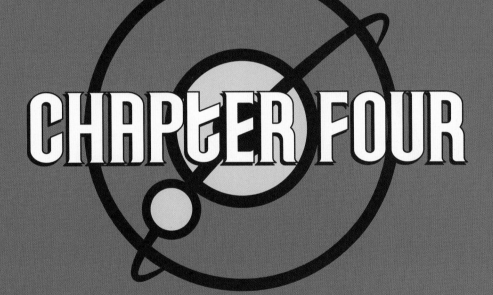

It wasn't what I expected. I mean--I don't know how I could have _expected_ anything specific. The Para-zone was the very definition of the unknown.

But I had touched it once, all those years ago, and stolen a piece of its power. I thought that was enough.

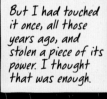

But seeing it there...open and waiting or me. I swear I've never wanted anything _so badly_ in all my life. Charlie.

My whole damn life...

1971

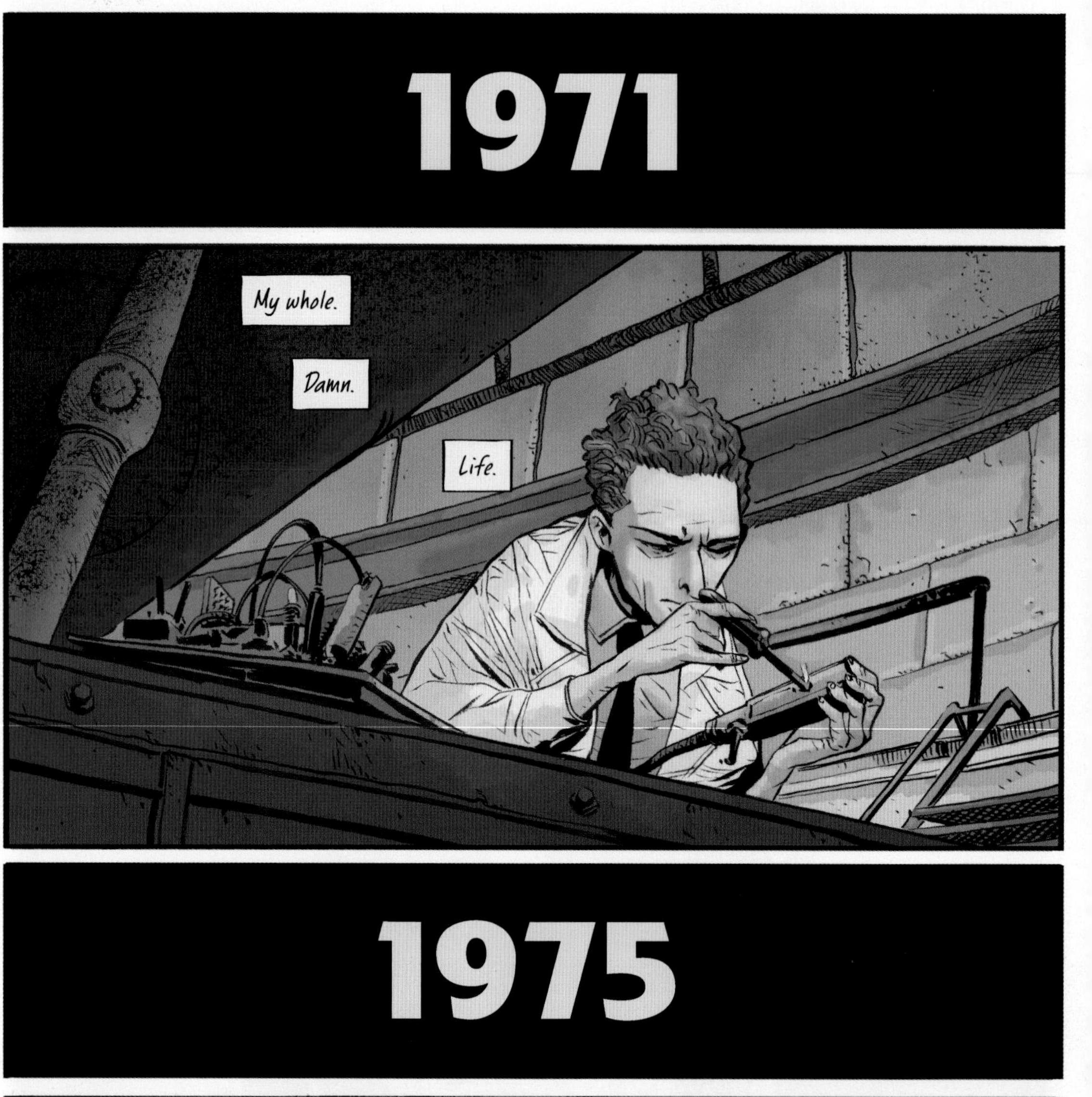
My whole.
Damn.
Life.

1975

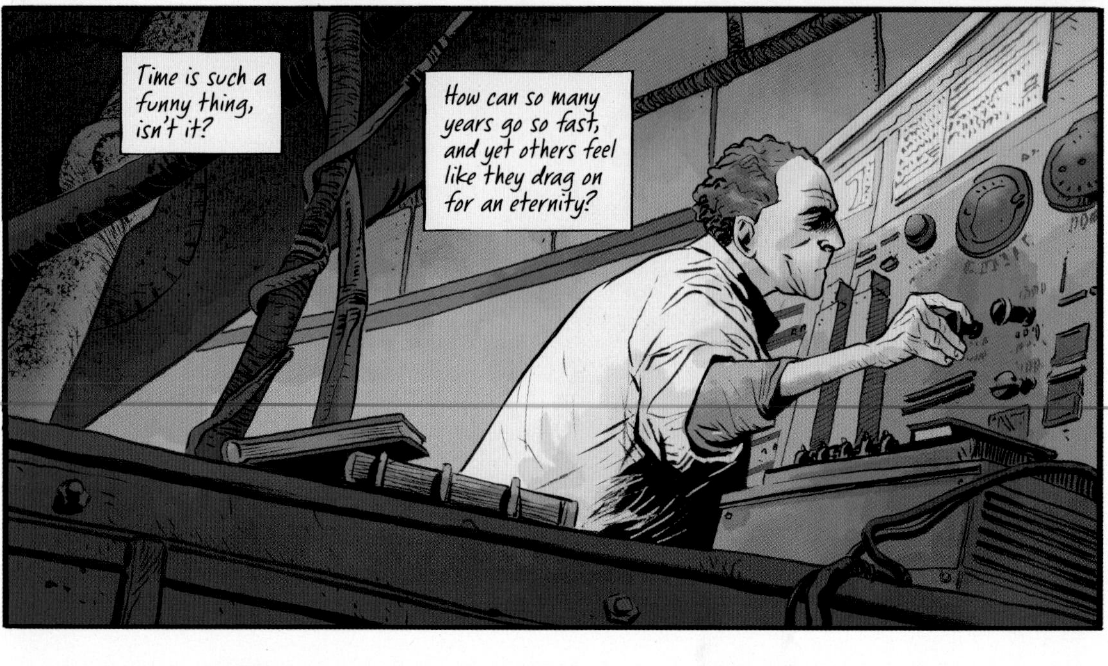
Time is such a funny thing, isn't it?
How can so many years go so fast, and yet others feel like they drag on for an eternity?

1981

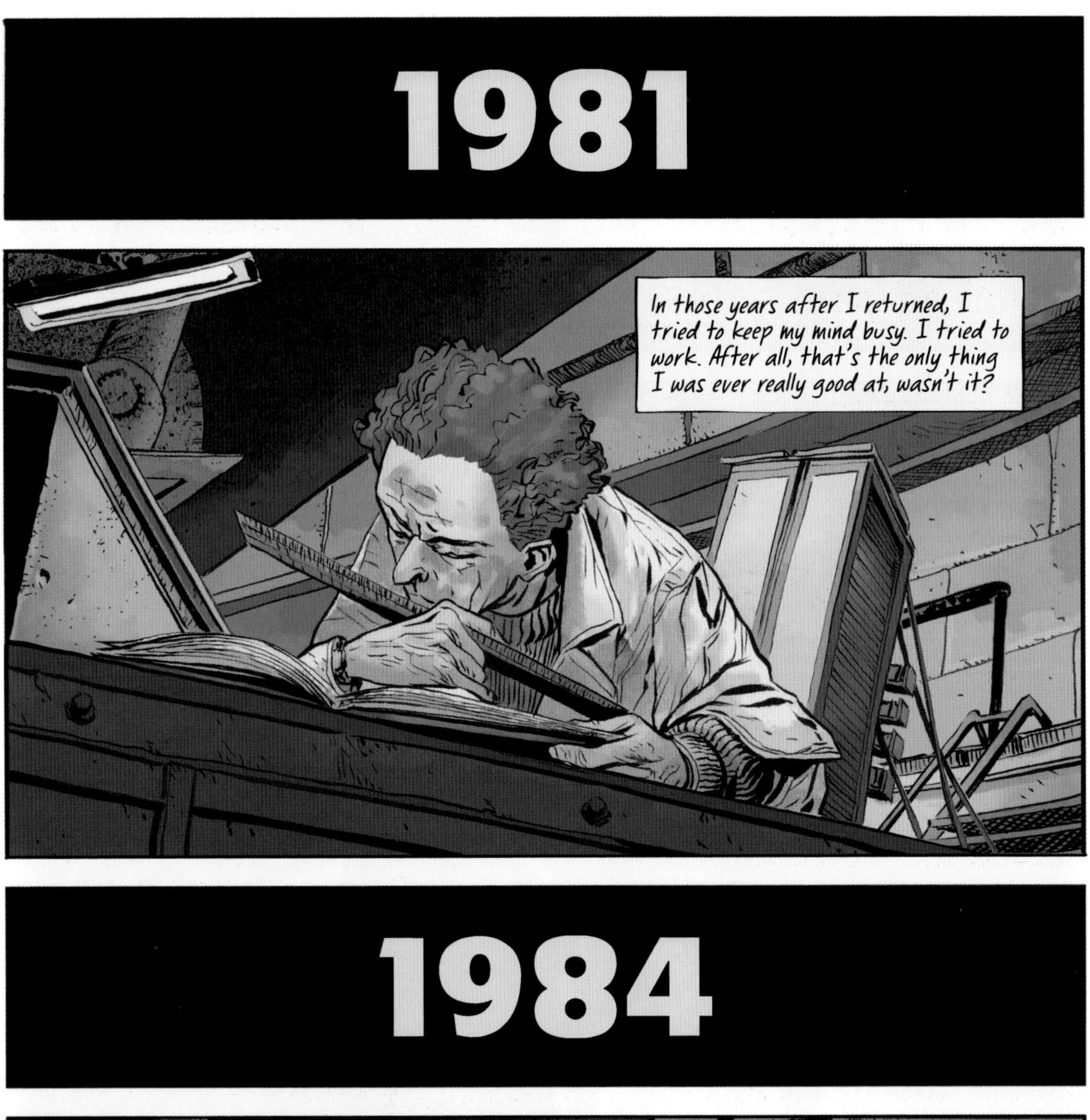
In those years after I returned, I tried to keep my mind busy. I tried to work. After all, that's the only thing I was ever really good at, wasn't it?

1984

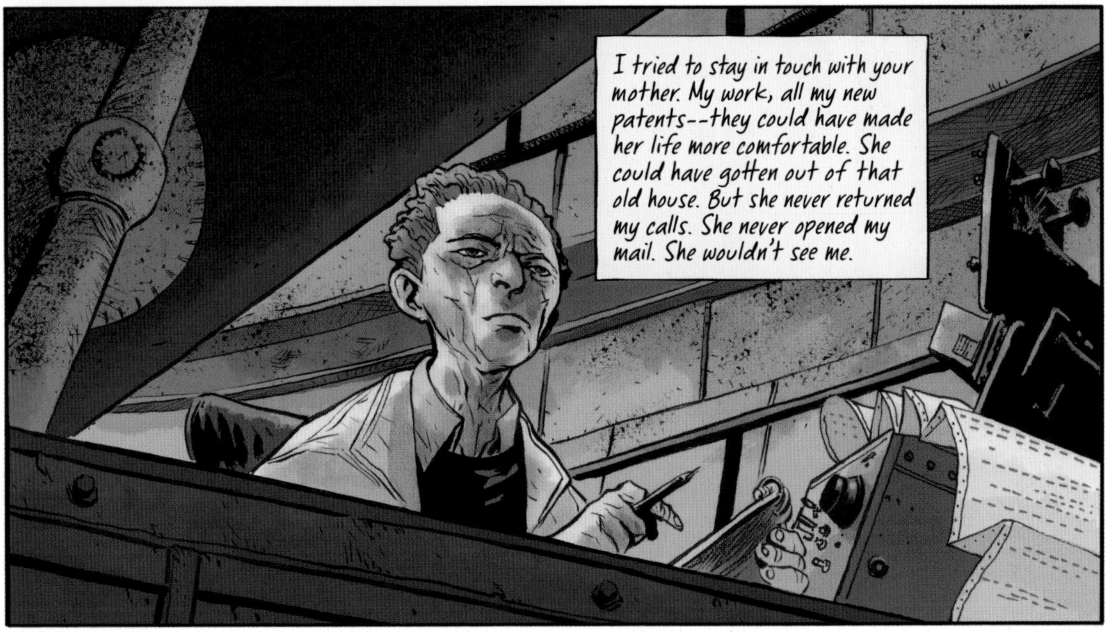
I tried to stay in touch with your mother. My work, all my new patents--they could have made her life more comfortable. She could have gotten out of that old house. But she never returned my calls. She never opened my mail. She wouldn't see me.

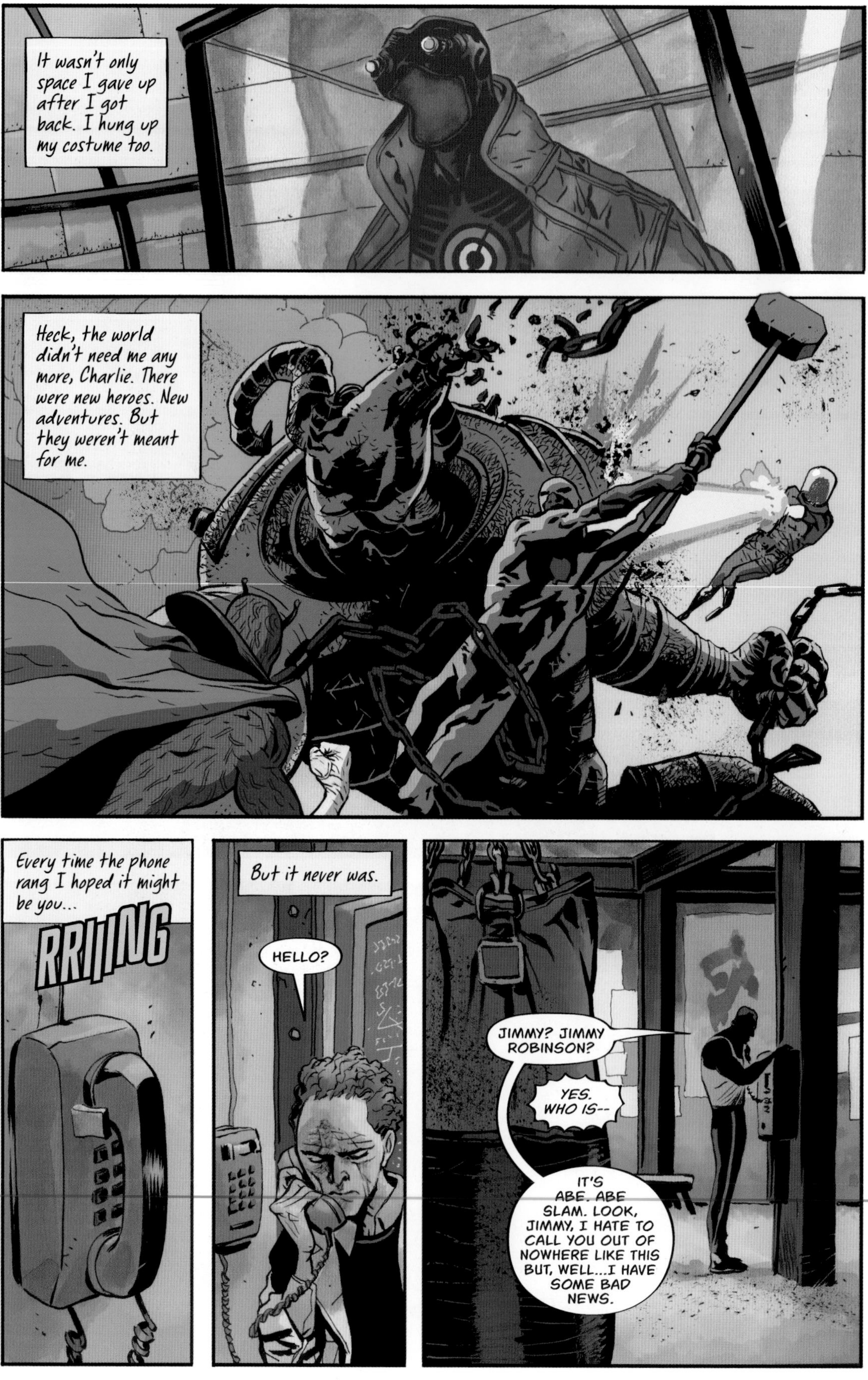
It wasn't only space I gave up after I got back. I hung up my costume too.
Heck, the world didn't need me any more, Charlie. There were new heroes. New adventures. But they weren't meant for me.
Every time the phone rang I hoped it might be you...
RRIIIING
But it never was.
HELLO?
JIMMY? JIMMY ROBINSON?
YES. WHO IS--
IT'S ABE. ABE SLAM. LOOK, JIMMY, I HATE TO CALL YOU OUT OF NOWHERE LIKE THIS BUT, WELL...I HAVE SOME BAD NEWS.

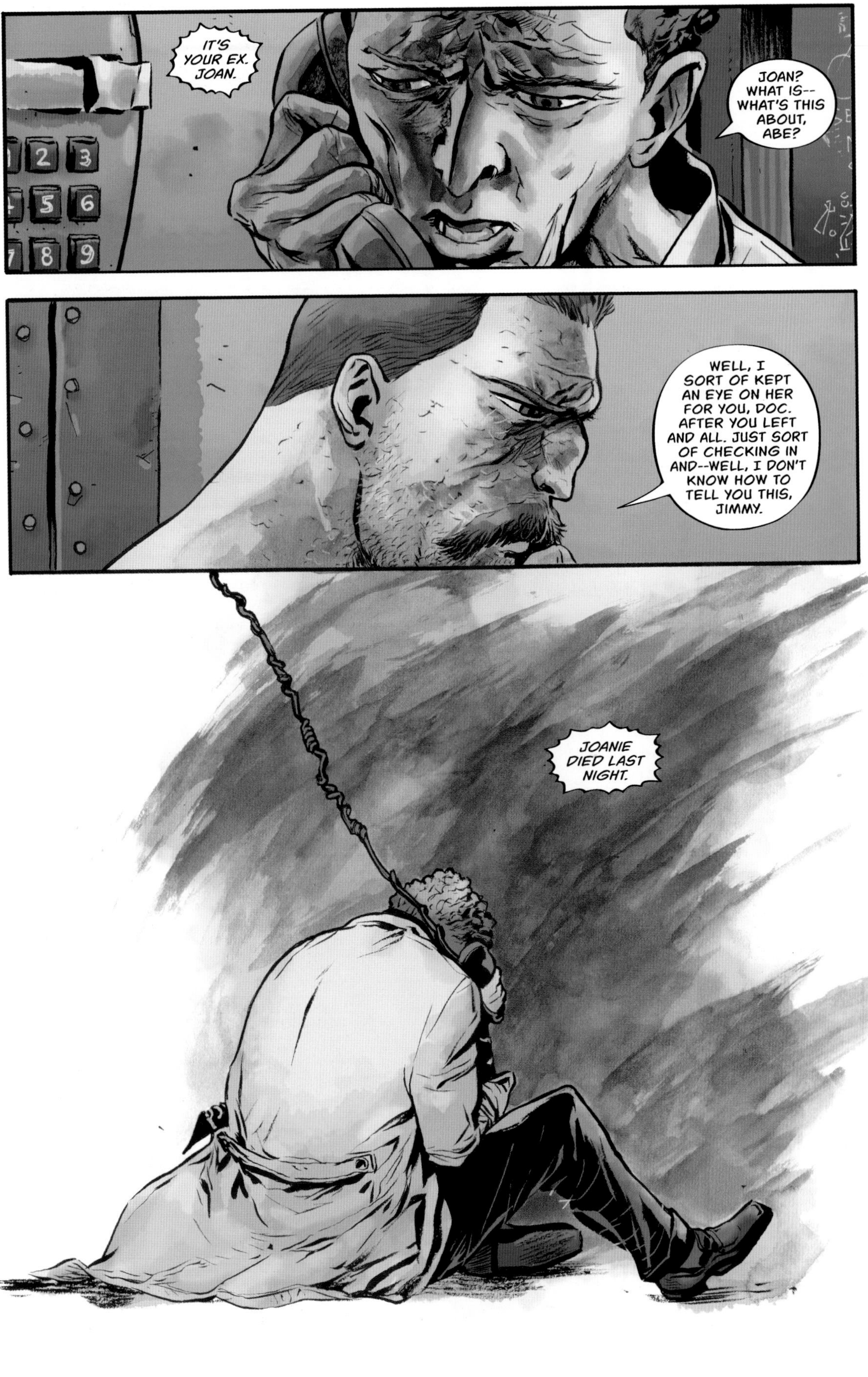
IT'S YOUR EX. JOAN.
JOAN? WHAT IS-- WHAT'S THIS ABOUT, ABE?
WELL, I SORT OF KEPT AN EYE ON HER FOR YOU, DOC. AFTER YOU LEFT AND ALL. JUST SORT OF CHECKING IN AND--WELL, I DON'T KNOW HOW TO TELL YOU THIS, JIMMY.
JOANIE DIED LAST NIGHT.

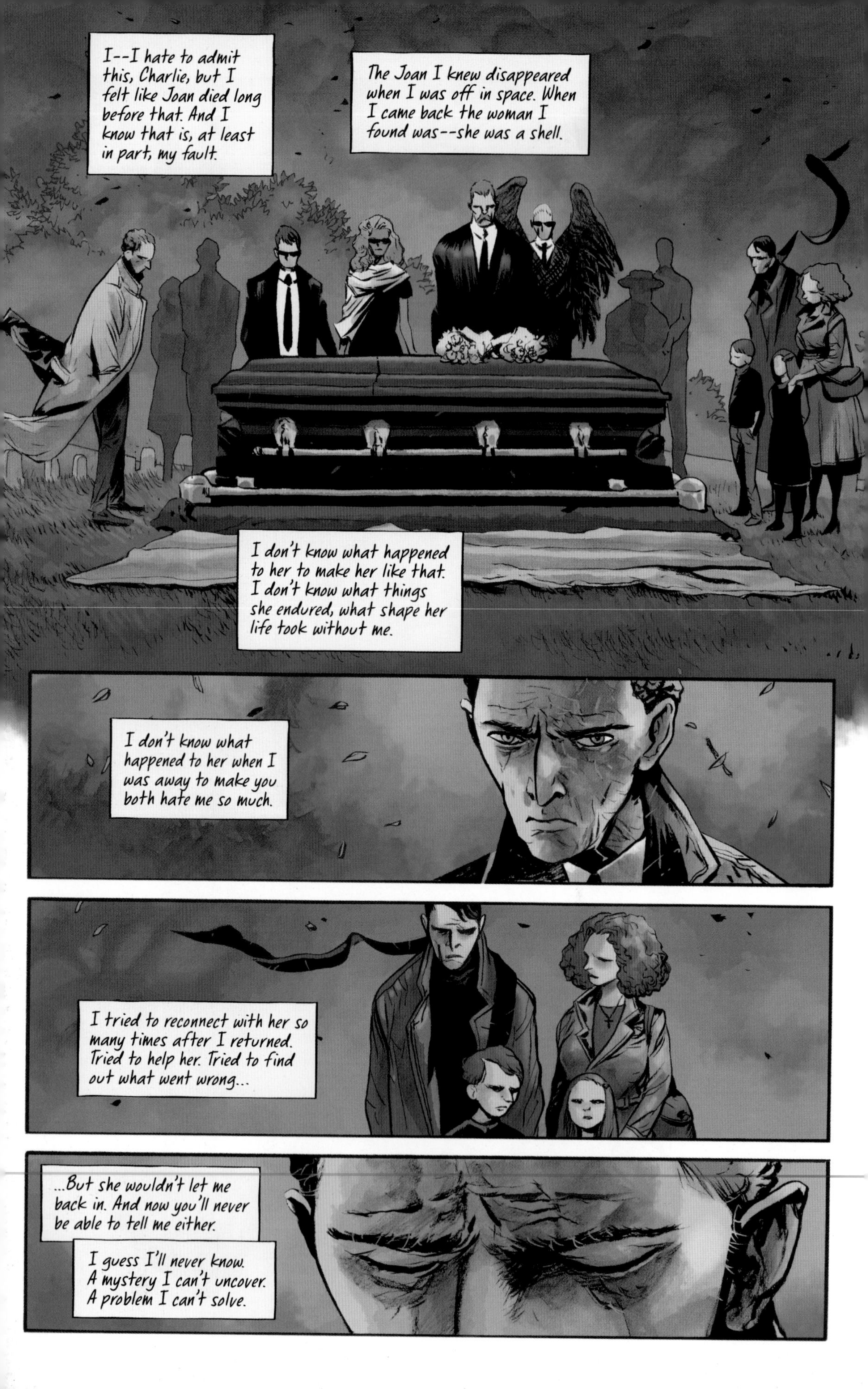
I--I hate to admit this, Charlie, but I felt like Joan died long before that. And I know that is, at least in part, my fault.
The Joan I knew disappeared when I was off in space. When I came back the woman I found was--she was a shell.
I don't know what happened to her to make her like that. I don't know what things she endured, what shape her life took without me.
I don't know what happened to her when I was away to make you both hate me so much.
I tried to reconnect with her so many times after I returned. Tried to help her. Tried to find out what went wrong...
...But she wouldn't let me back in. And now you'll never be able to tell me either.
I guess I'll never know. A mystery I can't uncover. A problem I can't solve.

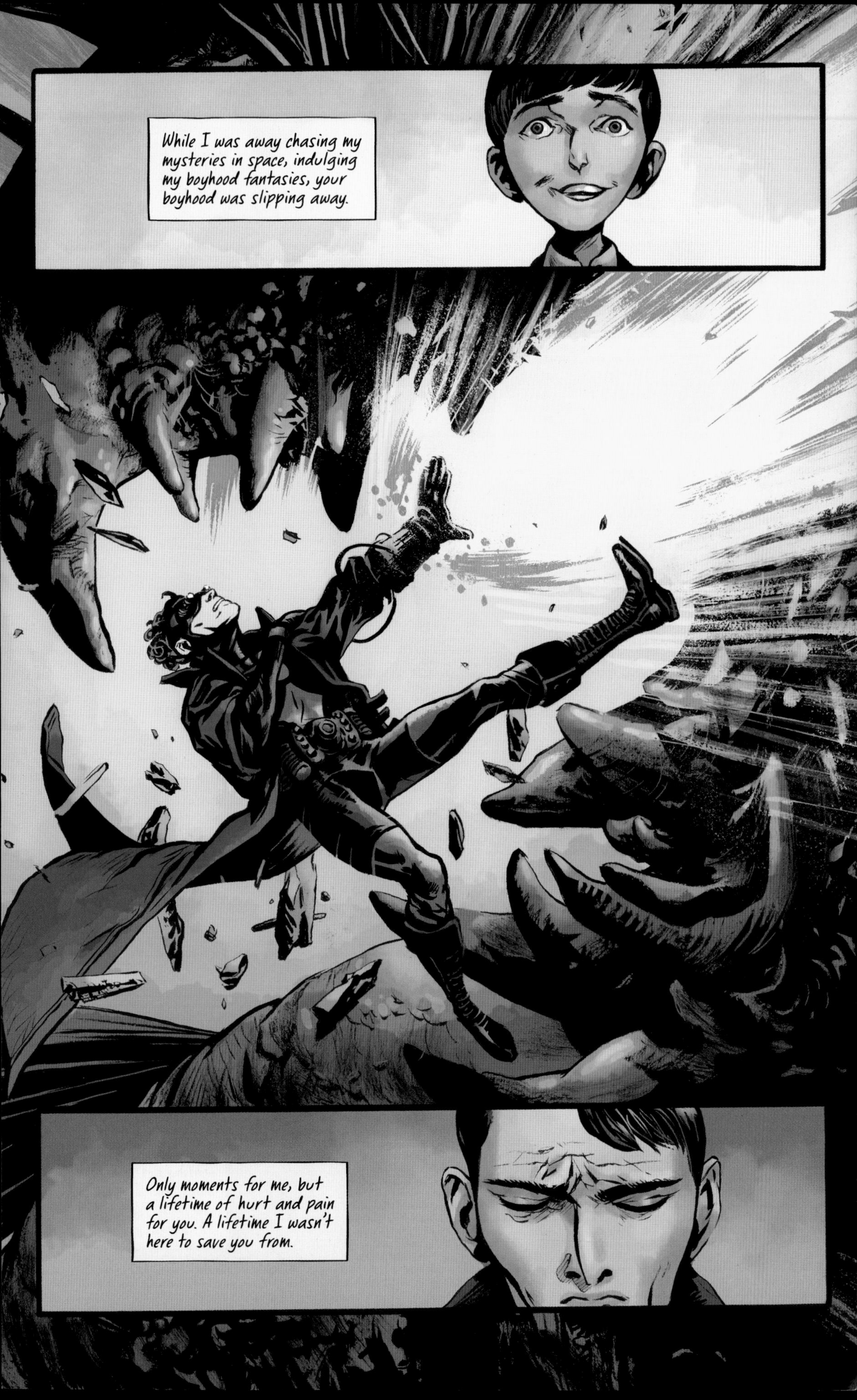
While I was away chasing my mysteries in space, indulging my boyhood fantasies, your boyhood was slipping away.
Only moments for me, but a lifetime of hurt and pain for you. A lifetime I wasn't here to save you from.

And I just _left_ your mother to try and navigate that life with you. I was off exploring new societies and seeing wonders no man had ever seen, and she--

Hell, who am I kidding, I left her long before that, didn't I? I was always in my lab. I was always working and she was--she was waiting.

And finally that waiting got to be too much, and I guess she collapsed under the weight of it.

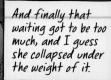

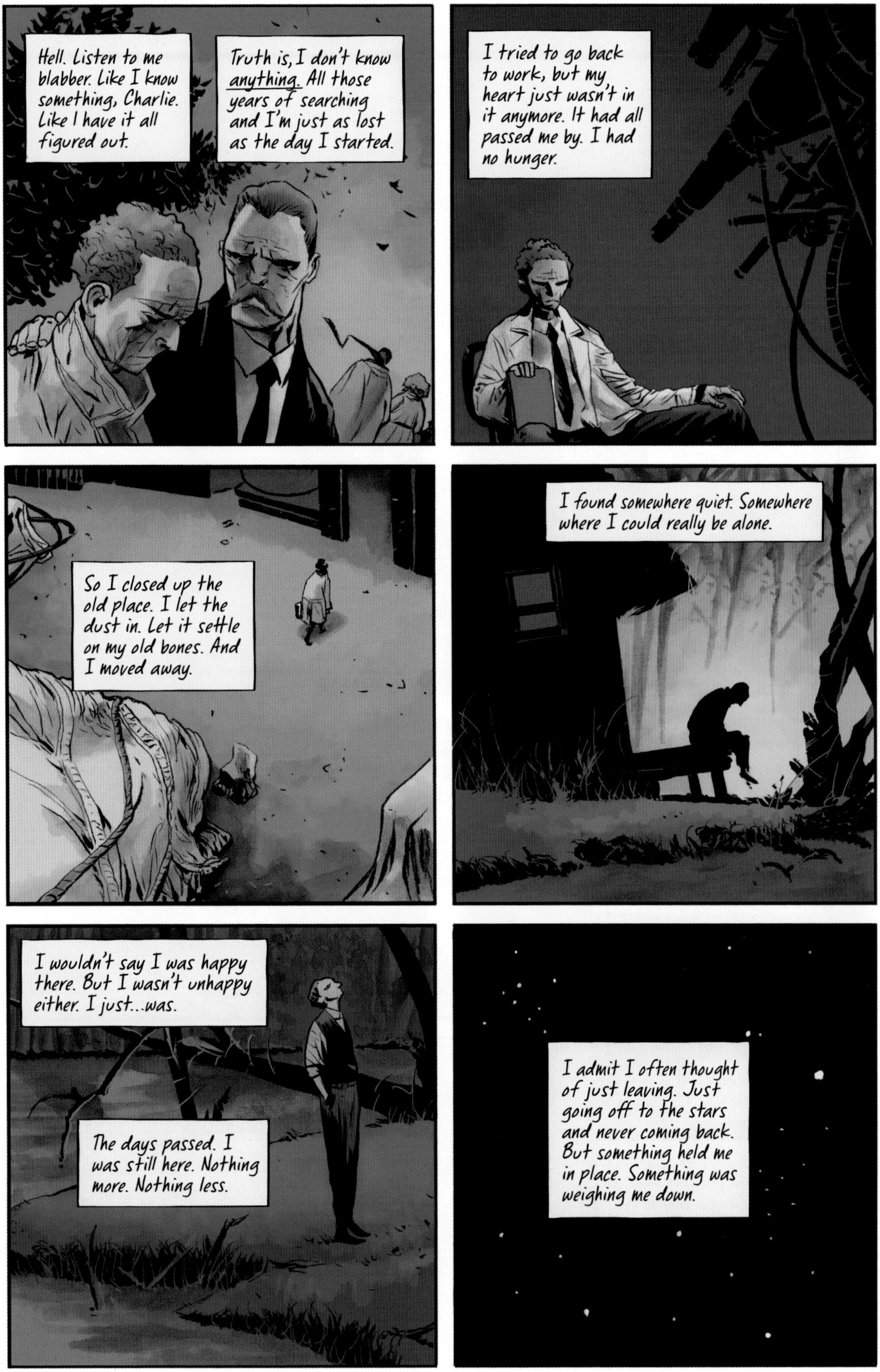
Hell. Listen to me blabber. Like I know something, Charlie. Like I have it all figured out.
Truth is, I don't know anything. All those years of searching and I'm just as lost as the day I started.
I tried to go back to work, but my heart just wasn't in it anymore. It had all passed me by. I had no hunger.
So I closed up the old place. I let the dust in. Let it settle on my old bones. And I moved away.
I found somewhere quiet. Somewhere where I could really be alone.
I wouldn't say I was happy there. But I wasn't unhappy either. I just...was.
The days passed. I was still here. Nothing more. Nothing less.
I admit I often thought of just leaving. Just going off to the stars and never coming back. But something held me in place. Something was weighing me down.

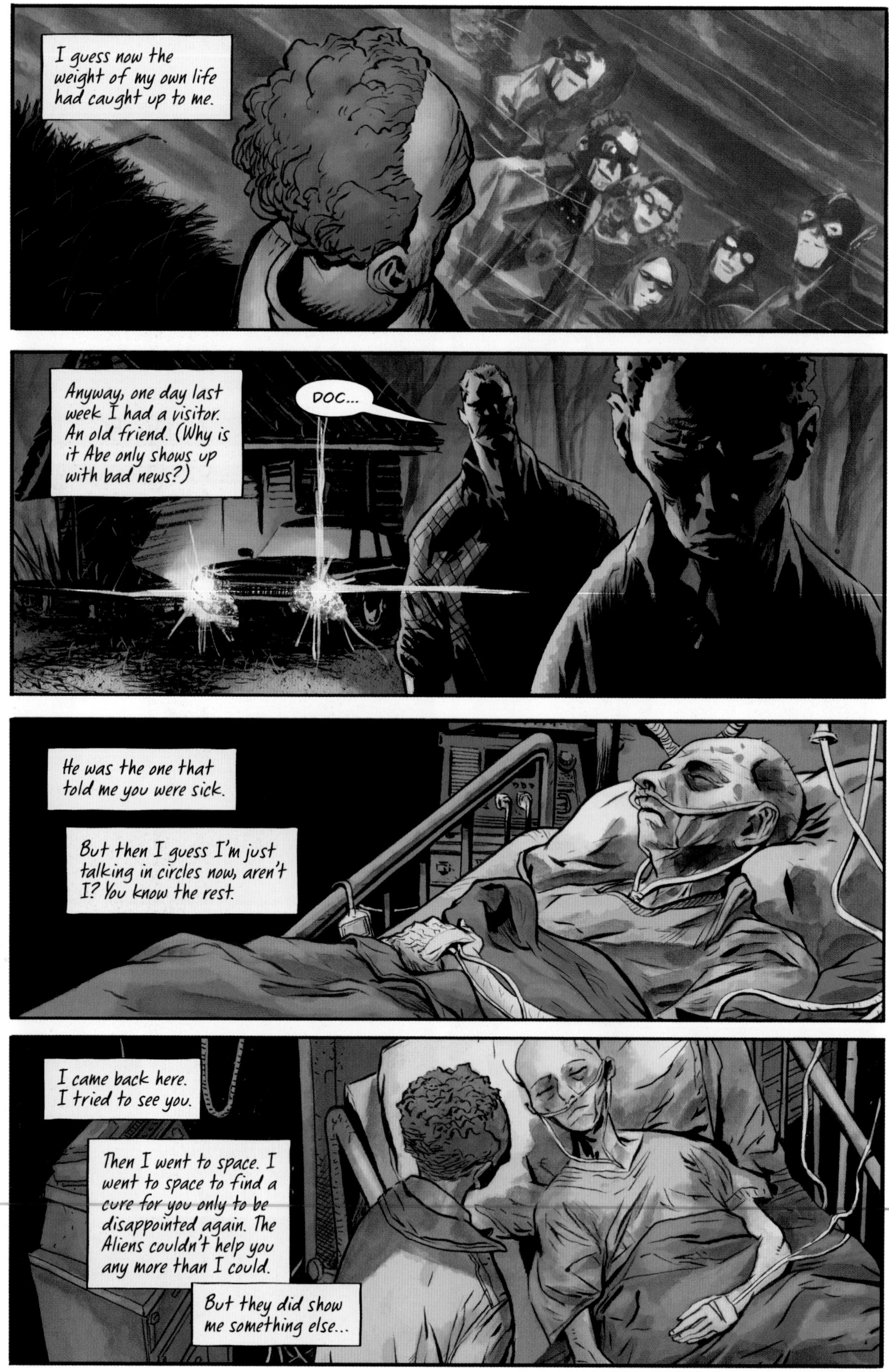
I guess now the weight of my own life had caught up to me.
Anyway, one day last week I had a visitor. An old friend. (Why is it Abe only shows up with bad news?)
DOC...
He was the one that told me you were sick.
But then I guess I'm just talking in circles now, aren't I? You know the rest.
I came back here. I tried to see you.
Then I went to space. I went to space to find a cure for you only to be disappointed again. The Aliens couldn't help you any more than I could.
But they did show me something else...

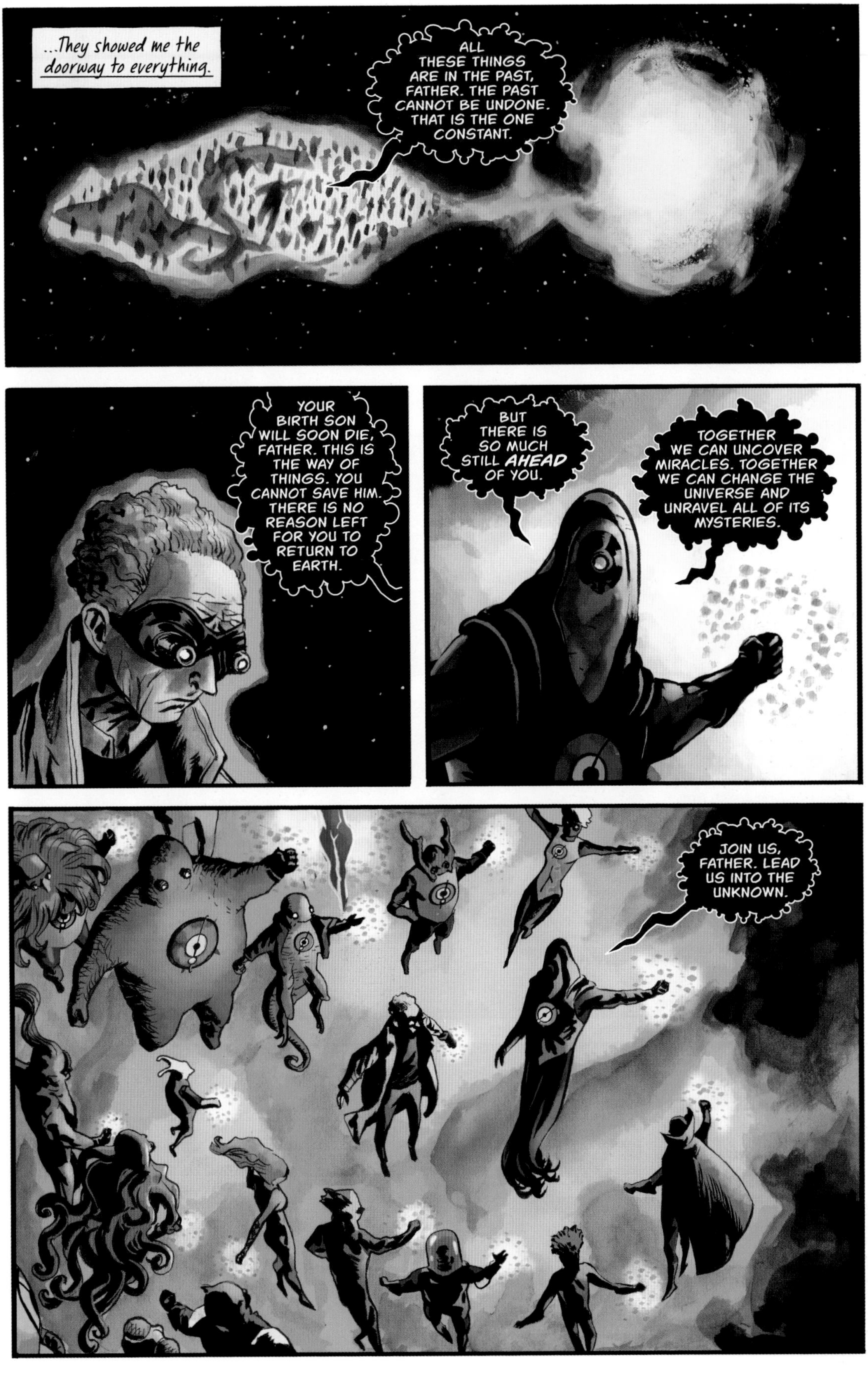

...They showed me the doorway to everything.
ALL THESE THINGS ARE IN THE PAST, FATHER. THE PAST CANNOT BE UNDONE. THAT IS THE ONE CONSTANT.
YOUR BIRTH SON WILL SOON DIE, FATHER. THIS IS THE WAY OF THINGS. YOU CANNOT SAVE HIM. THERE IS NO REASON LEFT FOR YOU TO RETURN TO EARTH.
BUT THERE IS SO MUCH STILL AHEAD OF YOU.
TOGETHER WE CAN UNCOVER MIRACLES. TOGETHER WE CAN CHANGE THE UNIVERSE AND UNRAVEL ALL OF ITS MYSTERIES.
JOIN US, FATHER. LEAD US INTO THE UNKNOWN.

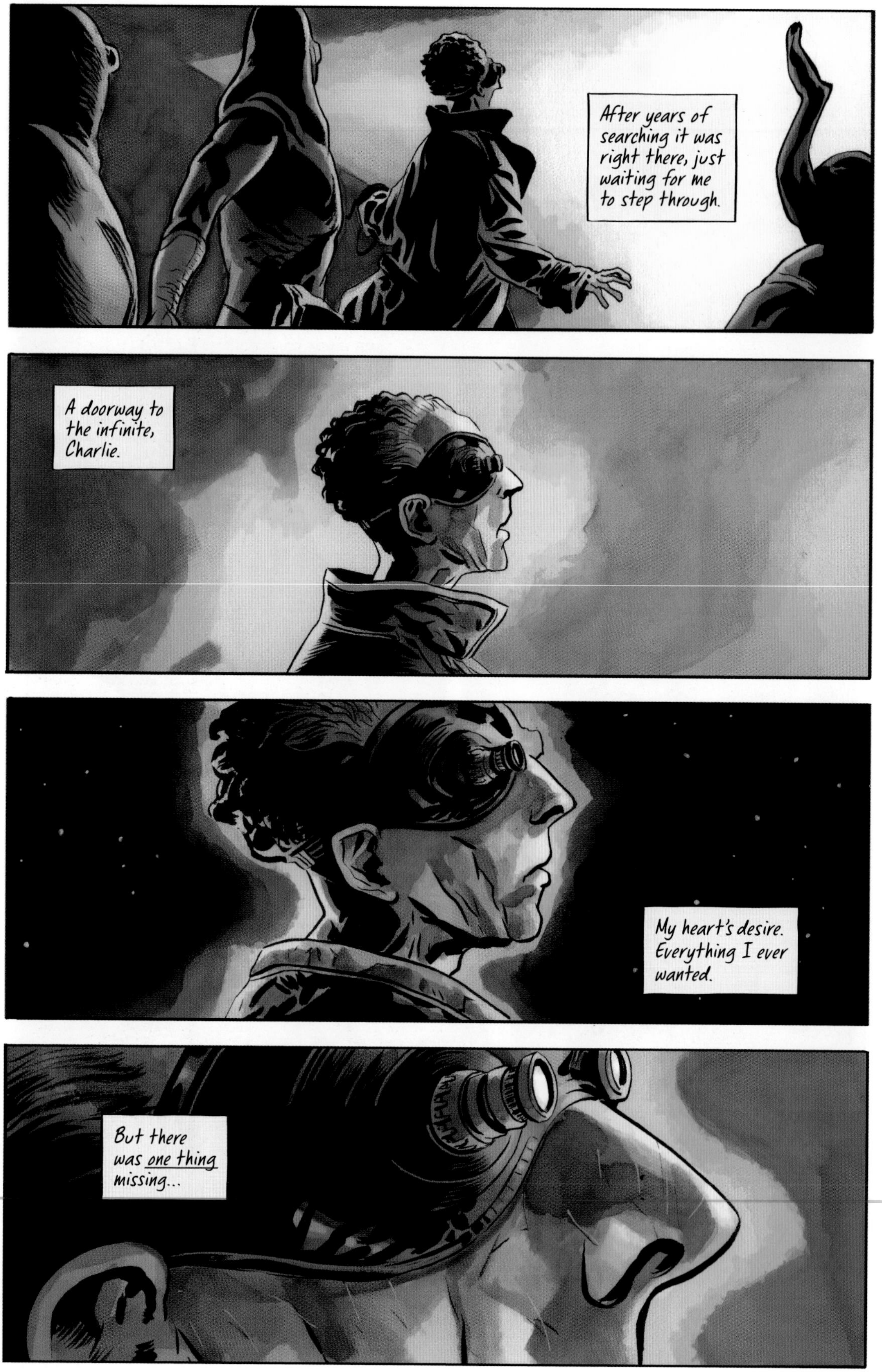
After years of searching it was right there, just waiting for me to step through.
A doorway to the infinite, Charlie.
My heart's desire. Everything I ever wanted.
But there was one thing missing...

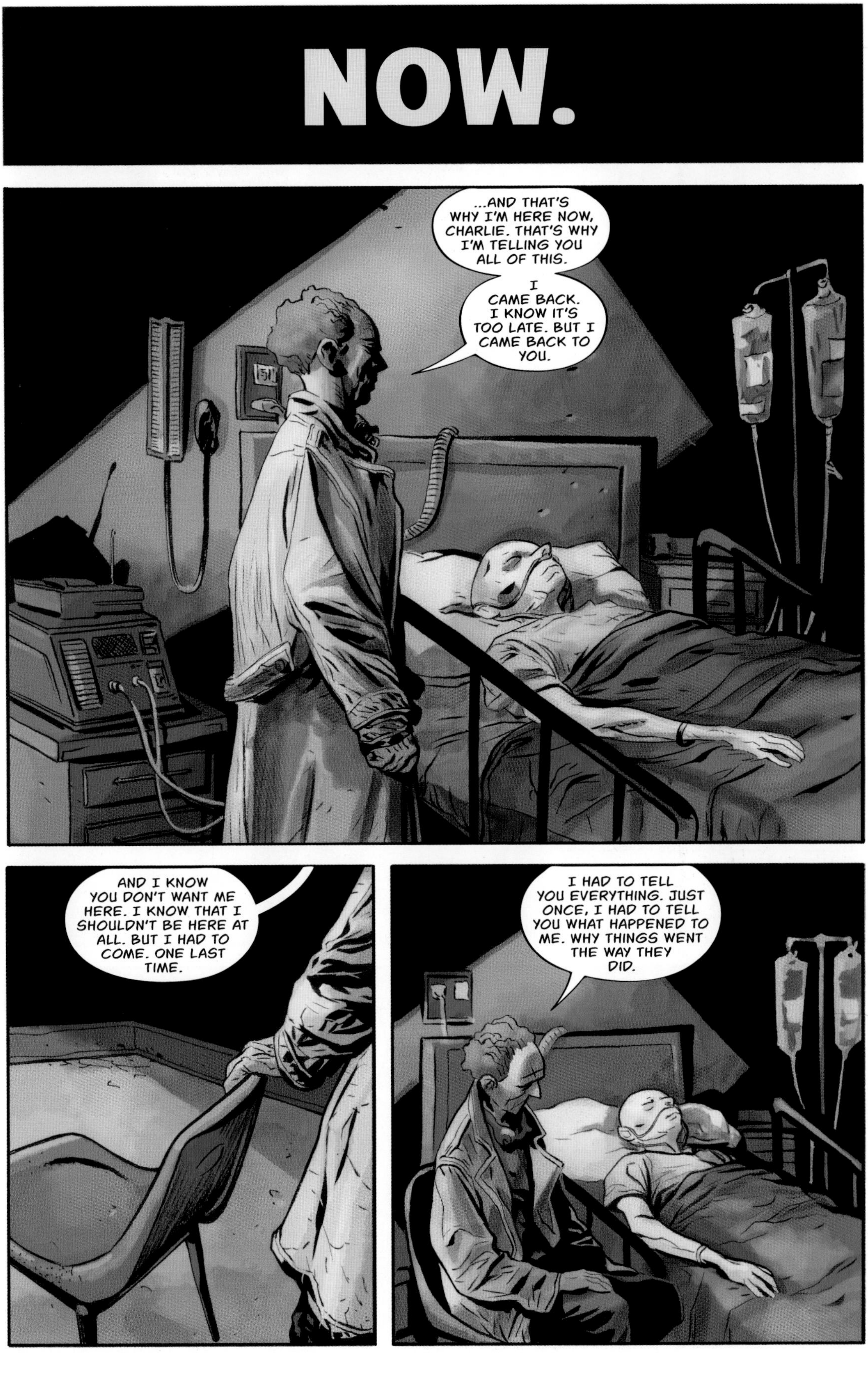
NOW.
...AND THAT'S WHY I'M HERE NOW, CHARLIE. THAT'S WHY I'M TELLING YOU ALL OF THIS.
I CAME BACK. I KNOW IT'S TOO LATE. BUT I CAME BACK TO YOU.
AND I KNOW YOU DON'T WANT ME HERE. I KNOW THAT I SHOULDN'T BE HERE AT ALL. BUT I HAD TO COME. ONE LAST TIME.
I HAD TO TELL YOU EVERYTHING. JUST ONCE, I HAD TO TELL YOU WHAT HAPPENED TO ME. WHY THINGS WENT THE WAY THEY DID.

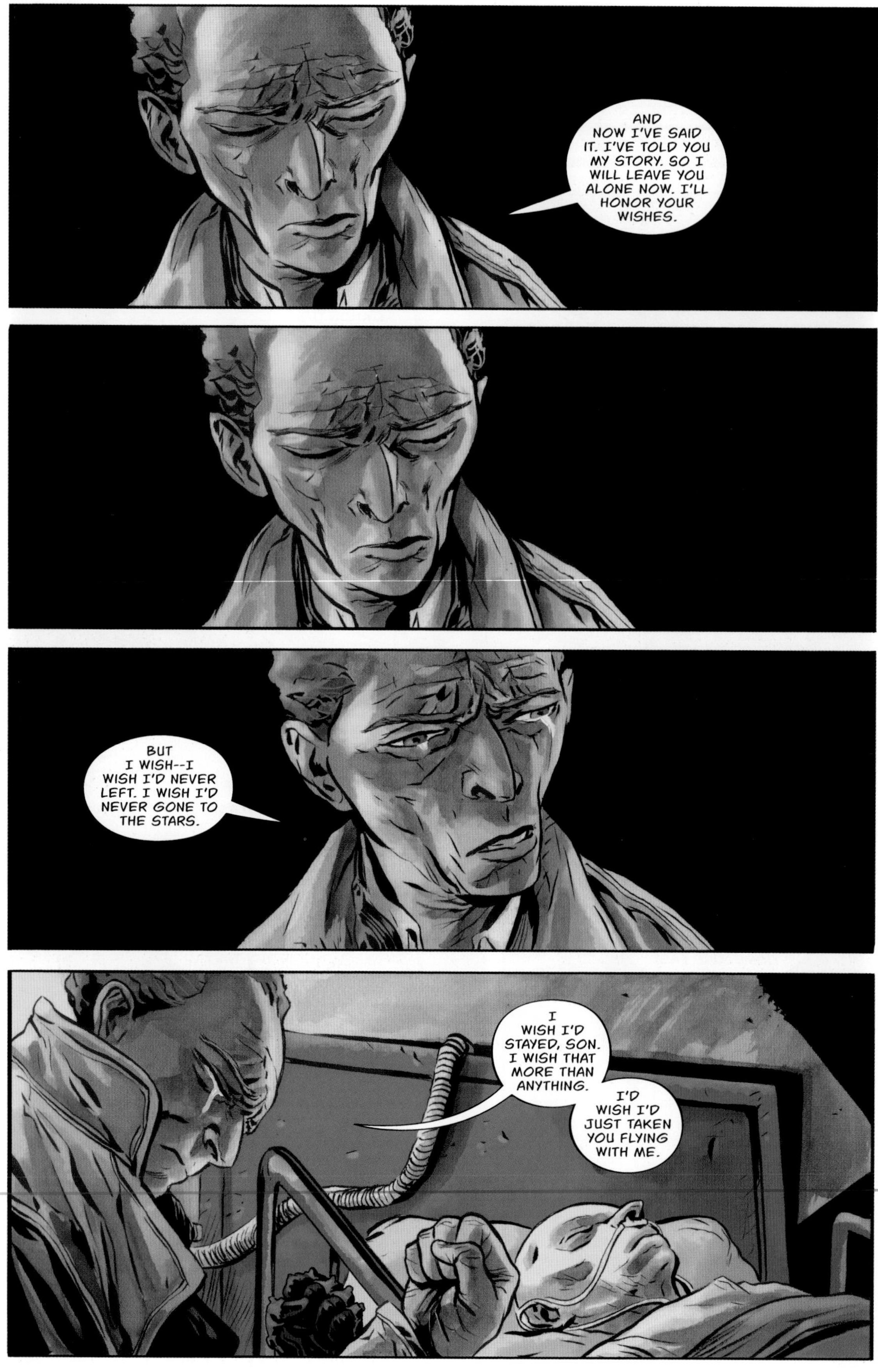
AND NOW I'VE SAID IT. I'VE TOLD YOU MY STORY. SO I WILL LEAVE YOU ALONE NOW. I'LL HONOR YOUR WISHES.
BUT I WISH--I WISH I'D NEVER LEFT. I WISH I'D NEVER GONE TO THE STARS.
I WISH I'D STAYED, SON. I WISH THAT MORE THAN ANYTHING.
I'D WISH I'D JUST TAKEN YOU FLYING WITH ME.

D--
DAD?
YES! IT'S ME, CHARLIE. I'M HERE.
TAKE ME NOW.
I--I DIDN'T HEAR THAT, SON. WHAT DID YOU SAY?
TAKE ME NOW, DAD... I'M READY.
You're ready.

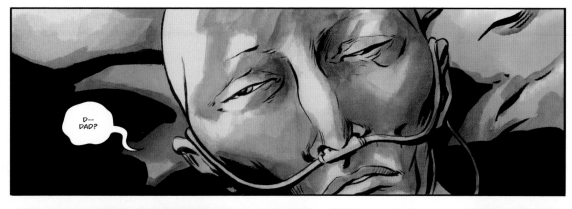

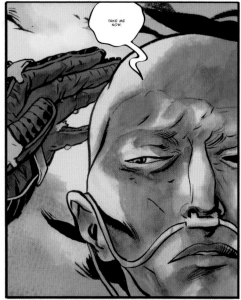

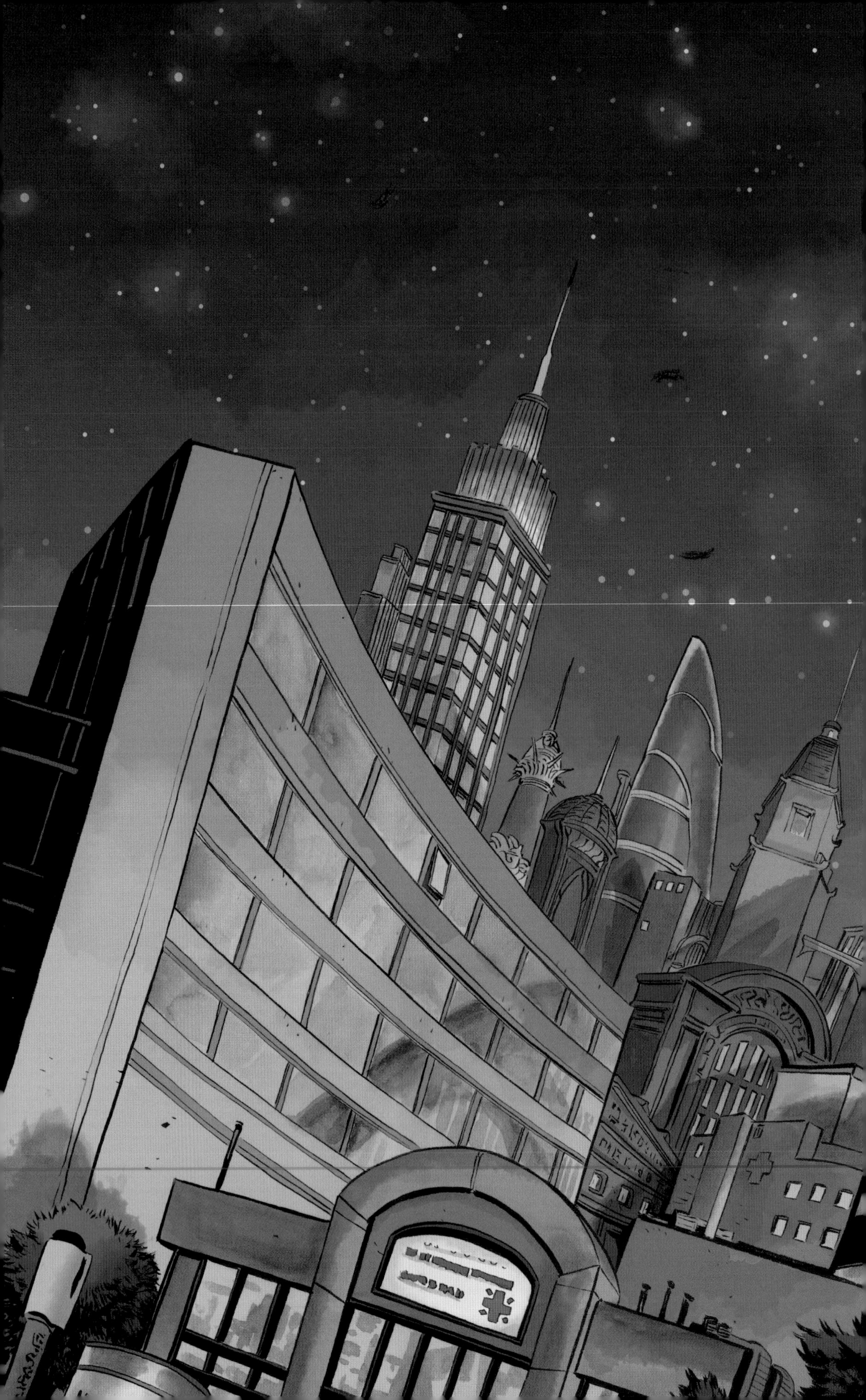

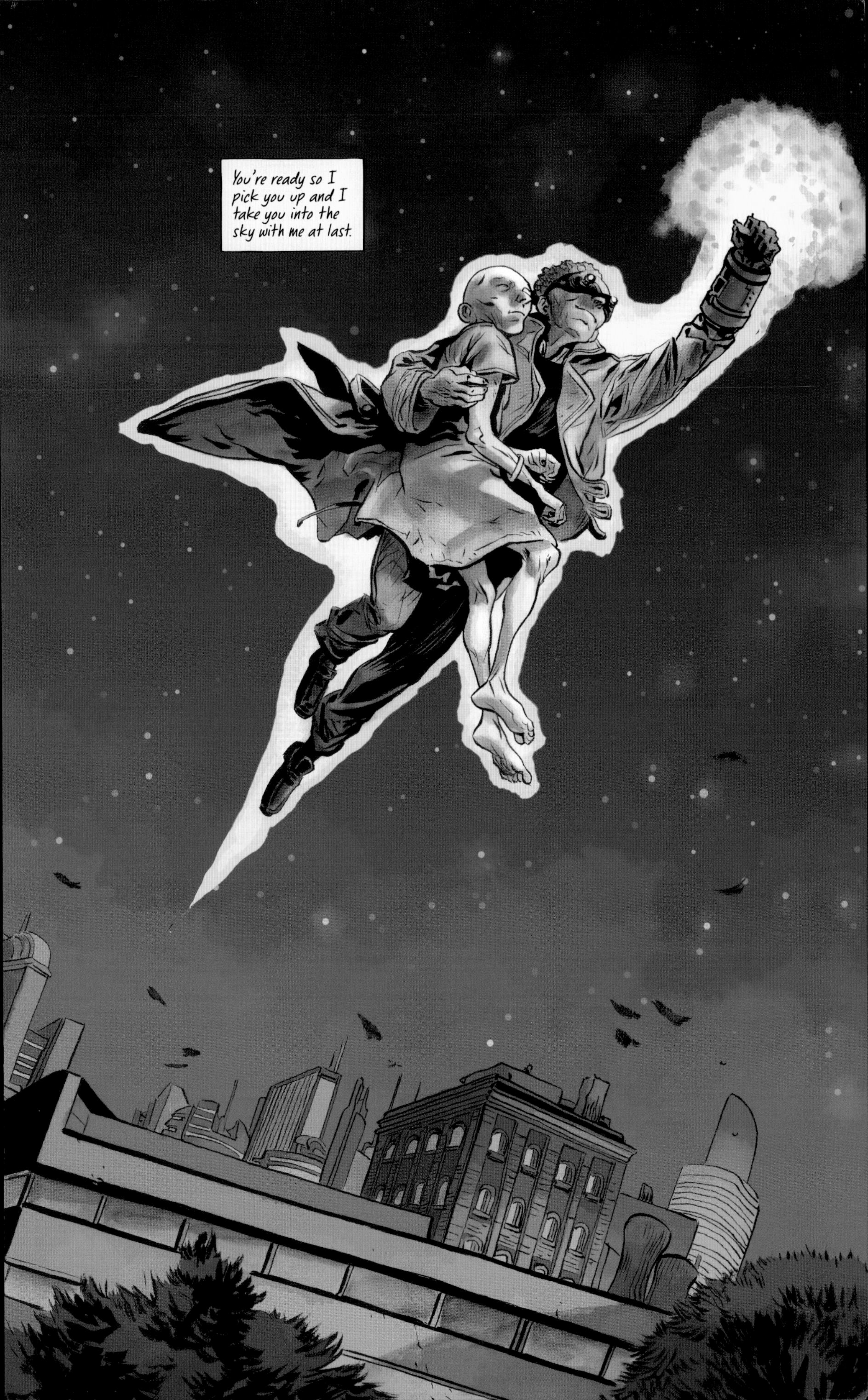
You're ready so I pick you up and I take you into the sky with me at last.

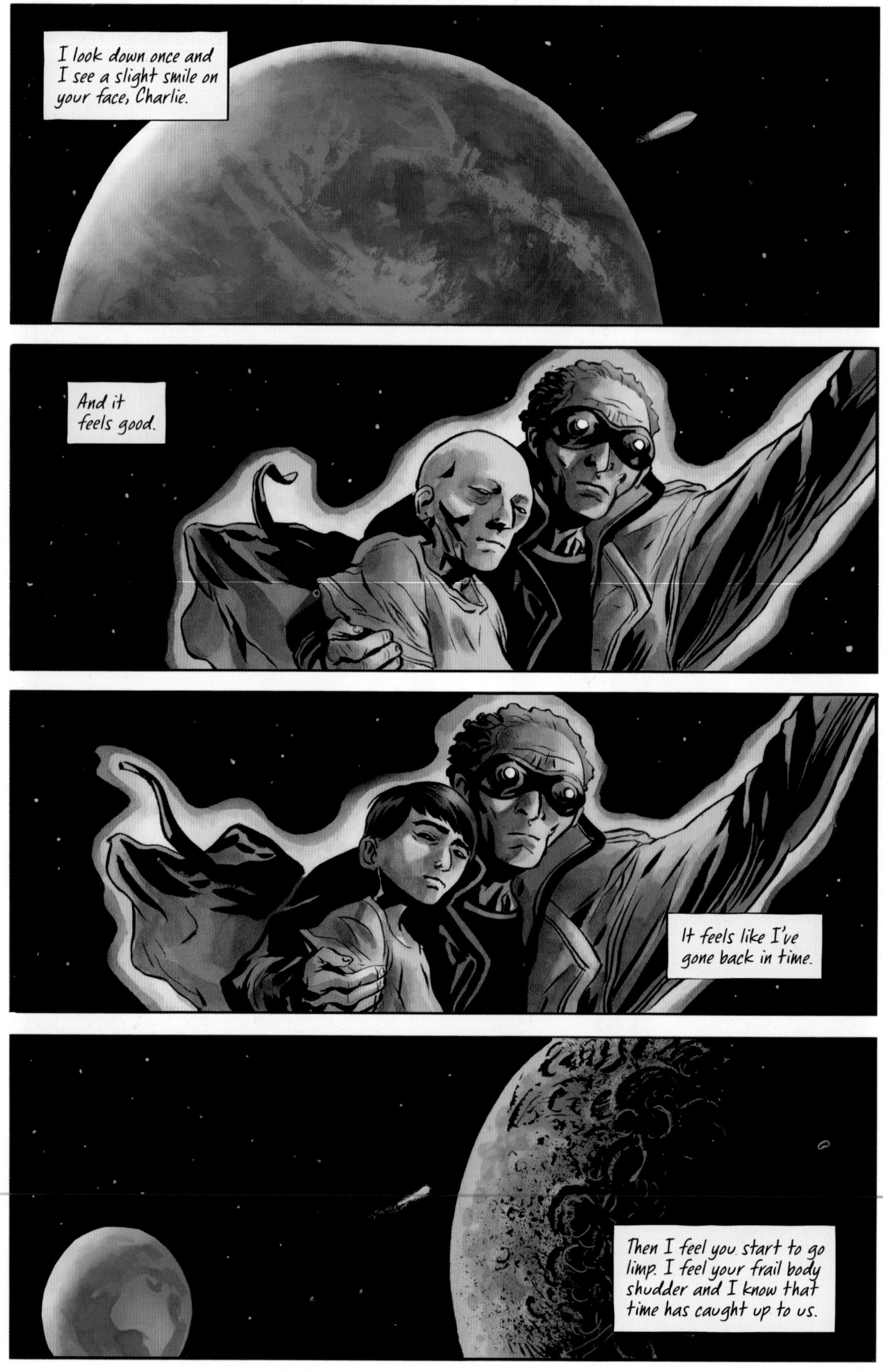
I look down once and I see a slight smile on your face, Charlie.
And it feels good.
It feels like I've gone back in time.
Then I feel you start to go limp. I feel your frail body shudder and I know that time has caught up to us.

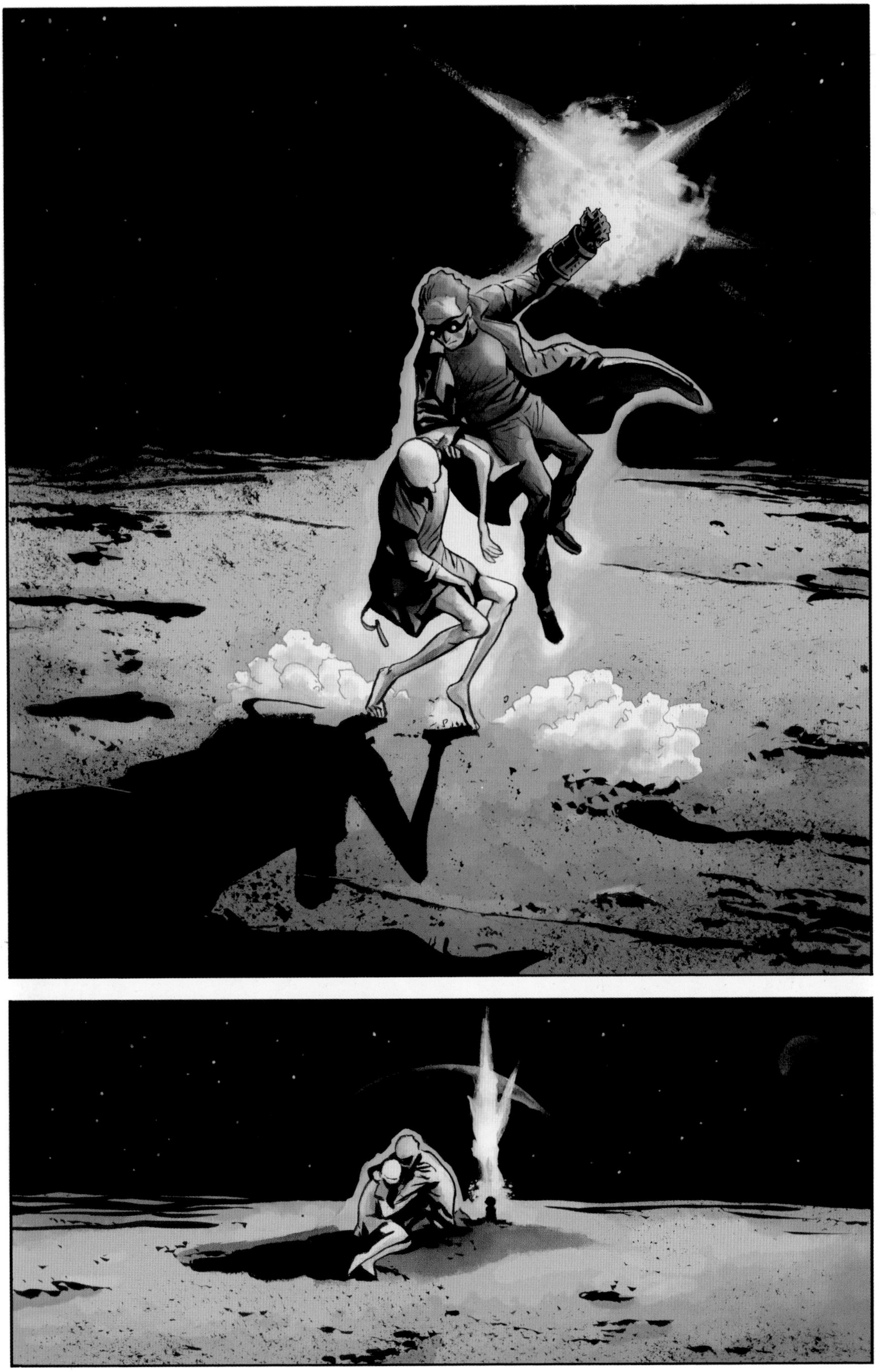

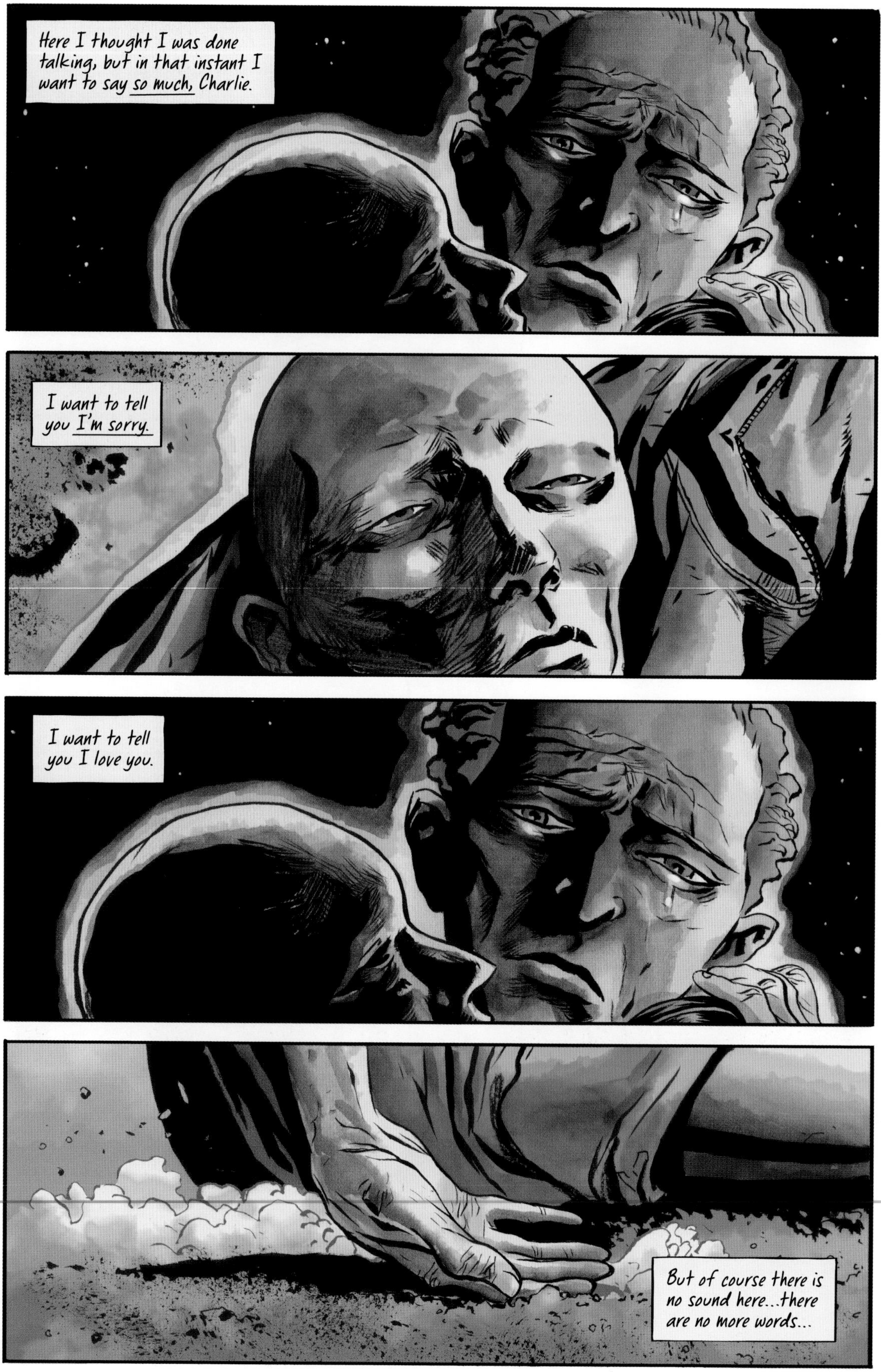

Here I thought I was done talking, but in that instant I want to say so much, Charlie.
I want to tell you I'm sorry.
I want to tell you I love you.
But of course there is no sound here...there are no more words...

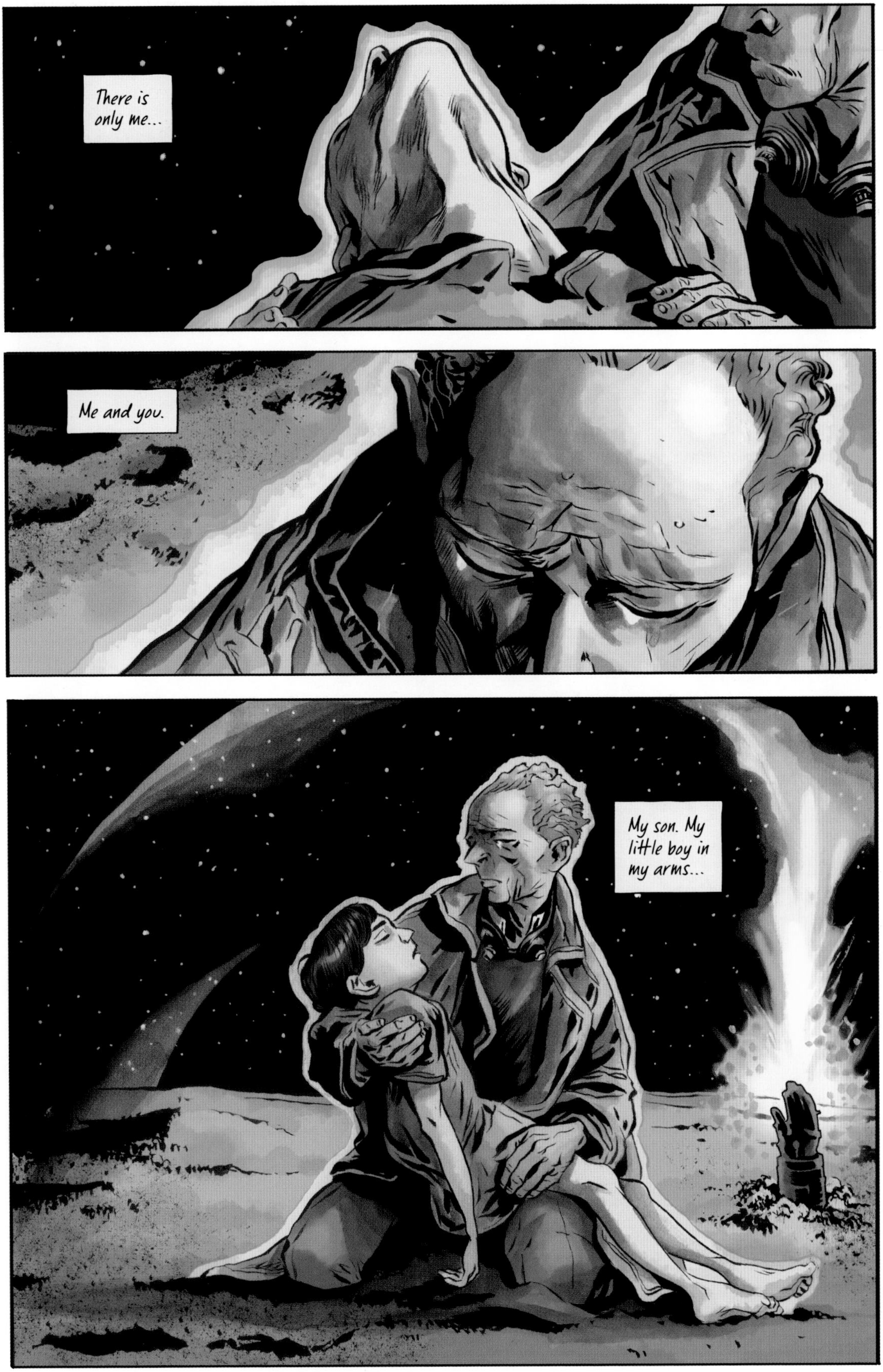
There is only me...
Me and you.
My son. My little boy in my arms...

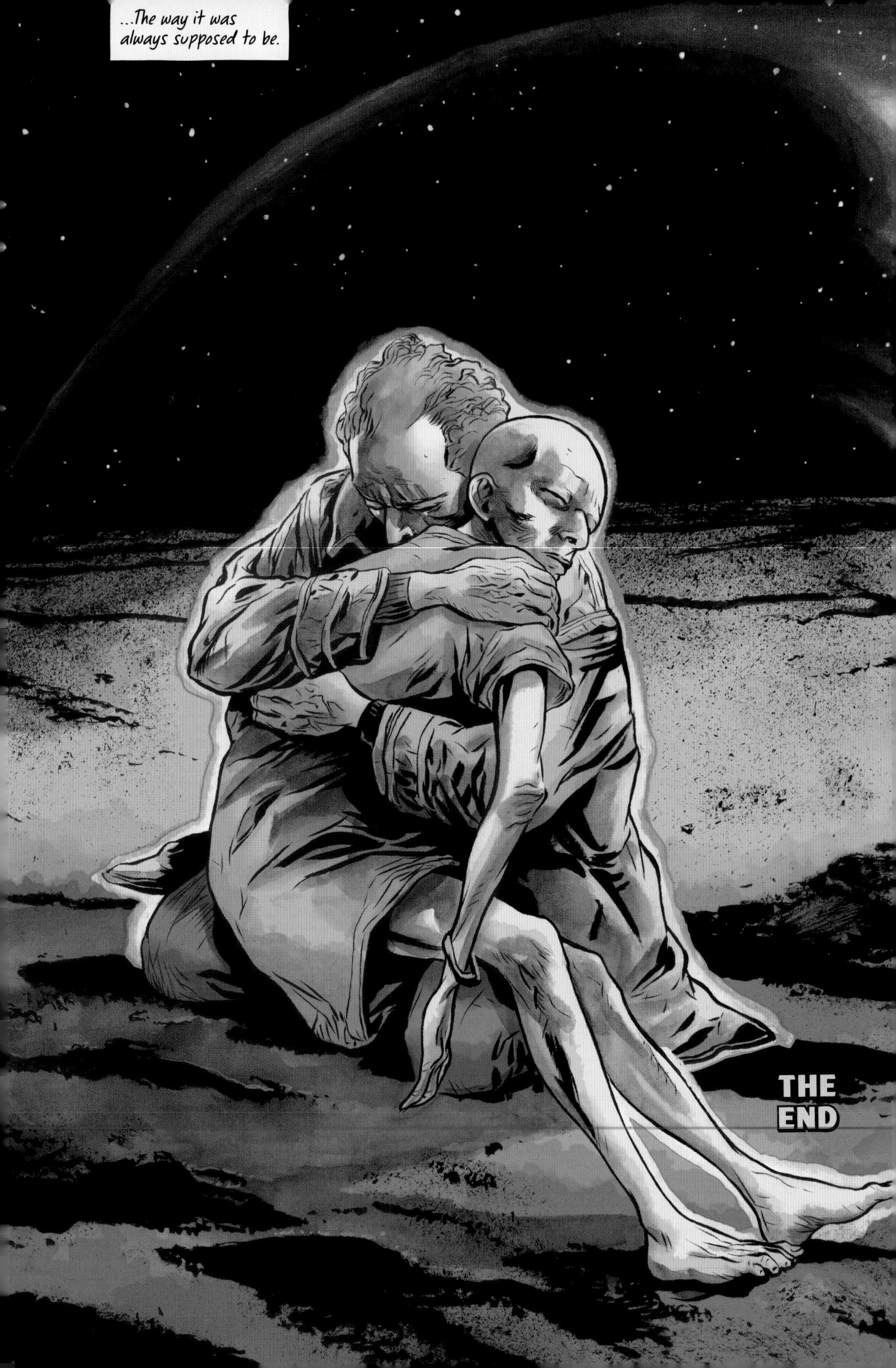
...The way it was always supposed to be.
THE END

DOCTOR ANDROMEDA

SKETCHBOOK

NOTES BY MAX FIUMARA AND JEFF LEMIRE

DOC 1986 - Late 50's

Jimmy's outfit

DOCTOR ANDROMEDA

Max Fiumara: Doctor Andromeda's original design was created by David Rubín, and then I added my take on it. I was interested in making something special with the costume shapes—something more notorious. Also I added some more science-y features to the costume like making the goggles look like a pair of tiny telescopic lenses.

With Jimmy's design I thought he needed to look older than he really was and also sad and dejected, so I made him wear clothes that would look like what he would wear from his past life.

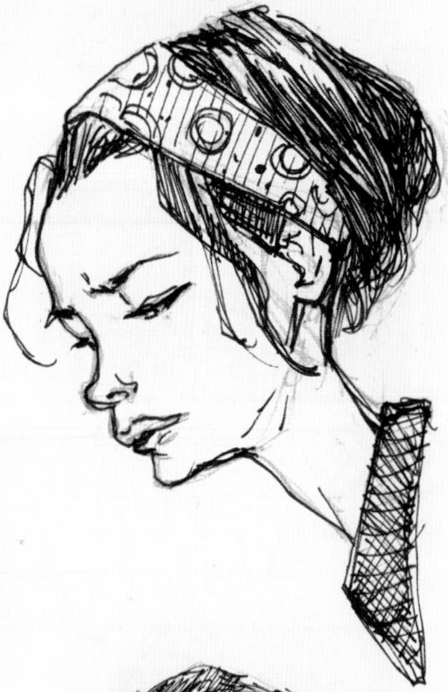

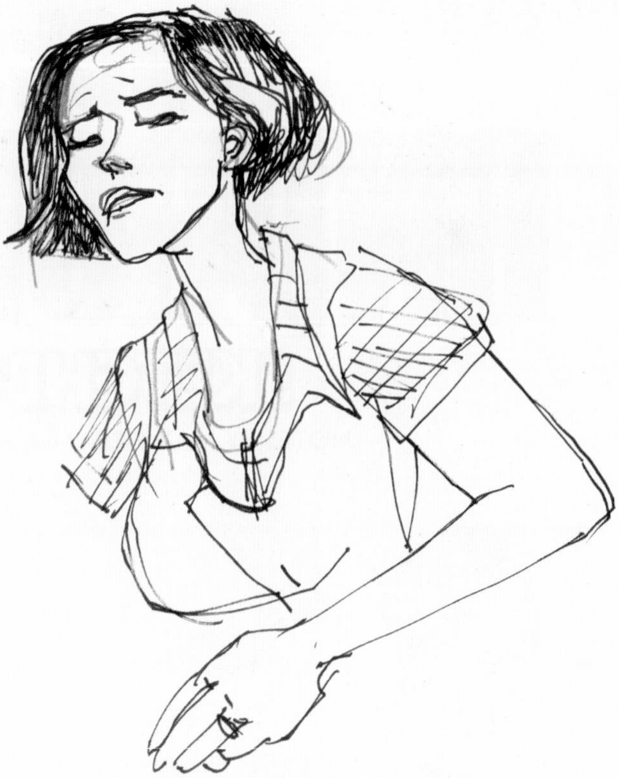

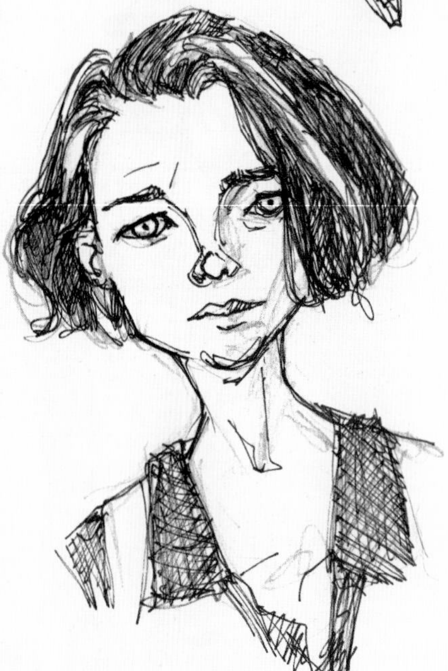

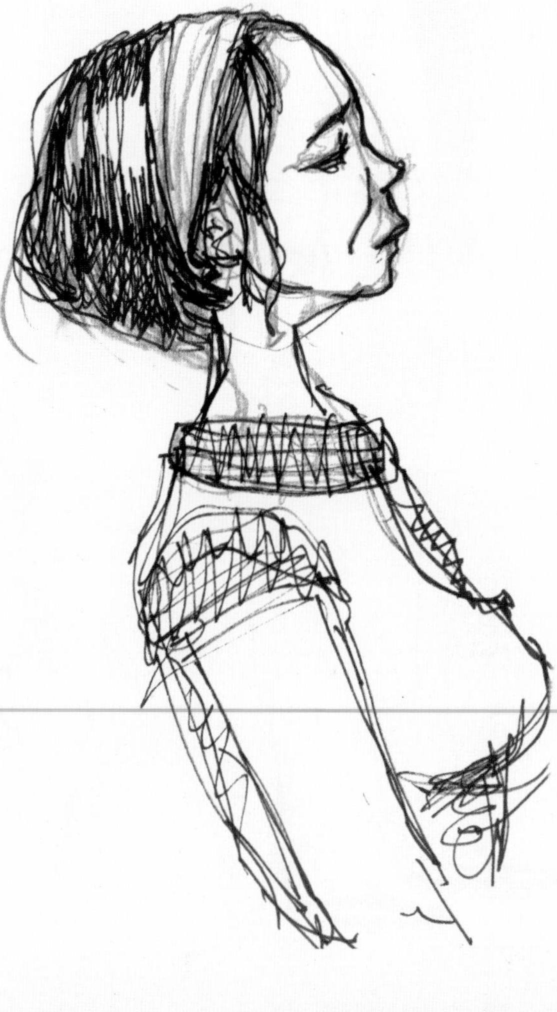

JOAN

MF: Joan is my favorite character. I wanted to make her strong at the beginning of the series and not so much at the end. She has to go through a lot of awful stuff in her life, so she needed to look tough, but also to have that look in her eyes that something is not right because of her husband.

Jeff Lemire: I was worried that Max wouldn't want to draw the 1940s New York that the script called for, but was pleasently surprised when he told me that this was his favorite era of American history. He really excelled at creating real characters, and having them page on the page in a realistic way.

(FACING) DOCTOR ANDROMEDA #4 PAGE 22

MF: Not much to say for this emotive scene. I just wanted to make a great, final shot of Doc accepting his reality while hugging the fragile body of his dead son in the emptiness of space.

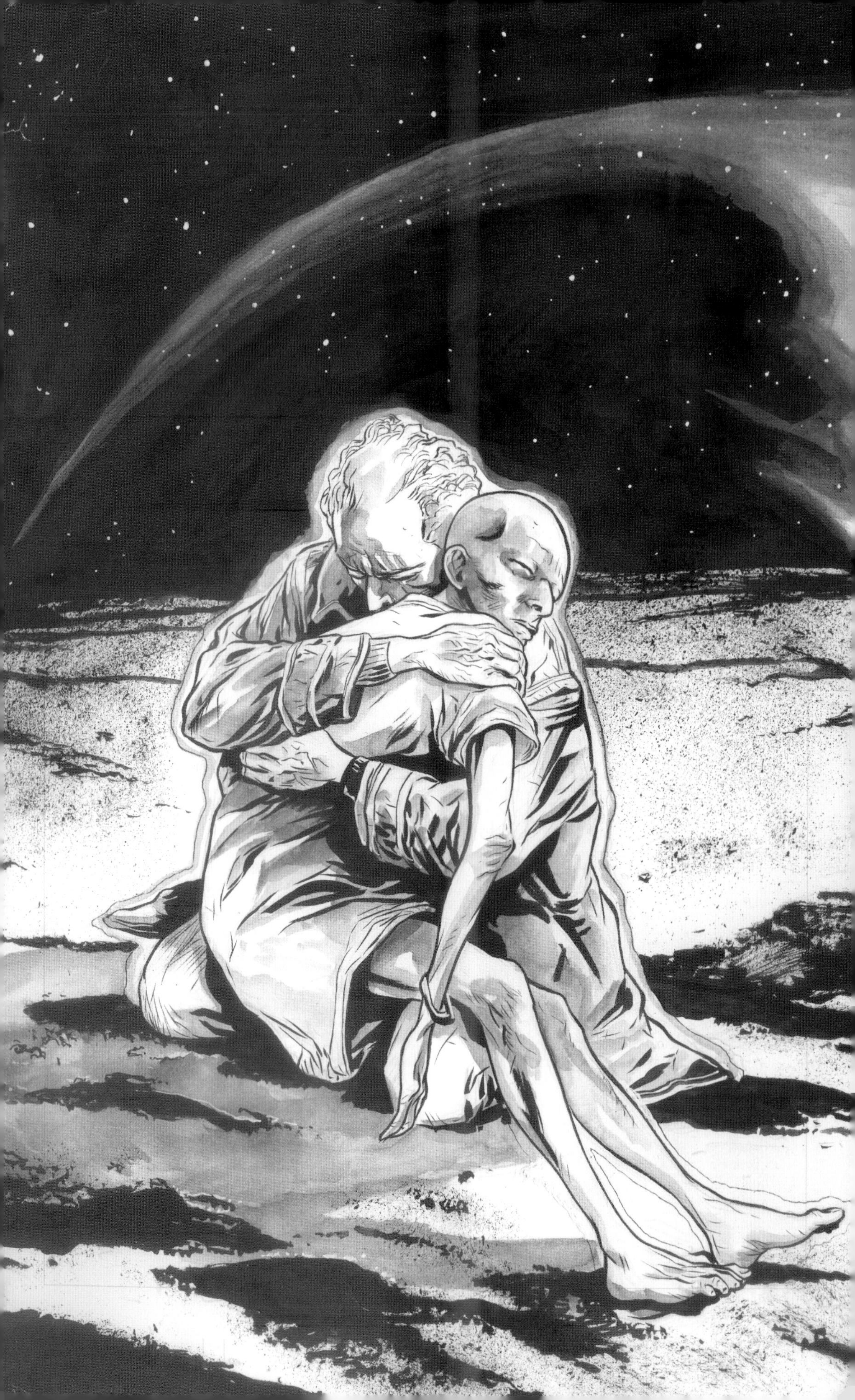

"If you think there's no room left in your life for another superhero comic, *Black Hammer* might just prove you wrong."—IGN

BLACK HAMMER™

ONCE THEY WERE HEROES, but the age of heroes has long since passed. Banished from existence by a multiversal crisis, the old champions of Spiral City—Abraham Slam, Golden Gail, Colonel Weird, Madame Dragonfly, and Barbalien—now lead simple lives in an idyllic, timeless farming village from which there is no escape! And yet, the universe isn't done with them—it's time for one last grand adventure.

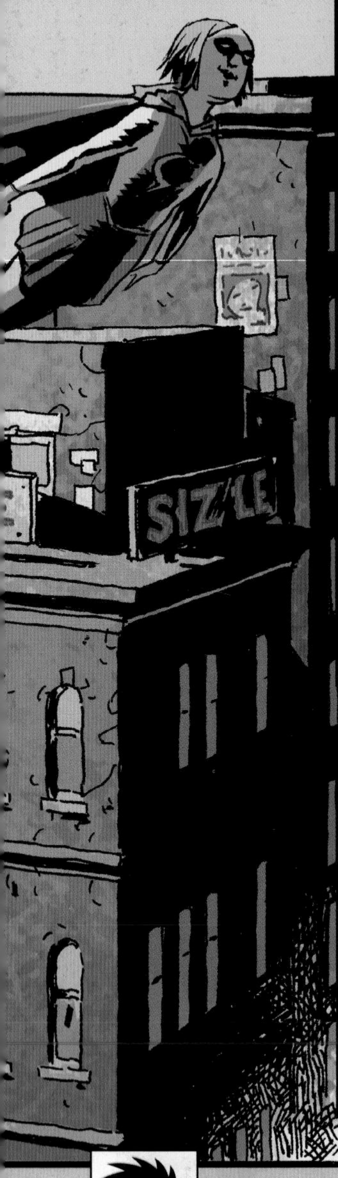

SIZZLE

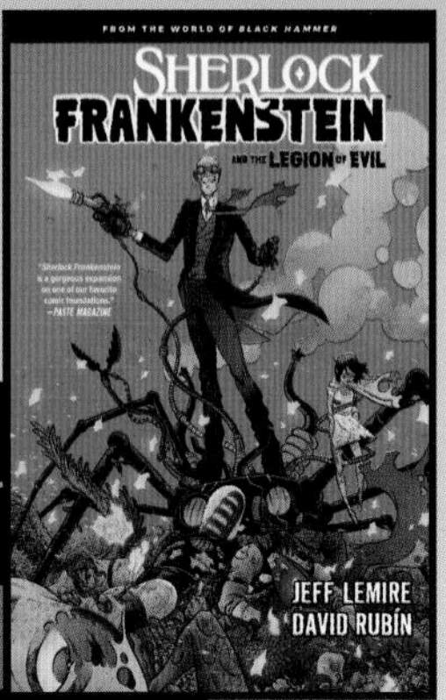

FROM THE WORLD OF BLACK HAMMER
SHERLOCK FRANKENSTEIN
AND THE LEGION OF EVIL
JEFF LEMIRE
DAVID RUBÍN

BLACK HAMMER
Written by Jeff Lemire
Art by Dean Ormston

THE WORLD OF BLACK HAMMER LIBRARY EDITION VOLUME 1
978-1-50671-995-5 • $49.99

THE WORLD OF BLACK HAMMER LIBRARY EDITION VOLUME 2
978-1-50671-996-2 • $49.99

VOLUME 1: SECRET ORIGINS
978-1-61655-786-7 • $14.99

VOLUME 2: THE EVENT
978-1-50670-198-1 • $19.99

VOLUME 3: AGE OF DOOM PART ONE
978-1-50670-389-3 • $19.99

VOLUME 4: AGE OF DOOM PART TWO
978-1-50670-816-4 • $19.99

BLACK HAMMER LIBRARY EDITION VOLUME 1
978-1-50671-073-0 • $49.99

BLACK HAMMER LIBRARY EDITION VOLUME 2
978-1-50671-185-0 • $49.99

SHERLOCK FRANKENSTEIN & THE LEGION OF EVIL
Written by Jeff Lemire • Art by David Rubín
This mystery follows a reporter determined to find out what happened to her father, the Black Hammer. All answers seem to lie in Spiral City's infamous insane asylum, where some dangerous supervillain tenants reside, including Black Hammer's greatest foe—Sherlock Frankenstein!
978-1-50670-526-2 • $19.99

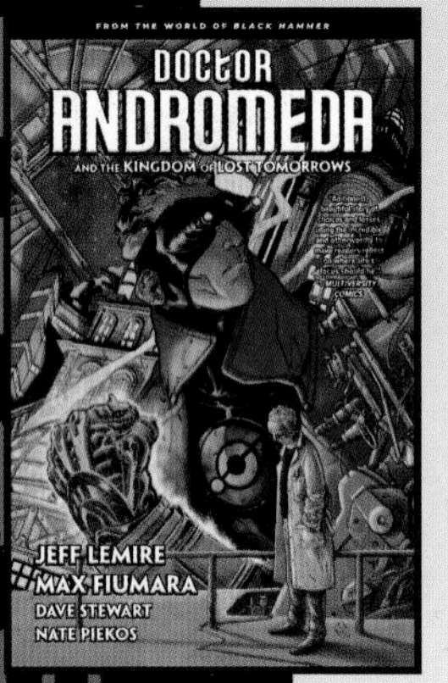

FROM THE WORLD OF BLACK HAMMER
DOCTOR ANDROMEDA
AND THE KINGDOM OF LOST TOMORROWS
JEFF LEMIRE
MAX FIUMARA
DAVE STEWART
NATE PIEKOS

DOCTOR ANDROMEDA & THE KINGDOM OF LOST TOMORROWS
Written by Jeff Lemire • Art by Max Fiumara
This dual-narrative story set in the world of *Black Hammer* chronicles the legacy of a Golden-Age superhero wishing to reconnect with his estranged son, whom he hoped would one day take the mantle of Doctor Andromeda.
978-1-50672-329-7 • $19.99

THE QUANTUM AGE: FROM THE WORLD OF BLACK HAMMER
Written by Jeff Lemire • Art by Wilfredo Torres
A thousand years in the future, a collection of superheroes, inspired by the legendary heroes of Black Hammer Farm, must band together to save the planet from an authoritarian regime, while a young Martian struggles to solve the riddle of what happened to the great heroes of the twentieth century.
VOLUME 1
978-1-50670-841-6 • $19.99

BLACK HAMMER: STREETS OF SPIRAL
Jeff Lemire, Dean Ormston, Emi Lenox, and others
A Lovecraftian teen decides she will do anything to make herself "normal," a bizarre witch guides her guests through her house of horrors, and an all-star slate of guest artists illustrate a bizarre adventure with Colonial Weird on the farm. Also features a complete world guide to the *Black Hammer* universe and its characters!
978-1-50670-941-3 • $19.99

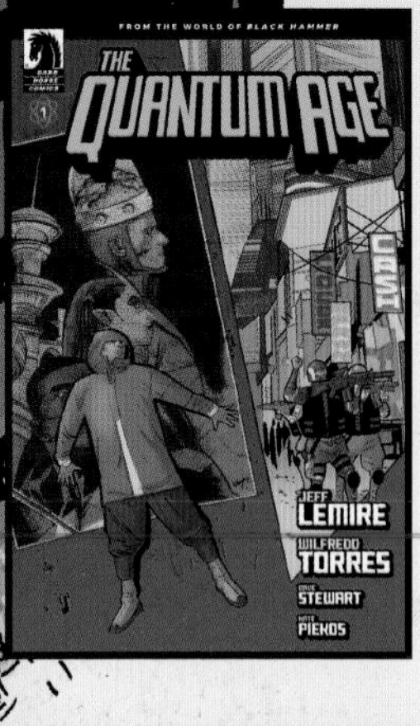

FROM THE WORLD OF BLACK HAMMER
THE QUANTUM AGE
JEFF LEMIRE
WILFREDO TORRES
DAVE STEWART
NATE PIEKOS

BLACK HAMMER '45: FROM THE WORLD OF BLACK HAMMER
Jeff Lemire, Ray Fawkes, Matt Kindt, and Sharlene Kindt
During the Golden Age of superheroes, an elite Air Force crew called the Black Hammer Squadron bands together to combat the Nazis, a host of occult threats, and their ultimate aerial warrior the Ghost Hunter.
978-1-50670-850-8 • $17.99

BLACK HAMMER/JUSTICE LEAGUE: HAMMER OF JUSTICE!
Written by Jeff Lemire • Art by Michael Walsh
A strange man arrives simultaneously on Black Hammer Farm and in Metropolis, and both worlds are warped as Starro attacks! Batman, Green Lantern, Flash, Wonder Woman, Superman, and more crossover with Golden Gail, Colonel Weird, and the rest of the Black Hammer gang!
978-1-50671-099-0 • $29.99

COLONEL WEIRD—COSMAGOG: FROM THE WORLD OF BLACK HAMMER
Written by Jeff Lemire • Art by Tyler Crook
978-1-50671-516-2 • $19.99

DARK HORSE BOOKS

AVAILABLE AT YOUR LOCAL COMICS SHOP OR BOOKSTORE
TO FIND A COMICS SHOP IN YOUR AREA, VISIT COMICSHOPLOCATOR.COM.
For more information or to order direct, visit darkhorse.com.